FOR THE LOVE OF W

This extraordinary book opens up the mysterious world of the *parea* – a lesbian secret society based in a small town outside Athens, which is so clandestine that the broader community has no notion of its existence. Though meeting to drink, dance and flirt in the most public night-spot in town, conducting intense sexual affairs under the noses of other customers, the *parea*'s members – many of whom are married with children and seem to have perfectly conventional lives by Greek standards – do not identify themselves as gay. Instead they use same-sex desire to renegotiate male and female identity, promoting their own idiosyncratic ideas about gender and sexuality and covertly challenging the chauvinism and heterosexual bias of Greek culture. Based entirely on first-hand fieldwork within the *parea*, Elisabeth Kirtsoglou's subtle and adventurous book reveals the friction of desire and disguise that dominates the women's complex double lives. Focusing on themes of lesbian initiation, friendship, passion and separation, the book weaves stories of love, sex and relationships into an intriguing and perceptive analysis.

Elisabeth Kirtsoglou is Lecturer in Anthropology at the University of Wales Lampeter.

FOR THE LOVE OF WOMEN

Gender, identity and same-sex relations in a Greek provincial town

Elisabeth Kirtsoglou

LONDON AND NEW YORK

First published 2004
by Routledge
11 New Fetter Lane, London EC4P 4EE

Simultaneously published in the USA and Canada
by Routledge
29 West 35th Street, New York, NY 10001

Routledge is an imprint of the Taylor & Francis Group

Typeset in Garamond by
Keystroke, Jacaranda Lodge, Wolverhampton
Printed and bound in Great Britain by
TJ International Ltd, Padstow, Cornwall

British Library Cataloguing in Publication Data
A catalogue record for this book is available from the British Library

Library of Congress Cataloging in Publication Data
A catalog record for this book has been requested

ISBN 0–415–31030–X (hbk)
ISBN 0–415–31031–8 (pbk)

CONTENTS

ACKNOWLEDGEMENTS

During the years it took me to complete this book I received help, support and encouragement from more than one person, in more than one country, region and institution. First and foremost I would like to thank the women of the *parea* for trusting me to present our experiences to wider audiences. I would also like to express my gratitude to Dimitris Theodossopoulos for being a constant source of warmth, encouragement, academic support and intellectual inspiration. My warmest thanks to Margaret Kenna, Jane Cowan and Victoria Goddard for their invaluable academic input. Special thanks to all my colleagues in the Archaeology and Anthropology Department of the University of Wales Lampeter for providing me with a stimulating and challenging academic environment.

This book is devoted to all the people who wish their voices could be heard.

1

FOR THE LOVE OF WOMEN

> I saw her suddenly: and I thought 'God, she is so beautiful'. I remember her in the dim light, warm and radiant and graceful, so alive. I was lost, abandoned in the sparkle of her eyes, gone. It was only a moment: a moment that lasted for so long. I wanted to embrace her, to close her in my arms tightly, in a desperate attempt to freeze time, to snatch the moment.
>
> (Zoi, Kallipolis 1997)

Documentations

This book is an ethnographic exploration of the social and performative realisation of gender identity as this is discursively and practically negotiated by a group of gay women in a Greek provincial town, which I call *Kallipolis*. Although the protagonists of this study engage in same-sex erotic relationships, they do not regard themselves as lesbians. Instead, they seek to promote a particular approach to gender and sexuality, according to which gender is a socially constructed category and sexual practices are not constitutive of identity. The members of this all female company maintain that they are a group, an affective community of friends bound by emotional ties who pursue erotic relationships with women, yet they wish to remain – in terms of their identity – unclassifiable.[1] Respecting their wish to resist common categories of self-ascription, I refer to these women throughout the book, as 'the *parea*' (the company), appropriating the expression they use to refer to themselves.[2]

My ethnographic textualisation of the life of the *parea* focuses on how its members employ certain culturally informed practices, such as dance and alcohol consumption, in order to articulate specific gender ideas and relations not only discursively, but also through aesthetically compelling public performances. The women of the *parea* reveal nothing about their sexual and ideological preoccupations to the other inhabitants of Kallipolis and present themselves as a 'company of friends'. None the less, the *parea*'s gendered performances take place at a highly visible space, a night-spot with live Greek music, frequented by virtually every adult in the town. The conscious decision of these women to engage in a constant politic of 'concealment and display' (cf. Herzfeld, 1987) by performatively locating themselves in this popular night-spot while fiercely protecting the opacity of their sexual lives, signals their ambition to remain fully integrated members of the social context within which they exist.

At the same time, the *parea* develops its own distinct group culture that entails public performances which take place within the framework of ritualised practices founded by the women of the group. The life of the company revolves around invented rituals based on conspicuous consumption of alcohol, food commensality and dance, that serve to mark specific events, such as the establishment or the end of an erotic relationship, and the initiation of a new member into the *parea*. Every such occasion is for the group a discursive and performative field for identity-making, in the framework of which the women draw upon familiar cultural material in order to compose an idiosyncratic idiom of personhood (cf. Sax, 2002: 4–5). In this sense, this work is concerned with an alternative context of gender (cf. Loizos and Papataxiarchis, 1991a: 4)[3] that is, however, firmly established within a specific cultural region.

My ethnographic involvement with this community of women does not attempt to present a social or historical account of lesbianism in Greece. The aim of this study is to demonstrate how a specific group of women with their particular sexuality negotiate their identity *vis-à-vis* the notions of gender prevalent in the society and culture that surrounds them. Kallipolis – my field site – and my informants alike are neither fully representative nor completely atypical examples of female homosexuality in Greece.[4] In this respect my book is as much about differences within (Greek, gay) women (cf. Moore, 1993; McNay, 2000: 1–2; Braidotti, 2002: 14) as it is about the shared experience of being a (gay) woman in a Greek province.

The unique narrative of my informants, which is nevertheless tied to larger categories of cultural, gender and class identity, is depicted in five ethnographic chapters which follow the life of the *parea* in its performative and discursive instances. The remaining part of this introduction is devoted to the explication of the cultural connotations of some of the *parea*'s practices, concluding with a note on methodology. In Chapter Two I present a theoretical overview that aims to situate my analysis in the corpus of regional and more general gender theory placing special emphasis on sexuality, the embodied dimension of subjectivity, and the relation between identity, performance and agency.

Chapter Three, the first of the ethnographic chapters, focuses on the ritualistic initiation of new members into the group. Incorporating new women into the *parea* is based on erotic attraction and usually follows a specific pattern that aims to ensure the establishment of an erotic relationship between a woman of the community and an outsider, as well as the successful integration of the new partner into the company. In this sense every initiation is simultaneously a courtship based on what Herzfeld calls 'effective performance', that is, a performance that 'uses form to draw attention to a set of messages' (1985: 47). Through alcohol, dance and food commensality, as well as through flirtation and the symbol of the 'effeminate' body, the women of the group enact an alternative gender model and assert the existence and growth of their collectivity.

Probably the most distinct set of practices in the *parea* is that pertinent to the different model of relatedness the women promote. Chapter Four concentrates on the two main forms of relatedness that exist within the *parea*, namely, friendship and erotic relationships. Friendship is regarded by my informants as the primal expression of emotional bonding. All the women have a 'best friend' who performs some of the roles usually encountered in familial relationships. Along with these friendships, one can safely argue that the group promotes a form of kinship based on personal choice and being entirely complementary to the 'erotic' self (cf. Weston, 1991/1997: 103–22). Through these friendships, the women construct strong emotional ties and employ their community both as a female network and as a framework for the creative redefinition of notions of kinship and identity.

The second part of Chapter Four is dedicated to erotic relationships. Erotic unions and flirting strategies are the two themes that consume most of my informants' time. Sexual expression in the group revolves around the idea of pleasure accomplished in passionate but nevertheless ephemeral unions. Their ideal relationship closely approximates Giddens' concept of the 'pure relationship' (1992) since it lasts as long as it satisfies both partners. In turn, the members of the *parea* measure satisfaction against the existence of passion and excitement. They do not wish to see their relationships transformed into loving and caring partnerships and thus once erotic passion ceases to exist a relationship is concluded. Since erotic behaviour in the context of the group depends on non-verbal as well as verbal communication, this section also examines dance and consumption as 'sites of social action' (cf. Cowan, 1990: 5).

Chapter Five is concerned with separation. The conclusion of an erotic relationship is treated by the *parea* as a highly ritualised occasion of collective regenerative mourning. In this chapter, I draw a parallel between the mourning practices of the group and those of a conventional Greek funeral. Without suggesting that the contexts of death and separation are identical, I am concerned with pain as a context for the construction of gender identity through the politics of suffering (cf. Seremetakis, 1991; Dubisch, 1995). One of my main concerns in this chapter is the use of narrative as a means of self-realisation (McNay, 2000: 27–9, 81–5; Braidotti, 2002: 22). Through long narrations that take place as part of the separation process, the women I studied rewrite their own personal history and that of the group and actively construct and disseminate ideas about gender and gender relations.

The women of the *parea* are, however, not only members of the group but also of a greater cultural community. Chapter Six documents their narratives as cultural persons who sustain and negotiate relationships with significant others, who do not belong to the *parea*. This chapter offers a series of portraits of women who struggle to remain part of 'both worlds', that of mainstream Kallipolis and the *parea*, arguing for the multiple and contextual character of identity (Corber and Valocchi, 2003: 2–3). The main purpose of this chapter is to illuminate the cultural conditions under which the women of the group resist as well as accommodate 'ideals and expectations defined for them' (cf. Goddard, 1996: 239). Through these narrative portraits, I wish to show instances of the dialectic relationship that exists between the *parea* and its social context by presenting my informants not only as women of the group but also as mothers, daughters and persons who hold multiple and at times conflicting identifications (cf. Moore, 1994).

Finally, the last ethnographic chapter explores the origins of the *parea*, a friendship group established initially by four women during their university years in Athens. Their stories, together with other narratives of women who do not strictly belong to the *parea*, reveal the episodic and biographical quality of gender identity, one that is socially constructed and often composed through random encounters of the actor with powerful societal idioms. In this chapter, I focus upon the institutionalised character of heterosexuality and I treat sexuality as 'a specifically dense transfer point for relations of power' (Foucault, 1976: 103), examining the relationship between gender and wider idioms pertinent to self-realisation.

Throughout this work, I treat gender as an identity that is socially constructed, 'tenuously constituted in time, instituted in an exterior space through *stylized repetitions of acts*' (Butler, 1990: 140, original emphasis). I claim that consciously or unconsciously, enacted gender performances serve to question as much as to crystallise conventional ideas and I pay specific attention to the role of the body as the material locus of subjectivity. I conclude the book by arguing that my informants' performances pertain to a culturally informed poetics of personhood according to which the self is always established competitively and in a defiant manner *vis-à-vis* some hegemonic discourse that threatens the actor's creativity, and places him/her in a paradoxical position of being at once powerful and powerless. The women protagonists of this work articulate sophisticated narratives of resistance (cf. McNay, 1992: 39; Alsop *et al.*, 2002: 83–4) from the margins of the Greek periphery. These narratives try to negotiate the lived contradictions of my informants' daily lives into a meaningful statement about the self, and the experience of being first and foremost a woman who happens to have a homoerotic sexuality in a largely heterocentric Greek provincial town.

Introducing the *parea*

Parea is a colloquial Greek term that stands for 'company'. An extremely versatile word, according to its contextual usage, it can mean anything from 'to keep company' (*kano parea*), a company of men and women, or a specifically male group. When married couples enjoy a night out together for instance they use the word *parea* (company) to refer to all those who share a table at a night-spot (Cowan, 1990: 155, 158). The term is also employed by people near Athens to suggest 'a group of male friends who regularly drink together' (Madianou-Gefou, 1992: 117) while, in the Aegean island of Lesbos, all male friendship groups that enjoy eating and drinking commensality are referred to as *parea* (Loizos and Papataxiarchis, 1991a: 17; Papataxiarchis, 1991: 166; 1992: 215–16). As a general definition, one could say that *parea* stands for a group of people (sometimes specifically male) who come together voluntarily (cf. Cowan, 1990: 159), usually in order to enjoy themselves through drinking, eating or dancing but also in other contexts. A *parea* can be stable through time and exist beyond the spatio-temporal bounds of commensality or not, while in most cases it is (or it pretends to be) an egalitarian schema.[5]

The women I studied refer to their group as 'the *parea*', or 'the girls',[6] and maintain that their company is an 'affective community' (*synaisthimatiki koinotita*) bound by strong emotional ties. The main corpus of the group is situated in a provincial town that I call Kallipolis, a town of approximately 200,000 inhabitants, large enough to have a university, a hospital, numerous schools, and an active trading centre. The women of the *parea* live and work in this community as fully integrated members, some of them married with children. They study or have their own businesses, work in the public sector or free-lance, and generally they are indistinguishable from the rest of the Kallipoliots. The *parea* is an egalitarian community with no specific leader or any system of patronage, and consists of approximately seventy women of mixed socio-economic, educational and age status.[7] The number of women affiliated to the group, however, is a much larger one since everybody who happened to be a member at some point in time is always considered a member irrespectively of whether she is physically present. Thus during the years that I was close to the community, women of different ages who lived in other towns kept returning to Kallipolis in order to spend some time with the *parea*, and were treated as if they never left.

The *parea* consists of persons who approximate the image of the 'middle-class-urban-educated woman', who – if unmarried – is able to pursue erotic relationships in a relatively free manner, dresses fashionably, and frequents – usually in the company of others – bars, cafes and restaurants (cf. Faubion, 1993: 174–6). The women of the community, and the majority of Kallipoliot women in general, are in this sense similar to their Athenian counterparts described by Faubion (1993). They are educated, very much 'modernised' and frequently economically independent but, nevertheless, still expected to be 'proficient housewives' (ibid.: 176). Most of my informants' female friends and relatives who are single and do not belong to the *parea*, are in search of 'serious' (*sovares*) erotic relationships that will hopefully end in marriage. Soon after a wedding reception of the standard type (cf. Argyrou, 1996), they will have to learn the art of balancing their lives between work outside the home and their domestic duties before they eventually have sons and daughters of their own. Some of the women of the group will also eventually marry. Some others, however, choose to disregard the increasing social pressure to 'open a house [i.e. create a home] of their own' (cf. Hirschon, 1989: 108; Cowan, 1992: 141–2) and prefer the friendship network of the *parea* to heterosexual conjugality.

Married or single, those who belong to the group, try and meet at night in a specific night-spot that I call *Harama*, and on other occasions for coffee, dinner, lunch and so forth.[8] At any moment of the day some women of the *parea* are gathered at some place, be it in a tavern or a home or even the private business of one of them, and one can spend time with friends literally on a 24-hour basis. The women of the group do not simply spend time together though, they also help each other in any way they can. The 'girls' know precisely each other's problems and they are heavily involved in each other's lives functioning as a large extended family (cf. Weston, 1991) that supports all its members emotionally, socially and even financially.

Most of these women's shared time is devoted to pleasurable talk, commensality and serious discussions. Some of them read a great deal, academic books and literature, and they usually transmit this knowledge to their friends. Thus, being a member of the *parea* means, among other things, discussing Foucault, contemporary art, cinema and international politics. A basic consequence of their general lifestyle is that to the eyes of the Kallipoliots, the women I studied are not outcasts[9] but instead are perceived as a circle of rather intellectual friends. The *parea* is in many ways, a network that enables the women to live a non-ordinary life, which is itself enabled by the alternative lifestyle of its members (cf. Adkins, 2002: 95).[10] The girls provide each other with the support and strength necessary to challenge one's place in society, and also with the cultural as well as financial means to achieve a degree of social mobility. Younger women often get the chance to study with the help of the *parea*, or to set up a stylish and successful private business, and older members – who already run their own businesses – frequently rely on the group's connections for a clientele and support. The community then fits Faubion's definition of the 'privileged marginals', in the sense that it is composed of (locally) 'distinguished women' who belong to an equally localised (not only, but also 'aesthetic') 'intelligentsia' (Faubion, 1993: 191).

In the context of the *parea*, the self undergoes what Faubion calls 'elaborate objectification' (1993: 163). The women of the group analyse themselves and others in a consistent and detailed manner, being quite capable amateur anthropologists, psychologists, philosophers and psychoanalysts (ibid.). Those with more experience teach the others, and everyone is thought to have something substantial to offer to the collectivity: for example, Lillian, the singer, spends hours analysing how a specific contemporary musical trend has roots in Byzantine music, while Aspa and Carolina who own a beauty parlour will offer, and often impose, their advice on the rest of the girls. Maro, who works in a health club as a physiotherapist, constantly argues about the value and power of meditation, while Emily, the lawyer, loves indulging in philosophical quests. Aphrodite, the 'capable bar manager' gave me repeated lessons on the 'psychology of the barman', and Irin, the doctor, is always preoccupied with alternative therapies. When all these women come together one might witness Emily talking about the medicalisation of the female body with Irin, who tends to view the person as 'a holistic entity'. In another instance, Aphrodite and Lillian might explain to Elena – who tries through the *parea* to establish herself as an interior decorator of recreational spaces – where the best place is to build a bar, or where a new club should have its dance floor. The transmission of knowledge, be it history of the arts, social analysis, psychology, sports or beauty tips is one of the *parea*'s basic features that enables its members to become 'legitimate autodidacts' who slowly but gradually establish 'their art of living' as a legitimate one in the context of provincial Kallipolis (Bourdieu, 1979: 25, 57).

Still, these women, despite their sophisticated attitude, feel that they have to play the politics of concealment and display (cf. Herzfeld, 1987). They struggle to remain visible and central to their greater community, yet they dearly protect the opacity of their lives. Nobody else but them and also very few close friends know that they sleep with women, that they drink in order to flirt and that behind each and everything they do there is one of the '*parea*'s codes'. Faubion argues that lesbian women in Greece do not 'pose a threat to the traditional sexual economy' (1993: 222). Indeed, homosexual women are hardly visible in Greece. Two women can live together, sleep together, hug each other and still remain unnoticed, and in so far as women are regarded as being 'phallically inactive', they may '"play" with one another' but these sexual encounters do not have any political consequence (Faubion, 1993: 221). Faubion is right in many ways when he claims that 'sexual liaisons between women . . . have for their part been less sinful than virtually incomprehensible' (ibid.). When I asked some of the Kallipoliots their opinions about lesbian women the answers I received varied from lukewarm acceptance to forceful condemnation, but rarely included a clear description of the phenomenon. The ambiguous and contradictory place that lesbianism occupies in Kallipoliot cultural imagery was evident in the embarrassment, disbelief, dismissal of the phenomenon, or even in the hostility with which my questions were at times confronted. Some men in their fifties informed me that lesbians are 'abnormal' (*anomales*), men-like women who do not wish to get married. In other instances, I was told that it was due to an unsuccessful sexual encounter with a man, or perhaps an unfortunate rape, that some woman stopped liking men and became lesbian. Biologistic explanations referring to genes and chromosomes were not infrequent either, mainly explaining homosexuality – both male[11] and female – as an inborn predisposition (cf. Faubion, 1993: 228).

Old-fashion 'sexological' accounts of women who belong to a 'third sex' were also interlarded into the repertoire of the local interlocutors. A man in his late sixties recently separated after some 10 years of marriage tried to capitalise on his ex-wife's[12] prolonged spinsterhood. She married him when she was in her forties and left him 10 years later because, according to her, 'he was hypochondriac and demanding, he left no money for the house because he was supporting his sister, assuming that she had to spend all her earnings but not his'. Their Kallipoliot circle – to which I gained access through the *parea*'s acquaintances – tended to support the particular woman. In turn, the ex-husband, probably in order to shift the focus from the accusation of being a poor provider and to gain some sympathy from common friends, 'confessed' to his ex-wife's closest kinsman that they separated because she was a lesbian. Upon the question, 'and how can you tell',[13] apparently asked by the woman's cousin, the man replied that 'she had a huge "padlock"' (*kleidaria*). The misunderstanding caused by the resemblance in Greek of the terms *kleidaria* (padlock) and *kleitorida* (clitoris) is perhaps more indicative than the claim itself of the vagueness of elderly people's knowledge of (gay) women's sexuality.

Extremely interesting is perhaps the opinion of some Kallipoliot men in their forties I spoke to, who tended to view lesbianism as a direct challenge to men, the institution of family and the current sexual economy, rather than as an independent sexual/emotional attitude. Chafetz has argued that same-sex relationships are reprimanded when seen as connected to social rebellion, thus pointing to disturbance of social norms and not sexual preference itself as the reason for societal condemnation (1990: 90; cf. McNay, 2000: 157). Confirming such a claim, the Kallipoliot men in question, argued fiercely that lesbians are against family and they try to defy 'the order of things', making an explicit connection between lesbianism and feminism.[14] Their arguments oscillated between disbelief and condemnation, on the one hand arguing that a relationship between two women is non-viable and merely consists of 'playing', while on the other professing that it is dangerous and anomalous. They thus talked about the difference between 'real' committed lesbians and women who might indulge in an unthreatening exploration. According to their views, although the latter is inconsequential, some 'real lesbian' may seduce an innocent woman into leaving her husband or boyfriend, filling her head with feminist ideas and persuading her to 'lift her head up' (*na sikosei kefali*), that is, to 'kick over the traces'.

Kallipoliot women in their fifties tended to close the discussion very quickly with statements such as 'the destiny of a woman is to marry and have kids', or 'these are anomalous things' (*anomala pragmata*) discouraging me from further questions. Younger women, however, in their thirties and forties had a more relaxed attitude, claiming that 'people do whatever they want in their beds and it is not up to us to judge them' (*o kathenas sto krevati tou kanei oti thelei. Emeis tha krinoume?*). What was most striking though is that most female informants[15] were certain of their own 'straight' sexuality. They stated that they were simply not attracted to women and expressed their adamant belief that a 'woman who is married and/or has children cannot be a lesbian', summoning motherhood as a proof of heterosexuality.

Another interesting and recurring male image of female homosexuality was one directly relating to pornographic films. Hard core porn movies are widely available in Greece to buy or to rent from local video-clubs, placed side by side with dramas, or at best on another floor under the rubric 'erotic' (*erotica*). Men rent *erotika* or *tsontes* as they are called colloquially, to watch in all male gatherings, alone, or even with girlfriends and wives.[16] Most such movies include in their standard repertoire one or more sexual encounters between women followed by, or shot simultaneously, or preceding encounters with men. Inspired by porn movies many men were very quick to tell me that they are rather aroused by the idea of two women having sex together. After a couple of sentences it was plainly clear that they imagined lesbian sex as the 'saucy part' of an otherwise heterosexual encounter, that would offer them the chance to 'watch' for their own pleasure.

The Kallipoliot image of female homosexuality was then, not homogenous. Different people according to their sex, age, educational, socio-economic status and personal experience, tended to put forward distinct opinions. The man-like woman, the sexually traumatised female, the anatomical curiosity, the abnormal person, the sexually deviant or the innocent explorer are, however, very far away from the girls' beliefs about themselves and their homoerotic experiences. In this context, it is not surprising that the women of the *parea* prefer to pass as friends exploiting the only type of homosexual relationship sanctioned by Greek culture. As they characteristically state: 'in the event of witch hunting we would not like to be the witches. We only wish to remain unclassifiable'. The girls consistently resist the labels lesbian, homosexual and bisexual and they construct their own subjectivities very much against existing stereotypes held by either ordinary Kallipoliots or western activists.[17] The women of the *parea* do not believe in the authenticity of grand narratives and profess that identity is something fluid and in a constant process of becoming, while they try to defy any straightforward link between sex, gender, identity and sexual practices (cf. Corber and Valocchi, 2003: 1). They claim that what ties them are 'sentiments' (*aisthimata*) of 'elective affinity'[18] (*eklektikis sygeneias*) and not a clear lesbian identity, while they conceptualise same-sex practices not as dictated by a stable erotic subjectivity, but rather in terms of fluid desire. Their politics of identity mainly emphasise status and a resistance towards well-defined categories and dominant essentialist stereotypes of gender.

It has been argued by Faubion that self-realisation in Athens is very much accomplished through an elaborate historical constructivism (1993). The *parea*, however, never talks about homosexuality in terms of ancient Greece. Although they are aware of the history of sexuality in the west, mainly through the writings of Foucault, and they argue for the constructed and institutionalised character of heterosexuality, they do not refer to Sappho or to the sexual practices of the ancient Greeks. This is indeed peculiar if one considers that the Greek island of Lesbos is employed for international lesbian gatherings and reunions. The girls' heritage-free narrative can be conceptualised in terms of the *parea*'s history explicated towards the end of the book, as well as with reference to the Greek educational system.

In his study of modern Greece, Mouzelis claims that the phenomenon of formalism – defined as the 'transformation' of 'substance into form' (1978: 138) – penetrates many aspects of Greek culture such as politics and education. According to Mouzelis, the formalistic character of Greek education is evident in the emphasis placed on the study of ancient texts, which nevertheless focuses on grammar and syntax (ibid.: 136–7).

> After six years intensive lessons in ancient Greek, the typical Greek pupil knows by heart all the irregular verbs and the complicated rules of grammar and syntax, but has hardly any idea of the philosophy and teachings of the great classical writers. It is not surprising therefore, that Greek gymnasium graduates, despite their longer schooling, seem so totally ignorant when compared with those of their counterparts who studied classics in Western Europe.
>
> (Mouzelis, 1978: 136)

Even during the 1990s, when specific attempts were made towards a less formalistic education, it was not peculiar for a learned high-school graduate never to have actually read the content of ancient Greek writers and poets. The main reason, however, that the girls never present themselves as lovers of antiquity and do not engage in systematic historical constructivism is not ignorance. As Hamilakis and Yalouri have argued, the classical past and ancient Greek antiquities have been consistently used in the construction of national identity (1996: 117). Through a rhetoric that emphasises continuity between modern and ancient Greece, 'classical heritage' has been one of the main themes of Greek nationalism[19] (cf. Hamilakis, 2003). In turn 'the nationalist use of the past is a complex phenomenon linked to other essentialist ideologies and practices and involves not only state bureaucrats and intellectuals but also social agents' (Hamilakis and Yalouri, 1999: 15).[20] The classical past has been consistently used by dictatorial regimes as a means of legitimising their power and authority as well as in their anti-communist politics (ibid., 1996: 125). Seen in this light, a rhetoric about Sappho and the homosexual practices of the ancient Greeks would seem to the girls as a direct claim to continuity between the modern and the classical past, and thus as a nationalist hegemonic discourse *par excellence*. The women of the *parea*, consistent in their vision of an identity that is not externally guaranteed, maintain their distance from such grand narratives with nationalist, conservative and essentialist overtones, preferring an experientially defined present over a systematically constructed abused past.

The everyday life of the *parea* and much of the present ethnography unfolds at a particular bar that I call *Harama*, where the girls go every night. The women of the group are friends with the owner and they have established with him a highly reciprocal relationship. The *parea* makes sure that the atmosphere of the bar is always good[21] while the owner, in return, charges them very little in relation to their overall consumption. *Harama*, the girls' favourite spot,[22] is a large bar with live Greek music – one of the many in town. Its advantage and disadvantage at the same time is that it plays 'cultured' music as opposed to other night-clubs that offer a more popular type of entertainment. This both brings a clientele and always creates the risk that the spirits of the participants are not as high as they might be in a place with more popular music, where people go specifically in order to engage in generous spending.[23] The *parea* thus makes sure that there is always *kefi* (high spirits) through dancing and drinking and by generally creating an ambience for the place. Thomas, the owner, returns them the favour by letting them drink almost for free and by offering them hospitality, since an accommodating space is very important for the existence of the *parea*.

The women of the group have literally domesticated *Harama*. Similar to the traditional coffee shop (*kafeneio*) in the case of male friendship groups, *Harama* is the natural habitat of the *parea* (cf. Papataxiarchis, 1991: 164–5). The company gathers around the bar just next to the rest of the clients who sit at the tables. The spatial distinction between the bar and the tables is a very important one for the dynamics of the space. The bar is conceptually and physically closer to *Harama's* 'backstage' (cf. MacCannell 1976: 92–6) – the people who work in the kitchen, the singers who rest there between shifts – as opposed to the tables that are occupied only by 'clients'. By choosing the bar, the women of the group ally themselves with the owner and the workers at *Harama*, distinguishing themselves from the 'ignorant' clients who are allowed to see only the carefully prepared 'front-stage' of the dance floor (cf. Boissevain, 1996: 14–17; Dahles, 1996: 242). Through the years the girls learned all the tricks of how to sell a damaged bottle of whisky, when to overcharge a client and, most importantly, what to do when the officials come to check that everything in the establishment is working legally.

Harama is in many ways the *parea*'s stage, since the women engage consistently in gendered performances accomplished largely through alcohol consumption and dance. In Greece the act of drinking is a gendered one and obeys certain rules that define it at different moments. Although both men and women drink nowadays, conspicuous consumption of alcohol is still related to the assertion of masculinity (cf. Herzfeld, 1985). The women of the *parea* consume vast quantities of alcohol, but not individually in the sense that they each buy their own separate drinks. Instead, they share rounds of shots of liquor ordered by one member (varying each time), and offered to the rest of the group. The act of *kerasma* (treating someone to a drink),[24] as Papataxiarchis argues, 'embodies the values of the gift' (1991: 158) and relates to an egalitarian ethos by establishing the ideals of reciprocity and commensality in a masculine context (Papataxiarchis, 1991, 1992; Madianou-Gefou, 1992). Practising drinking commensality is thus for the *parea* one of the many fields for the enactment of masculinity.

The women of the *parea* maintain an appearance that ranges between casual 'unisex' and the highly effeminate. In turn, this aesthetic ideal, encountered in other lesbian communities as well (cf. Green, 1997: 169), introduces a break between what Butler (1990) calls the gender of the performer and the gender of the performance. By adopting the masculine ethos of drinking commensality and cultivating their feminine appearance, the girls mingle differing performatives and achieve a highly desired fusion. On the other hand, they do not only consume in masculine ways. They frequently gather together and talk about their girlfriends and relationships while at the same time they 'read the coffee cup', a distinctly feminine, divinatory practice (cf. Cowan, 1990: 69). Through their consumptive habits, they thus open the way towards a kind of gender syncretism which is an integral part of the group's ideological project.

The second site of gender performativity of the *parea* is dance. Although there are several dances that one can perform in a night-spot with Greek music, the most prominent and frequent ones are *tsifteteli* and *zeimbekiko*. *Tsifteteli* is an oriental rhythm performed as a belly-dance, and, although nowadays it is danced to by both men and women, it is considered to be a female rhythm. The dance involves sensuous and sometimes explicitly sexual movement of the body and it is almost always performed in pairs. When danced by a man and a woman, the man usually maintains a rather straight position avoiding too many embellishments and is said to 'escort' the woman. On the other hand, two women who dance *tsifteteli* are free to synchronise their movements and often have physical contact. The explicit gendered connotations of this specific dance make it highly popular among the girls of the *parea* who use *tsifteteli* in order to flirt, to flatter one another and generally enact femininity and desire.

The second dance that is preferred by the *parea* is *zeimbekiko* (plural: *zeimbekika*). *Zeimbekiko* is a powerful solo dance with such rich masculine significations that it started being performed by women only during the last decade or so, and in urban settings. In more traditional contexts, or back during the 1960s and 1970s, the reaction to a woman dancing to a *zeimbekiko* was so strong that in some places the musicians would stop playing for her and leave their instruments aside. As Cowan notes, *zeimbekiko* is the performance of *mangia* 'a tough, swaggering yet also introspective style of masculinity' (1990: 173). The *mangas*, the tough guy, is a persona born out of the specific socio-historical circumstances of post-1922 Greece. After the military defeat of the Greek army in Asia Minor in 1922 and the compulsory exchange of populations between Greece and Turkey under the auspices of the Lausanne treaty (1923) (cf. Hirschon, 1989: 6–14) more than a million Greek-speaking refugees landed in Greece. With them, they brought a specific oriental musical tradition that developed into what is known as *rembetiko* music.[25] The *rembetiko* is associated with a specific urban subculture of hashish smokers and petty thieves, many of them but not exclusively refugees, who mainly lived in Pireaus the Athenian port and a specifically working-class area.

> A *rebetis* or *mangas* was a person who lived outside the accepted standards of the traditional Greek society and who showed contempt for the establishment in all its forms: he didn't marry . . . bitterly hated the police and considered going to jail a mark of honour.
>
> (Petropoulos in Butterworth and Schneider, 1975: 11, quoted in Cowan, 1990: 174)

Zeimbekiko is the dance of *mangia par excellence*. Without specific steps, it rests on the originality and the talent of the dancer who engages in an almost esoteric pursuit of the perfect, controlled, intense performance that exists only for himself (Cowan, 1990: 175). For this reason the *zeimbekiko* dancer requires the dance floor exclusively for himself:

> Putting his lit cigarette between his lips, eyes on the floor, body tense and slightly crouched, arms loosely out to the sides, he begins to move slowly, deliberately around some fixed imaginary point on the floor . . . breaking the heavy tension of the dance with explosive outbursts of energy as in sudden leaps, hops, turns, squats. No one else gets up to dance; it would be an insult and a trespass on his impending emotional release . . . The man danced for himself.
>
> (Petrides in Butterworth and Schneider, 1975: 28–9, quoted in Cowan, 1990: 175)

Up until the 1970s and early 1980s, the person who wanted to dance a *zeimbekiko* usually made a request to the band, or as it is called in Greece 'an order' (*paraggelia*).[26] The band would acknowledge his request by announcing the name of the song and specifying that it is a *paraggelia*. Subsequently, the musicians would start playing the song and only the person who requested it had the right to go to the dance floor with his *parea*.[27] He would dance alone and his friends would crouch forming a circle or a semi-circle around him, and clap their hands as he performed difficult and acrobatic embellishments. To violate somebody else's special request by attempting to dance to it, was considered a major insult: so much so that, back in the 1960s, a man called Koemtzis stabbed some other customers who had thus insulted him in a *skylladiko* (*bouzouki* bar).

Most of the characteristics of the *zeimbekiko* remain intact today apart from two main features. Especially in towns and in places like *Harama* many people can dance a *zeimbekiko* simultaneously, while some of those dancers can be women. Although *bouzoukia* (night-clubs, which played Greek music that grew out of the *rembetiko* culture) were popular from the 1950s, Greek music (and specifically the old *rembetika*) became extremely trendy among people of various ages and socio-economic strata during the 1980s. Part and parcel of this new celebrating ethos that prevails in urban settings is a more active involvement of women in the production of *kefi* (high spirits). The expressive dancing of *zeimbekiko* is now practised by women as well as, if not more so than men, and consumption of strong alcoholic spirits is open to both genders. Nevertheless, *zeimbekiko* never lost its performative power and gendered connotations completely. Many young people in Greece admit that 'women do not dance *zeimbekiko* well', or praise an accomplished female performer by saying that 'she danced this *zeimbekiko* in a masculine way' (*andrika*).

Similarly to the young men of Sohos, the women of the *parea* dance *zeimbekiko* mainly in order to perform either *kapsoura* (infatuation with a woman), or in order to assert themselves according to the ethos of *eghoismos* (self-regard) (Herzfeld, 1985). As a Sohoian informant said: 'you dance either from anxiety or from enthusiasm . . . A desire, a past long gone, something upsets you, and you put it in your body. You are in love, crazy with love, and you don't understand a thing that's happening' (Cowan, 1990: 177). The girls of the *parea* maintain that they dance *zeimbekiko* because 'it has a certain weight' (*ehei varos*). As Martha, one of my informants epitomised:

> *Zeimbekiko* is not just a dance. It is a means of expressing a very specific masculine energy. It combines important and conflicting sentiments: indifference and at once total involvement, control and abandonment, dominance and submission. When you dance a *zeimbekiko* you feel like a king, like a God. All that is large becomes small and all that is small becomes large.

For the girls, *zeimbekiko* is in many ways, the dance of *eghoismos*, an extremely powerful masculine idiom of self-assertion always performed, as Herzfeld argues, on behalf of a collectivity be it one's family, village or region (1985: 11). The women of the group perform *eghoismos* on more than one occasion, mostly on behalf of the group as a whole. With special reference to dance, Cowan (1990: 177) pointedly argues that:

> however much the dancer [of *zeimbekiko*] dances for himself he only does so in a public setting. This stylised choreographic articulation of the lone self is always posed to a watching audience, and it is those youthful male peers who witness and, by their supporting gestures validate his performance. As a public performance of the inner self, *zeimbekiko* is externally directed; it is both a form and a forum for display [*epidiksi*].

The audience in the case of the *parea* is not only the women of the group, who indeed validate each other's performances, but all the Kallipoliot celebrants who happen to be present at *Harama*. By dancing in front of them, 'figuratively and sometimes actually', the girls also dance '*against* them' (Cowan, 1990: 177, original emphasis) thus using dance as a central feature of their politics of 'concealment and display' (cf. Herzfeld, 1987). It is then, mainly through dance and consumption, that the women of the *parea* present every night their selves 'in front of life', rather than simply 'within life' (Herzfeld, 1985: 11). By means of these self-presentations, the girls engage in an intersubjective process of creatively redefining genderhood, through practice as well as discursively. Hence, this book can be said to be about performances and their self-making power (cf. Sax, 2002) in the context of a group of women, whose 'efforts to imagine and to put into practice new ways of being . . . inevitably reflect, as they engage with, the contradictory dimensions of their everyday reality' (Cowan, 1991: 202).

Fieldworking

Although the fieldwork upon which this study is based was conducted between 1996 and 1998, my affiliation with the *parea* stretches back as early as 1994 and, in the eyes of the community, when I started my research I was already considered a member of the group. As several social analysts have pointed out, insider knowledge of a community is extremely helpful for it facilitates the establishment of higher levels of trust between the researcher and the social actors (cf. Finch, 1984; Dunne, 1997: 24). With special reference to the *parea*, the women do not allow anybody who has not been initiated into the group to closely follow their everyday lives.[28] My prior connection to the community was then, most certainly, the only reason I was allowed to be there as a researcher.

As I have already noted, the girls of the *parea* unanimously wish to keep their agenda private. None the less, when I suggested to them that I would write about the life of the group, they saw this as an opportunity to address themselves to a wider audience. They made it explicit, however, that it was my responsibility to ensure that nobody would be able to identify the community. 'You know very well, that what we are trying to achieve is the embodiment of dissonance and ambiguity' (*i ensarkosi tis diafonias kai tou amfilegomenou*), Rosita claimed. 'If they find out about us, they will target and classify us' (*tha mas valoun sto stoxastro, tha mas katigoriopoiisoun*), Aphrodite added and Maro agreed: 'From then on we will become history, a dead script in the library of some English university' (*nekro gramma sti vivliothiki kapoiou panepistimiou tis Agglias*). As Emily epitomised: 'Write about the *parea* and let the world know that somewhere there exist some women who dare imagine a different life. Write about our lives and our beliefs and our stories, but don't sell us down the river by giving away our real identities'.[29] Respecting their wish, I changed all their names, including that of the town, and I was careful to obscure even small details such as the driving distance from Kallipolis to Athens. As a result all the spatial and biographical information provided in the book is an approximation of the original. Still, I was careful not to tamper with the social connotations of any information referring to socio-economic and educational status.[30] Seen in this light, both my presence inside the group and the subsequent process of ethnographic documentation were always permeated by a 'sense of complicity' (Marcus, 1998: 126). For I was part of 'a women's world', that very much depended on a 'conspiracy of silence' as well as a strict politics of exclusion (cf. Abu Lughod, 1986: 27).

Apart from the concealment of their identities, the women of the community posed no other restrictions to me. Nevertheless, there were certain times when the girls resisted my ethnographic gaze (cf. Dubisch, 1995: 104). While I usually was unquestionably part of the group's 'backstage' (cf. Abu Lughod, 1986: 15), occasionally the women just refused to provide me with extensive narratives and postponed discussions concerning specific areas of their personal lives. The lived tension between unconditional inclusion on the one hand and the erection of boundaries – albeit temporal ones – on the other, was a part of the fieldwork which served to remind me that my ethnographic understanding of the community could not be achieved in a 'neutral manner'. As is true about all forms of social interaction, the research process was always 'negotiated and tested in an ambiguous and stressful field of interpersonal relations' (Jackson, 1998: 5). It was on the basis of these interpersonal relations that the women of the *parea*, especially those I was close with before the beginning of the research, often demanded that I behaved not as a researcher but as part of the group. As a result, the times when I was trying to keep notes while the girls insisted that I danced a *zeimbekiko* instead, were not rare.[31] Indeed as Marcus suggested: 'the scene of fieldwork and the object of study are . . . essentially coterminous, together establishing a culture situated in place and . . . learned about by one's presence *inside* it in sustained interaction' (1998: 113, original emphasis).

During the time I participated in the group's daily life, I observed, listened and urged the women to reflect extensively upon their ideas and practices (cf. Hammersley and Atkinson, 1995). Studying a community in Greece, however – being Greek myself – meant that I had to inquire into and record a familiar cultural context in a way that as a social actor I had never done before. This culture was undoubtedly not foreign to me. However, looking at it from the angle of the ethnographer entailed a deconstruction and a denaturalisation of my own daily experiences (cf. Panourgia, 1995). In many ways fieldwork was as much about 'my life' as that of 'those written about' (Denzin, 1997: xi).

It has been suggested that previous familiarity with the culture that one studies entails a desensitisation of the ethnographer (cf. Hastrup, 1987; Dubisch, 1995). Although this is true in many ways, it is also the case that as a researcher I often felt I did not fully belong either to the *parea* or to that 'abstraction called Greek culture' (Loizos, 1994: 78). Instead I was living, feeling and experiencing the fieldwork situation from the standpoint of a 'third culture' (Hastrup, 1987: 105), that of the ethnographer who sought to capture what was unfolding before her. For the knowledge I was searching for 'could only be represented through action, enactment or performance' (Fabian, 1990:

6, quoted in Pool, 1994: 22). Indeed, as Fabian has argued, the ethnographic information I was pursuing was 'not enacted', but 'produced' on the spot in the performances of the women of the *parea* (ibid.). It was knowledge established through action, instead of being already present in 'some cognitive reservoir' located either in the girls' heads or in mine (Pool, 1994: 22).

Seen in this light, my fieldwork was not about 'collecting facts', 'perceiving reality' or 'transforming encounters into data' (Ellen, 1984: 10; Crapanzano, 1977: 72). As all researchers, I too belong to multiple communities and hold multiple and conflicting identities that render objectivism a mere impossibility (Rosaldo, 1993: 193–4). In fact, it has been suggested that the discourse of objectivity is inevitably linked to a language of power (Abu-Lughod, 1990: 150; Herzfeld, 1987: 17) and 'gives ethnographers an appearance of innocence' that distances them from the political implications of their study (Rosaldo, 1993: 168–9). As Hastrup has noted, fieldwork is 'fundamentally confrontational and only superficially observational' (1992: 117). If the researcher adopts the stance of the distanced observer and moves away from the dialectical process between self and other (cf. Fabian, 1985: 20), then practice becomes a 'spectacle' (Bourdieu, 1977; Hastrup, 1992: 119) and fieldwork is reduced to observation instead of being an 'insight' (Hastrup, 1992: 119). According to Clifford, once social analysis moves away from 'visualism', the possibility of a cultural poetics – an 'interplay of voices' – is revealed (1986: 11, 12). Accepting an account of a social situation is always 'relational', thus I treated the process of fieldwork as 'social interaction, and dialogue', as a site of interindividual life and intersubjective experience (Jackson, 1998: 6). Throughout the period of my research, I adopted a reflexive stance that emphasises situatedness and partiality (Marcus, 1998: 198), being aware that the 'line between observer and observed' is inevitably blurred in an ethnographic dialogue (Dubisch, 1995: 115). An indispensable part of the fieldwork was to follow closely the group both physically and emotionally for lengthy periods of time. As a result, what I collected was 'experiences' which were subsequently transformed into ethnography, encounters with the women of the community rather than observations of their lives (cf. Crapanzano, 1977).

Having accepted the 'partiality of all claims to knowledge' (Marcus, 1998: 198) one cannot dismiss a basic methodological question, raised and explored extensively within the academic community, namely, the representational value of the ethnographic text as well as its epistemological validity and verisimilitude[32] (Radway, 1988; Fiske, 1994; Todorov, 1977; Stake, 1994; Geertz, 1973). There is a common consent by now among ethnographers that since discourse is always productive, a given 'text cannot be repeated without change in its meaning' (cf. Denzin, 1997: 36). Texts do not merely describe or reflect situations. They are situations in their own terms with a separate life (Clark and Holquist, 1984: 204; cf. also Denzin, 1997: 38; Derrida, 1976). The specificity and individuality of the writer are always present in the ethnographic text (Okely, 1983: 172; Ramazanoglou and Holland, 2002: 115), to the extent that ethnography itself has been characterised as an allegorical performance (Clifford, 1986). This does not mean, however, that ethnography does not have a representational value. For the ethnographic text and its composers (the author, the people studied and, to a great extent, the scholars whose ideas are summoned in a given ethnographic analysis) remain always part of a greater social and historical matrix. Ethnography, albeit subjectivist, is always a product of social interaction historically and politically situated in a given reality, and so is its audience. The ethnographic text's verisimilitude is then given in its 'ability to deconstruct the reproductions and simulations that structure the real' (Denzin, 1997: 13). The ethnographic reality, as a discursive text, represents 'not what actually happened beyond any doubt', but what one feels that happened (ibid.: 127), or in other words, just one standpoint and not a final account of reality (Smith, 1989; Harding, 1991; Ramazanoglou and Holland, 2002: 47–57). Aligning with these approaches that treat ethnographic analysis as relational and provisional, I often structure the ethnographic textualisation of this study around narratives that concentrate on individuals and the specific instances of their lives (cf. Abu Lughod, 1993: 27). Narrative as a form of social analysis has been mostly suppressed and marginalised by classic norms of ethnography (Rosaldo, 1993: 128). 'By [the classic writers'] aesthetic standards, truth was a mainly serious business: plain, unadorned, not witty, oblique and humanly engaging' (ibid.: 128). Contemporary ethnography, however, uses narrative as a way of bringing forward intercultural differences by allowing the informants to speak for themselves (Fisher, 1986; Dubisch, 1995). The narratives I recorded were not only verbal though. They were more often embodied tales that expressed 'personal sentiments about interpersonal situations' (cf. Abu Lughod, 1986: 27). In this sense, my ethnography is an ongoing story telling about the self/narrator/performer and the other/audience, but mostly about the relationship between the two.

While constructing the ethnographic text I had, however, to deal with a burning question: 'How does one document the stories of people who are sophisticated enough to speak for themselves'? (Dubisch, 1995: 15; cf. also Faubion, 1993; Marcus, 1988; Ramazanoglou and Holland, 2002: 112–15). I had to find a way of conveying these complex narrative instances of culture without 'objectifying' my experience (Clifford, 1986). Quoting the women was one way of ensuring that they were the true protagonists of the book. Occasionally treating myself as an informant was another means of questioning the ethnographic 'economy of truth' (Clifford, 1986: 7) through producing a highly subjective account of the research time (cf. De Certeau, 1983). Thus I decided to relate some of the women's verbal and bodily stories through my narration. As a result some of the ethnographic text that comprises this book is 'transported' out of my field notes. These paragraphs, like the narratives of the women themselves, appear in italicised form to indicate that they were written at a time different from that of the actual 'production' of ethnography. The purpose of developing this personal writing style was mainly to admit that ethnography is ultimately about the personal narrative of its author (Jackson, 1998).

All written texts, and ethnography is no exception, are 'moral and cultural productions' (Denzin, 1997: 39) that imitate reality instead of capturing it (Barthes, 1985; Denzin 1997: 42). The ultimate purpose of this book is thus not merely to depict the real (Fisher, 1986) but to uncover the subjective, the particular and the experiential. It is a 'performance text' that emphasises presentation and improvisation (Denzin, 1997: 116) ethnographically accounting for a group of women 'from the inside', while simultaneously seeking to 'reflect upon the epistemological grounding of such an account' (Marcus and Fisher, 1986: 26). The present ethnography is therefore allegorical (Clifford, 1986). Its aim is not to privilege one interpretation as the 'final, overriding version of the world' (Denzin, 1997: 55; cf. Ramazanoglou and Holland, 2002: 57–8), but rather, to acknowledge that fieldwork is a social drama (Hastrup, 1992: 118). The women I studied textualise their reality by inscribing it into ritualised performances (cf. Derrida, 1976; Clifford, 1986: 117). I do the same by writing. Whose form is more 'legitimate' is, sadly, something we know already. Whose form is more powerful, however, remains to be seen.

2

THEORETICAL REFLECTIONS

Gender and Greek ethnography

Largely examined in the contexts of marriage and kinship, gender has always been an important subject in the ethnographies of Greece (Loizos and Papataxiarchis, 1991a: 3–4; Cowan 1990: 8). Given that the early anthropological explorations of Greece developed within the frame of a larger project that strove towards the establishment of a conceptual unity of the Mediterranean cultures, the study of gender was initially tied to the theorisation of the cultural and moral values of 'honour and shame'.[1] On the basis of these values, anthropologists argued in favour of the cultural continuity of different *circum*-Mediterranean societies and tried to explain a number of cultural idioms and institutions in terms of the honour and shame code (Goddard, 1994: 60). According to this code, the position of a family in the social arena depends on the effective preservation of the reputation of its individual members (Dubisch, 1995: 196). The reputation of men, defended chiefly in the public sphere, relates to the energetic protection of their families' interests, as well as of the chastity of their wives, sisters mothers and daughters (ibid.). The honour of women, on the other hand, is seen as being related to the cultivation of shame, depending not only on their actual moral integrity but also on their reputation of being virtuous (Dubisch, 1995: 196). According to the cultural code of honour, a woman's reputation is less threatened if she stays in or close to the house, avoids gossip and fulfils her role as a mistress of the house, while a man's honour is 'claimed' and 'evaluated' in the public realm (ibid.: 197).

It has been argued that within this framework gender was repeatedly discussed, but not against the rich corpus of gender theory (Goddard, 1994: 58–9), a practice resulting in the ethnographic production of a fairly fixed set of representations of masculinity and femininity (Cowan, 1990: 9). The honour and shame literature was particularly criticised for portraying women as passive and subordinate (Goddard, 1996: 15) while maintaining an active, gendered distinction between the domestic and public realms (Dubisch, 1995: 196).[2] Although – especially since the late 1970s – the ethnographic studies of Greece grew increasingly independent of the honour and shame axis, gender was still seen as being largely realised through kinship and, at least for women, in the domestic sphere (cf. Loizos and Papataxiarchis, 1991). With reference to the anthropology of southern Europe in general, Goddard argues that the centrality of family and marriage in ethnographic studies is largely due to a tradition of anthropological training 'anchored in African systems of lineage' (1994: 68). The 'domestic model' of gender as Loizos and Papataxiarchis (1991a: 5) call it, can probably be traced back to the honour and shame tradition that promoted not only a behavioural but also a spatial separation of men and women (Dubisch, 1995: 196). The household as the site of domestic life and procreation *par excellence* was regarded as morally and physically linked to women (cf. du Boulay, 1974; Hirschon, 1978; Dubisch, 1986; Loizos and Papataxiarchis, 1991a), while men were portrayed as destined to realise themselves in the public sphere.

The rigid dichotomy between domestic and public against which gender was examined in Greece rested on a number of ethnographic assumptions that influenced not only the way identity was conceptualised but also the manner in which sexuality was portrayed. The focus on family and kinship meant that women's (and men's) sexualities were viewed, in Greek ethnography, as being realised through marriage and – more specifically for women – procreation. Furthermore, female sexuality in particular acquired a highly ambiguous status largely due to its implication for the honour of men and the reputation of the household as a whole. Inasmuch as female chastity was exhibited through aversion towards sexual activity and energetic attempts 'to disguise the physical attributes of [one's] sex' (Dubisch, 1995: 196), female informants often denied their own sexuality (cf. Handman, 1983; Hirschon, 1978; du Boulay, 1986). At the same time, since women's extra-curricular sexual activity was perceived as a threat to the men's honour, female sexuality was in a different context overemphasised often by the same informants (du Boulay, 1974). In turn, the sanctioning role that motherhood plays in female sexuality in the Greek context (Loizos and Papataxiarchis, 1991b: 223) created a strong ethnographic link between sexuality and procreation (ibid.).

The main weakness of such a one-dimensional theorisation of gender and sexuality is that it neglected the existence of contexts alternative to kinship that play an important role in the production of gender and sexual identities (Loizos and Papataxiarchis, 1991a: 4). As Goddard has argued with reference to Mediterranean societies in general, the overemphasis on kinship and the cultural values of honour and shame 'privileges heterosexuality and marginalises alternative sexualities as individuals and relationships are saturated with idioms derived from kinship' (1994: 83). Indeed, homosexual relations between either men or women in Greece is a topic that lacks ethnographic substantiation. Faubion accounts for male homosexual behaviour in Athens, noting that the notion – and practice – of male homosexuality is often trapped in the conventional bipolar model of the penetrating versus penetrated (1993: 220; cf. Loizos, 1994; Yannakopoulos, 2001: 172). Women on the other hand, can enter the masculine 'public' domain and as long as they do not abandon their domestic world, their energetic behaviour is valorised (Cowan, 1990; Faubion, 1993).[3] Conversely, Greek men are 'haunted' by the possibility of being associated with female behavioural roles and attributes, since such an identification could have possibly effeminising effects with devastating results on their masculinity (Loizos and Papataxiarchis, 1991b: 223; Herzfeld, 1985). Female homosexuality is, in turn, absent from ethnographic accounts; it is a sexual behaviour that although existent (as this book demonstrates) is largely overlooked and unrecognised by virtually all institutions (cf. Faubion, 1993; Loizos and Papataxiarchis, 1991a). As Faubion argues, homoerotic behaviour between women in Greece remains politically unthreatening so long as it is not considered specifically sexual (1993: 221).

Undoubtedly, the reasons for the invisibility of female homosexuality stretch far beyond the lack of ethnographic data on the subject. Nevertheless, the preoccupation with kinship and parenthood as central idioms for the construction of gender identities obscured the fact that different groups of people might hold distinct and even antithetical views with reference to gender realisation (cf. Cowan, 1990, 1991, 1992). In fact, as Goddard has argued, the tradition created by the honour and shame literature placed too much emphasis on 'consensus and cultural homogeneity' (1996: 14). In the context of the association of women with the household and of men with the public sphere, most of the ethnographers who specialise on Greece fostered a complementarity-based approach with reference to the roles of the sexes. The co-operation of women, as the agents who run the household, with men, who represent and defend it in the public arena, is seen by most ethnographers as a prerequisite for achieving a successful household (*noikonyrio*). Success in both the public and private spheres effects an affluent household, an achievement that brings prestige to both men and women, and is conceptualised by many ethnographers as an indication for the complementarity of gender roles in Greece (du Boulay, 1974, 1983; Salamone and Stanton, 1986; Papataxiarchis, 1992 among others).

The complementarity-based approach attempted to question the conceptual link between power and the public sphere. Most ethnographers in this tradition attempted to exemplify the domestic power of women – who are indispensable agents of the overall success of the household – as no less important than that of men. Nevertheless, the relationship between power and prestige gained through the successful running of a household was eventually questioned (Dubisch, 1986), particularly since 'complementarity implies equality' (Cowan, 1990: 11). Indeed, examining the majority of Greek ethnographies, one could argue that it is women who are imagined and constructed in Greek culture to complement men and from this point of view complementarity most certainly describes gender relations in this particular cultural context. As Cowan argues, offering specific ethnographic substantiation, instances of complementarity should not be disengaged from the generally asymmetrical relations found between the sexes in Greece (ibid.).

The ethnographic association of women and men with the domestic and public spheres, respectively, was increasingly disputed by ethnographers who stressed the possibility of ethnographic bias (Hirschon, 1984; Dubisch, 1986, 1992; Cowan, 1992). The portrayal of women as domestic and restricted was criticised by Dubisch who pointed to the powerful public performances of female pilgrims on the island of Tinos (1995: 195). Hirschon has also argued that the ethnographer's own (western) perceptions of power and its link with the public context have hindered and explicitly shaped the ethnographic analyses of Greece (1984: 19). Salamone and Stanton have also claimed that the household (*noikokyrio*) should not be viewed exclusively as the domestic domain for it extends to both private and public spheres (1986). As such, the domestic realm cannot be viewed as less social and therefore invested with less power (Dubisch, 1986).

It can be safely argued that the ethnographies of Greece grew less and less concerned with an analysis of gender based on complementary oppositions. As Herzfeld argued, such theoretical schemata separated women and men, and represented gender as a set of fixed roles and categories (1986a). At the same time, the all-pervasive domestic model of gender and sexuality was effectively questioned by Loizos and Papataxiarchis who promoted a particularistic view of gender (1991). The papers included in their edited volume provided ethnographic validation for the existence of alternative discourses and contexts in relation to gender-realisation (ibid.). Acknowledging the diversity of Greek culture, many ethnographers became increasingly uncomfortable with the portrayal of Greek society as one homogenous matrix (Faubion, 1993; Herzfeld, 1986; Loizos and Papataxiarchis, 1991a; Panourgia 1995), claiming that one can no longer 'assume consensus about the meanings of male and female in contemporary Greece' (Cowan, 1991: 201). In the Greek ethnographic context gender is thus steadily escaping its conventional conceptualisation as a set of fixed and inescapable roles. A more substantial theorisation of the relation between gender and power is pursued, while the contextual and performative character of identity is more widely acknowledged (Loizos and Papataxiarchis, 1991a; Loizos, 1994; Herzfeld, 1985; Cowan, 1990; Dubisch, 1995; Danforth, 1982, 1989). The ethnographic textualisations of Greece become increasingly concerned with the 'differences within' (Moore, 1993) establishing the existence of masculinities and femininities in the region (cf. Loizos, 1994). Within the bounds of this ethnographic trend, the present work offers a unique documentation of gender performativity and accounts for alternative discourses on sexuality in Greece. Gender is viewed here as multiple, fluid and context-dependent, as a series of performances that uncover no essence, no essential truths behind them. I propose that gender identity is best understood as the creative orchestration of performative layers that sometimes crystallises, and at other times, subverts the hegemonic notions of genderhood.

The ethnographic depiction of the life of the *parea* and particularly the women's performances reveal the existence of alternative narratives on gender that nevertheless depend on familiar cultural idioms of masculinity and femininity. It is for this reason that throughout the book I do not hesitate to employ comparative ethnographic examples of both men and women in order to illuminate the meaning of my informants' idiosyncratic performative utterances. In this sense, my work is concerned with performative texts, whose meaning is established intersubjectively, and which comprise rather than merely express the cultural selves of their protagonists as well as of my own self who came to be so critically involved in this process of textualisation.

Homosexualities

Although homosexual practices have been documented in different cultures and across historical periods, the category 'homosexual' is a relatively recent, western invention (Somerville, 1997). According to Foucault (1976) and other social analysts (MacIntosh, 1968; Weeks, 1979, 1987; Somerville, 1997; Greenberg, 1997) sexual practices did not define individual identities before the nineteenth century. Homosexuality as a term implicated in the engendering of a specific gender and sexual identity evolved between the seventeenth and nineteenth centuries (Green, 1997: 124). Fashioned in 1869, the word homosexual gained considerable currency among sexologists and academics towards the end of the nineteenth century, and marked a new era in the conceptualisation of homoerotic relations (Jivani, 1997: 13). For the first time a strong link was established between sexual practices and sexual identities that rendered the homosexual 'a personage, a past, a case history . . . a species' (Foucault, 1976: 43). From this period sexuality was medicalised, psychoanalysed, biologised, normalised and finally naturalised in a binary frame that distinguished between homosexual and heterosexual bodies, between productive and unproductive sexualities and finally between individuals (cf. Giddens, 1992; Foucault, 1976; Somerville, 1997). The model of sexuality constructed by the sexologists of the late nineteenth and early twentieth centuries was based on a discourse of scientific reason and objectivity. Nevertheless, as it was argued, it promoted in fact a hierarchical model of a sexually divided society (Jackson, 1987: 52) where homosexuality was established as the predicament of certain people and heterosexuality was identified with normality (Weeks, 1987: 35).

With particular reference to women, the creation of the term 'lesbian' coincided with specific social and political changes. Studies in North America and Britain reveal that until the nineteenth century romantic friendships between upper-class women were not only socially legitimate but also acknowledged as a suitable kind of emotional training for marriage and heterosexuality (Faderman, 1981). With the emergence of the feminist movement, women started pursuing their own economic independence, and relations with other women, beyond heterosexual marriage, were becoming increasingly possible (Faderman, 1981; Green, 1997: 126). The category lesbian, timely constructed by the sexologists, contributed significantly to the prohibition of romantic friendships and the creation of an artificial distinction between 'normal' (i.e. heterosexual) women and 'congenital inverts' (i.e. lesbians) (Faderman, 1993: 33; Gunter, 1998: 86).

It can be said that the sexological literature legitimised a number of western folk beliefs and served the interests of dominant groups by canonising sexuality (Jackson, 1987: 52), thus proving that 'gender is a site of ideological struggle', intrinsically related to power (Cowan, 1991: 201, 1990). The study of different cultures, however, indicates the existence of heterogeneous sexual activities. Homosexual behaviour – connected with or disconnected from a homosexual identity – has been registered by many ethnographers (Herdt, 1981, 1994; Nanda, 1990, 1994; Roscoe, 1994; Johnson, 1997; Kulick, 1998; Shepherd, 1987; Kendall, 1999; Blackwood and Wieringa, 1999; Green, 1997; Dunne, 1997). One of the most important theoretical insights gained through such studies is that homosexual activity was often thought of and analysed within a western cultural framework (Whitehead, 1981). Cultural notions of homosexuality, dominant in the west, frequently coloured the way researchers approached homosexual behaviour and consequently gender in other cultures (cf. Roscoe, 1994). Meticulous ethnographic research, however, demonstrates that sexuality-based classifications are far from universal (cf. Herdt, 1994; Whitehead, 1981; Wieringa and Blackwood, 1999) and thus, a binary gender model cannot account for the cultural variations observed with reference to sexual conduct or identity (Roscoe, 1994; Nanda, 1994).

The extraordinary diversity of notions concerning sexuality and gender strengthens the argument that sexual practices need to be contextualised before their meaning can be effectively explored, let alone generalised (Whitehead, 1981). Particularly when it comes to lesbian studies, ethnographers have documented a wide variety of discourses on sexuality and identity (cf. Wieringa and Blackwood, 1999). Multiple and contradictory ideologies exist even within communities that generally share a common definition of female homosexuality (Green, 1997). Racial, social, cultural and generational factors prevent ethnographers from treating all forms of homosexual expression the same, or from speaking about one homogenous lesbian or gay community (de Lauretis, 1994: 29; Whitehead, 1981). As Plummer notes, it is 'intellectually naive' and 'politically conservative' to deal with homosexuality as a simple category (1992: 12). The diverse and heterogeneous experiences and identities within the gay trajectory, many authors argue, simply cannot be forced into a unified explanatory scheme (cf. Plummer, 1992; de Lauretis, 1994; Greenberg, 1997). Homosexual desire and/or homosexual acts not only cannot define (sexual) identity *per se*, but also there are times when they appear disengaged from the very identification of the actors with a homosexual role (Caplan, 1987). Identification with a lesbian identity for instance, rather than simply being anchored in specific sexual practices or desires, is for many, part of a much more complex process of belonging or dealing with female oppression (Rich, 1980; Green, 1997: 17).

Within the field of lesbian studies, the theoretical acknowledgement of the instability of the category 'lesbian' – like that of the category 'heterosexual' – fuelled a wider debate in relation to issues of identity and ethnographic representation. Wieringa and Blackwood (1999) have argued that the meaning of the terms gay or lesbian is not necessarily shared cross-culturally. The category 'lesbian' born in the west and at a specific historical moment, cannot effectively encompass various forms of same-sex behaviour and does not necessarily constitute a universally shared identity marker (ibid.: 19; Greenberg, 1988: 484). Apart from the ethnographic use of the term lesbian the adoption of a lesbian identity is another perplexing issue that troubles feminist theorists. The lesbian movement, as it has been developed in the west, aimed at the construction of a stable collective identity in its attempt to de-medicalise and reclaim the category 'lesbian' (Stein, 1997: 380). Many lesbian communities believed in the authenticity of both womanhood and lesbianism (cf. Green, 1997: 10; Stein, 1997) finding themselves on the edge of fostering a totalising discourse on identity. A number of feminist theorists pointed out that to classify oneself as a lesbian means the privileging of one identity, one subject position above others; it necessarily excludes a number of options, thus promoting a fixed and unified model of the self (Weeks, 1987: 31; Butler, 1991; Wieringa and Blackwood, 1999; di Leonardo and Lancaster, 1997). Not all those who engage at one point or another in some forms of homosexual practice wish to identify themselves as gay or homosexual either for personal or for political reasons (Weeks, 1987; Fuss, 1991: 5). Furthermore, as Fuss has argued, 'how does one know s/he is gay' (1991: 6) since 'sexual identity is less a function of knowledge than performance . . . less a matter of final discovery than perpetual reinvention' (ibid.: 6–7).

Identity categories are notoriously unstable and each person occupies more than one at any given moment of their lives (di Leonardo and Lancaster, 1997: 67; Butler, 1991: 14). Still, the term lesbian is a viable political emblem mainly because it calls for the endorsing of the differences within women by disempowering the system of intolerance towards non-normative sexual choices (Wieringa and Blackwood, 1999: 21; di Leonardo and Lancaster, 1997: 3). When theorising same-sex behaviour, however, one has to acknowledge that s/he is dealing with 'homosexualities', rather than homosexuality, multiple and variant sexual expressions that carry distinct meanings and can only be analysed in their cultural, social and historical context. Homosexual behaviour, like any other form of sexual behaviour, desire and identification, cannot but be intimately connected to specific socio-historical contingencies that give rise to certain possibilities of identities and discourses. The normative, artificial and hierarchical distinction of sexuality into homocentric and heterocentric is a discourse mostly cultivated in the west and in this light it has to be analysed and deconstructed.

Sexuality, sex and gender

The medicalisation of sexuality in the west through the development of what Foucault called 'scientia sexualis' (1976: 71) is not unrelated to the growing influence of social Darwinism towards the end of the previous century (Caplan, 1987). The idea that survival is intrinsically bound with sexual selection, privileged biology and tied sexuality to reproduction (Weeks, 1987). Sexual differentiation, perceived in the Darwinian model as a sign of evolution, led sexologists to the characterisation of certain bodies as anomalous and subsequently to their dismissal (Somerville, 1997). According to Jackson, the 'scientific model' instituted by the sexologists of the twentieth century universalised and naturalised heterosexuality and female submission (1987: 71). Sex and subsequently gender were thus examined within a naturalist and essentialist framework. At best, sexuality was conceived as a representation of what is real, objective and natural while maleness and femaleness were rendered universal (Abramson, 1987: 195, 197).

The view that sexuality is a universal human drive was central to the promotion of the idea that heterosexuality is the only normal sexual expression (Caplan, 1987; Weeks, 1987; Ross and Rapp, 1997). Exclusive heterosexuality is thus, far from being chosen, a socially produced instituted process intimately related to a number of other institutions (Cucchiari, 1981: 38–9; Plummer, 1992; Dunne, 1997). According to Foucault, modern industrial societies transformed sexuality, through the policing of sex, into an 'economic' and 'political' behaviour (1976: 25–6), an observation which amply demonstrates that 'sexuality is not a drive but an especially dense transfer point for relations of power' (ibid.: 103). By effectively questioning the idea of sexual repression, Foucault saw sexuality as a culturally shaped form of human behaviour mobilised by power, rather than as an innate biological force (1976; Giddens, 1992).

Foucault's conclusion that sexuality is the aftermath of power relations firmly established in a specific historical period, is shared by a number of scholars. Anthropologists were especially qualified to argue that sexuality is a culturally specific and contextual form of human expression (Elliston, 1999: 244). What is sexual in one context might not be in another (Caplan, 1987) while sexual behaviour is not only shaped by social contexts but also evaluated by them (Elliston, 1999: 244). Undoubtedly, sexuality cannot 'escape its cultural connection' (Caplan, 1987: 25); it is a cultural construct and not merely a biological idiom (de Lauretis, 1997; Giddens, 1992; Ross and Rapp, 1997) that relates to issues of race, class, and the exercise of power (Somerville, 1997; Caplan, 1987; Seidler, 1987; Giddens, 1992). According to McNay, the portrayal of sex as natural leads to the consolidation of diverse bodily functions into a 'unifying notion of natural heterosexuality' that obscures the relation of sexuality and power (1992: 29). The conceptualisation of sexuality as pre-social does not only hinder the appreciation of its complexity as a sphere invested with power (Jackson, 1987). The 'naturalisation' and 'biologisation' of sexuality often go hand in hand and indeed facilitate the promotion of other scientific discourses such as scientific racism (cf. Somerville, 1997; Alsop *et al.* 2001: 20–7), while the marking of bodies is clearly related to phenomena such as ethno-nationalism and political violence (Johnson, 1997: 12).

Most branches of gender and feminist scholarship now agree that the construction of sexuality is an always-unfinished process that involves a series of intersubjective identifications. Within this framework, sexuality can be understood as a 'lived relationship and not an essence whose content is fixed' (Ross and Rapp, 1997: 163). I would also argue that sexual identifications are not only conceptually or symbolically reworked by the subject but also practically established consciously or unconsciously. In this sense, sexuality is not only a culturally constructed regulatory ideal, but also a practically or performatively instituted idiom or, in other words, not simply a subject of discourse but also a matter of practice.

The cultural character of sexuality is a central theme in any discussion of sex and gender, and especially with reference to the relationship between these two categories that has not always been simple. More specifically, the preoccupation of some of the representatives of the feminist scholarship to establish that gender is socially constructed introduced in effect a dichotomy between sex and gender (cf. Yanagisako and Collier, 1987). In this framework, gender was not regarded as resting on a biological basis itself but it was nevertheless seen as the cultural illustration of biological sex difference (Moore, 1994: 12, 1999). The distinction between sex and gender, mainly established in the 1970s, was intended to challenge these models that viewed gender as the continuation of some 'natural' sex and therefore as being itself rooted in 'natural' difference (cf. Butler, 1991: 27). In effect though, it reintroduced a dichotomy between nature and culture obscuring the fact that both categories rather than being pre-social or ahistorical entities, are deeply rooted in specific discursive contexts (MacCormack, 1980). To paraphrase a notable argument put forward by Strathern (1980), there is no nature as the blueprint of culture and no culture as the elaboration of naturally fixed givens. Collier and Yanagisako argued against the distinction between sex and gender pointing out that biological differences although existent (not only between women and men but also between women and between men) do not necessarily form the basis for the categories male and female cross-culturally (1987: 15).

> Rather than taking for granted that 'male' and 'female' are two natural categories of human beings whose relations are everywhere structured by their difference, we ask whether this is indeed the case in each society we study. . . . Although we do not deny that biological differences exist between men and women (just as they do among men and among women) our analytic strategy is to question whether these differences are the universal basis for the cultural categories 'male' and

> 'female'. In other words, we argue against the notion that cross-cultural variations in gender categories and inequalities are merely diverse elaborations and extensions of the same natural fact.
>
> (Yanagisako and Collier 1987: 15)

In this sense, gender differences are not merely the effects of discourse on some fixed natural facts. For if gender was the social representation or construction of sex this would mean that sex is absorbed and replaced by gender (Butler, 1997a: 534, 1993: 5). In so far as gender is not the cultural elaboration of sex, it cannot also be its discursive origin (Moore, 1999: 154–5). The theoretical isolation of sex from gender depoliticises both categories (Wieringa and Blackwood, 1999: 14) while effectively neutralising the body that becomes a mere surface upon which the discursive effects of culture are inscribed (McNay, 1992: 22, 2000). The historical and constitutive importance of the body in the theorisation of sex and gender and ultimately of subjectivity is indeed notable. Thus before presenting a theoretical framework within which gender and identity can be effectively explored, I intend to briefly examine the role of the body as a site of performative establishment and reflexive enactment of gender subjectivities.

The body

The need to speak about the embodied dimension of subjectivity has been noted by numerous scholars. Social theorists now agree that the body, far from being a natural and ahistorical object is a culturally constituted 'lived anatomy' (Moore, 1994: 22), heavily involved in the fashioning of gender identity (Cowan, 1990; Grosz, 1994; Moore, 1994; Butler, 1990, 1993, 1997; Giddens, 1992; de Lauretis, 1994). The centrality of the body in much of contemporary theory is directly related to its former position in the dominant philosophical paradigm of the Enlightenment (McNay, 1992). The discursive construction of the body as natural and thus distinct from the symbolic processes that take place in the mind is rooted in the Cartesian conceptualisation of the subject that rested on the hierarchical opposition between mind and body[4] (ibid.: 12–13). Long before the natural sciences objectified the body, the seeds of its exclusion from the symbolic realm were planted by Cartesian dualism that opened the way for the objectification and medicalisation of the body and, finally, for its rejection as a proper object of study for the humanities and social sciences (Grosz, 1994: 8, 9).

Through the body and its biological and reproductive activities women were linked to nature, and the mind/body distinction became incorporated and even facilitated the male/female opposition (Grosz, 1994; McNay, 1992: 18). The early feminist reaction to the perception of women as tied to nature through reproduction was to think of the body as a constraint, an 'obstacle that had to be overcome' for the sake of the establishment of equality (Grosz, 1994: 16).

Within this early perspective the body was identified as the material basis for women's oppression, however, its discursive naturalisation was not sufficiently questioned. In its attempt to denaturalise it, the first wave of social constructionism treated the body as a neutral surface that accepted the effects of discourse, unlike language which was perceived to be the uncontested territory for the politics of gender construction (ibid.: 17). Criticising this 'linguistic monism', theorists like Judith Butler came to pose burning questions: 'if everything is discourse, what about the body?' (1993: 6). For if the body is merely a surface upon which the effects of discourse are inscribed, then it has to be pre-discursive and thus purely natural (Butler, 1993, 1997a: 535). Clearly, such a theorisation of the body reintroduced, in effect, the naturalistic biases it sought to deconstruct.

Foucault is undoubtedly one of the most prominent theorists who dealt with the body not as an essentialist notion but as a site of political struggle (Braidotti, 1991). Showing how the body has become both an object and a target of power, Foucault engaged in an analysis of a political rather than a physical anatomy (1976; 136, 138). Without denying the material dimension of the body, and by concentrating on the productive effects of disciplinary power, Foucault stressed both the political and cultural character of the body (cf. McNay, 1992: 30; Braidotti, 1991). Most importantly, through his conceptualisation of the body as a field of power relations, he 'redefined subjectivity in terms of bodily materialism' (Braidotti, 1991: 78). Foucault demonstrated that the 'man [*sic*] of modern humanism was born' out of 'meticulous but often minute' disciplinary techniques which he called 'the microphysics of power' (Foucault, 1977: 139, 141). Furthermore, with the concept of bio-power, Foucault successfully linked the disciplinary construction of bodies with the historical contingencies of industrial societies. He claimed that from the seventeenth century onwards, power was directed towards life instead of death:

> there was an explosion of numerous and diverse techniques for achieving the subjugation of bodies and the control of populations marking the beginning of an era of 'bio-power' . . . This bio-power was without question an indispensable element in the development of capitalism.
>
> (1976: 140)

Foucault's work on the body received two major criticisms: the first related to the lack of a sufficient theorisation of human agency and is connected to his portrayal of the body as a passive surface upon which the effects of power are inscribed (McNay, 1992: 12, 2000). The second criticism relates to Foucault's 'gender blindness' in examining the specific character of many of the disciplinary techniques that produced a specific model of the female body and sexuality (ibid.: 11, 18). Despite the critiques, Foucault has definitely marked a new era in the study of embodied subjectivity. Creatively reworked, his lack of focus on individual autonomy, although problematic as it stands, could potentially demonstrate what Braidotti calls 'the non-coincidence of the subject with his or her consciousness' (1991: 282). With special reference to the construction of gender identity, Foucault's theory of the body illustrates how the process of gendering does not always require the mediation of consciousness, but it can be to a certain extent the direct result of power relations (Foucault, 1980, in Braidotti, 1991: 77).

Although Foucault's view of the body continues to be widely acknowledged, the idea that the body is a passive entity is being consistently attacked (Gatens, 1990: 152). The body is now regarded by most theorists not as a 'biological *tabula rasa*' but as a social, cultural and historical site (Grosz, 1994: 18; cf. Braidotti, 2002: 20–1), not an 'anatomical destiny' but one's 'primary position in reality' (Braidotti, 1991: 219). At a social level, the body and more particularly the female body is often representative of cultural boundaries (Goddard, 1996; Okely, 1983; Hirschon, 1978, 1989: 146) thus constituting an intersecting point of the material and the symbolic (Braidotti, 1991: 282, 2002: 25; Moore, 1999: 168). Human bodies 'in-corporate social meaning' through daily practice (Cowan, 1990: 23) and are thus a means of making sense of and internalising cultural values (Bell, 1992: 97). Hence, it can be argued that embodiment pertains to the fashioning of gender subjectivity albeit not as its only location, but rather as one of the crucial fields where gender is constituted and realised (Moore, 1994).

Grosz (1994) summarises all the above ideas offering a plausible theoretical approach to the body that can be briefly outlined: in her view, the body has to be conceptualised outside the binary frame of body versus mind and outside singular models (ibid.: 21). According to Grosz, there is not one representative (and thus normative) body, but bodies that encompass difference, richness and variability. Corporeality can no longer be associated with one sex while biologised and essentialist accounts of the body only succeed in marking it as an opposition to culture (ibid.: 22, 23). For her, the body is a cultural product, one that is neither solely 'public, self or other, natural or cultural' (ibid.: 23) but a concept occupying all those positions (1990: 46) and thus a 'transitional entity' (McNay, 2000: 32). Viewing the body as a sociocultural artefact while acknowledging its materiality, further illuminates its relationship with sex and gender, not as one of nature and culture but as a mutually productive interface. As Strathern argues with reference to Melanesian culture, 'persons are not axiomatically conceived as single-sex' (1988: 122). In other words, the body is not the natural basis for the establishment of sex and gender cross-culturally. Instead, it can be understood as the site where sexual conditions and relations are constituted. In this sense gender can be regarded as a 'corporeal style' (Butler, 1990: 140), one that is consciously or unconsciously enacted.

Undoubtedly the issue of reflexivity remains a major one here. According to Bourdieu the subject can never become fully aware of its social construction

(1977). Bourdieu devised a theory of practice according to which 'objects of knowledge are constructed' around the principle of the habitus (1990: 52). The habitus, Bourdieu argues is an historical effect which itself creates more history by producing individual and collective practices (1990: 53). The concept of habitus (originally exemplified by Mauss[5]) accounts in Bourdieu's approach for 'structuring principles' inscribed in the 'body' and 'thought', established and exemplified through practice (1977, 1990: 53). The body has in a sense a practical knowledge that can never be fully reflected upon or verbalised, or intentionally transformed since it lies 'beyond the grasp of consciousness' (1977: 94). The habitus can be collective inasmuch as it is regarded as the site of social distinctions, although Bourdieu acknowledges 'personal style' as well (cf. Moore, 1994: 79).

There are two major problems identified in Bourdieu's approach: first the lack of recognition of reflexivity (cf. Cowan, 1990), and second the fact that his scheme does not fully acknowledge internal multiplicity (cf. Moore, 1994; McNay, 2000: 72). With reference to the notion of reflexivity and as far as gender is concerned, it would be tremendously difficult to argue that the process of gendering is not compulsory (cf. Butler, 1993: 231). Femininity and masculinity are not entirely a matter of choice but 'a forcible citation of a norm' (ibid.: 232), realised in 'posture, in the gestures and movements of the body . . . in the opposition between straight and bent . . . directness and restraint, reserve and flexibility' (Bourdieu, 1990: 69–70). Nevertheless, as Cowan argues, there are contexts where the actor becomes increasingly aware of her body, 'reflexively conscious' of the fact that 'she is a body and she has a body' (1990: 24). In a detailed discussion of Bourdieu's writings McNay argues that Bourdieu produces a much less determinist account of the body than Foucault. Examining the importance of praxis and Bourdieu's idea of the 'field'[6] she maintains that his theory offers a more balanced interpretation of 'how the autonomous subject emerges from constraint' (2000: 72).

With reference to the second point, given that the self always occupies more than one category, the body can be seen as the intersection point of different discourses and practices, a corporeal manifestation of multiplicity and even ambiguity. Bourdieu himself maintains that the process of embodiment is never finished (cf. Moore, 1994; Bourdieu, 1990). It is thus possible to think of the gendered body not only as a medium for the constellation of social values, but also as a field where gender ideals undergo a constant, albeit subtle, transformation. From the beginning of its existence the embodied subject is in a constant dialogue with a possible array of socio-cultural, material and symbolic spatio-temporal contexts. Any difference in the construction of the body entails a differentiation in the construction of the self as embodied (Synnott, 1993: 37). In other words, it is likely that the process of embodiment entails both a reiteration and a reformulation of gender ideas and relations.

Towards a performative approach to gender

The present work adopts a performative approach to gender, for I believe that the theory of performativity with all its faults and weakness allows for the conceptualisation of gender not as a fixed category but as an intersubjective process. Hence, in this last section I intend to outline a framework for the understanding of gender with special reference to the women-subjects of this book.

It can be argued that gender is not simply a fixed attribute of the person, but the point of interaction between subjective experience, cultural ideals, social values and power relations. In this sense, the construction of gender identity is implicated in the fashioning of subjectivity as a whole (cf. Goddard, 1996: 239). It is safe to claim that any kind of identity, including gender, is not unchanging, pre-social or immune to historical contingencies but constituted both practically and discursively in an intersubjective manner (cf. McNay, 1992; de Lauretis, 1994, 1997; Moore, 1994). Practice, what people do, all forms of human action (Rabinow, 1996: 6) and also what people often refrain from doing, is heavily involved in the construction of identity. So long as gender is practically as well as discursively instituted it has no fixed essence (Kirkham and Attfield, 1996; Butler, 1990). Every time gender is enacted it is both interpreted and realised contextually (cf. Moore, 1986; Butler, 1990, 1993, 1997a). When the subject is engaged in a certain form of performativity, s/he simultaneously constitutes a given performative idiom and is constituted by it (Butler, 1990). That is, s/he informs a certain socio-cultural image and is shaped by this image through internalising it and identifying with it (Johnson, 1997).

The conceptualisation of gender as performative rather than expressive (cf. Kirkham and Attfield, 1996; Butler, 1990) implies a dramaturgical approach not only to gender identity but also to the self (Greenberg, 1997). Social life can be seen as a theatre (Dubisch, 1995) where not only masculinities and femininities but the very awareness of the self is developed and tested through performance. Within the framework of such a performative approach to gender and identity, Judith Butler introduced the notion of performativity (1990, 1993, 1997a). According to Butler, performativity is not an act but the rehearsal of a 'norm' or a 'set of norms' that acquires an 'act-like status' (1997a: 538). Butler maintains that gender is always a 'doing' by a subject that does not exist 'prior to the deed', and in this sense performativity is not deliberate (1990: 25, 1994: 2). To the extent that gender performativity is constitutive, a means by which discourse materialises and produces what it names (Butler, 1990, 1997b), 'gender is a construction that regularly conceals its genesis' (1990: 140).

Through emphasising the fluidity and poetic character of performance (cf. Battaglia, 1999), the theory of performativity focuses on the possibility of challenging normative gender and is thus characterised as a theory of resistance

(Moore, 1999: 156). The main criticisms it has received revolve around the emphasis on ambiguity and individual agency. With reference to individual agency, it was noted that the theory of performativity implies that gender identity is partly culturally constructed and partly fashioned by the individual through mixed performances that introduce a break between sexual practices, sexed bodies and gender identities (McNay, 1992: 71; Moore, 1999: 156; Butler, 1990, 1993, 1997a). The counter-argument, often informed by anthropological data, is that gender identity is not always a subject of conscious choice (McNay, 1992: 71; Moore, 1999: 158). Nevertheless, I believe that this criticism is based on a misinformed reading of the performative approach that conflates performance and performativity. Butler draws a distinction between performativity and performance (1993). Performativity for her is more than enacting gender; it involves the repetition of norms 'which precede, constrain and exceed the performer' (1993: 234). What Butler strives to avoid through the notion of performativity is the promotion of a strategic kind of reflexivity, thus establishing the fact that gender is not always subject to the conscious will of the actor, or to a cognitive monitoring of the self (cf. Butler, 1993, 1997a). Butler argues that 'there is no volitional subject . . . who decides which gender it will be today . . . gender is not a performance but a performative in the sense that it constitutes as an effect the very subject it appears to express' (1991: 24).

The second criticism focuses on the idea that the notion of ambiguity employed by performative approaches does not have the explanatory potential to exhaust the issues of sex and gender (Moore, 1999: 156; McNay, 2000). Ambiguity is indeed a central theme in performativity theory since gender performances often entail the deconstruction and reassociation of the semiotics of gender (cf. Battaglia, 1999: 128). Gender identity is seen in this theoretical framework as performative in the sense that it is instituted through corporeal and discursive means (Butler, 1990). In turn, various practices of gender-bending, like cross-dressing, are seen as parodic performances that reveal the originality of normative gender as illusory (Butler, 1990: 137, 1991: 23) and break the continuity between body, practice and identity. Judith Butler, reflecting upon 'drag performances' or parodies of gender as she calls them, states:

> If the anatomy of the performer is already distinct from the gender of the performer and both of these are distinct from the gender of the performance, then the performance suggests a dissonance not only between sex and performance, but sex and gender, and gender and performance.
>
> (1990: 137)

Nevertheless, performative theory does not imply that the ambiguity of parody is only about the resistance and deconstruction of normative gender as suggested in the critiques (cf. Moore, 1999: 156). The flexibility and ambiguity of performance reifies cultural ideals as much as it induces their questioning. In order to ethnographically substantiate my argument I shall refer to Kulick's (1998) work with Brazilian transvestites, one of the most eloquent anthropological enquiries into the performative character of gender. According to Kulick, the 'travestis' of Salvator – to use the local term – are unique as far as they combine female physical characteristics with a male homosexual subjectivity (1998: 6). Through ingesting hormones and injecting considerable amounts of industrial silicone directly into their bodies, the 'travestis' achieve female bodily features. At the same time, they refuse to undergo a sex-change operation and they do not regard themselves as women. In his ethnographic work, Kulick demonstrates that the 'travestis' draw on a specific cultural system within which the possession of a certain type of genitalia is a secondary source of gender identification to the use of these genitals (1998). In other words, males become men through penetrating and homosexuals through allowing themselves to be penetrated. Here, sexuality rather than sex is the key element around which the gender system revolves (Kulick, 1998: 227). This scheme is by no means unique to Brazil. The idea that somebody is effeminised by being penetrated can also be found in Philippines (cf. Johnson, 1997), in Turkey (Tapinc, 1992) and in Greece (cf. Loizos, 1994; Yannakopoulos, 2001). It is probably this penetrator–penetrated schema that produces what Kulick calls three modes of gender identification: that of the man, that of the woman and that of the homosexual who is 'structurally equivalent' to women although biologically distinct (1998: 226, 229). Kulick criticises the interpretation forwarded by many theorists that 'travestis' belong to a third gender. In fact he maintains that they share the same gender (although not the same sex) with women, and through performing femininity they further substantiate rather than invert the traditional gender roles of their cultural context.

At least four basic theoretical implications arise from Kulick's ethnography. First, anatomical sex is not always the primary source of gender identification (cf. Butler, 1990). Second, gender is not only socially constructed but performatively established, either through the appropriation of a certain sexuality (cf. Kulick, 1998; Johnson, 1997) and/or through the exhibition of certain behavioural traits (cf. Herzfeld, 1985; Loizos and Papataxiarchis, 1991a). Third, sexuality, like gender, is culturally constructed since sexual practices and erotic desire have never 'sprung into being ex-nihilo' and 'cannot exist in a vacuum' (Caplan, 1987: 10, 25; di Leonardo and Lancaster, 1997: 1). Finally, as Kulick argues, a gender system that revolves around sexuality where biological males who do not behave like men, are not men, produces 'transsexual subjectivities' (1998: 227). It is precisely this observation that relates to the fourth theoretical implication of Kulick's study, namely that gender performances not only challenge but also crystallise normative notions of masculinity and femininity, inform them, and are informed by them (Kulick, 1998: 9).

An example from my own material might further strengthen this argument. When two women dance a 'female' belly dance while simultaneously and aggressively flirting with each other, the continuity between the anatomy of the performer and the gender of the performance is – in the context of Kallipolis – indeed broken (cf. Butler, 1990; Kulick, 1998). According to Butler such a performative instance deconstructs the naturalised and allegedly unified experience of gender through a perpetual performative displacement that manifests the fluidity of identity itself (1990: 137, 138). Butler maintains that such parodic performances are not mimic instances of some 'original' but they expose the fact that the heterosexual 'original' is a copy (ibid.: 139), and although parody in itself is not exactly subversive, it allows a recontextualisation and resignification of identity. The parodic repetitions of gender expose the illusion that identity is something beyond practice, that it involves an essence, a substance or a depth (Butler, 1990: 146). Although parodic performances are strategies of subversive repetition that displace gender, they simultaneously substantiate and reify gender markers (Butler, 1990, 1993).

With special reference to dance, Cowan has demonstrated how 'by engaging in the social and bodily practices of dance events celebrants literally embody particular ideas and relations' (1990: 233). Although Cowan has not focused on parodic or mixed performances, she offers ample ethnographic substantiation to the argument that dance situations are sites for the 'articulation of social identities and relationships' (ibid.: 89). In the case of the group I studied, dance is a context where familiar signs of femininity and masculinity are employed in order to effect a mixed performance, resulting in the stabilisation of these signs as well as indicating the fact that they are made rather than given.

Mixed performances thus at once crystallise gender and reveal its fragility and its ultimate dependence upon practice for its social existence as a lived category. Most importantly though, as parodies, these performances enable a recontextualisation of gender as the effect of practical (i.e. lived) signification. Parodic performances deal with meaning. They are readings of certain cultural texts and at the same time they are textualisations of gender. What Butler calls displacement of gender idioms is achieved precisely through the retextualisation of masculinity and femininity through such performances. For the actors engaged in them deconstruct gender as they read it, and reconstruct it again only in a scrambled fashion. These reconstructions do not escape gender itself. After all, in order to achieve a syncretic outcome some basic norms have to be acknowledged as such. For the 'pastiche' effect to be realised one has to accept that one is mingling 'masculine' and 'feminine' elements and by accepting it these elements remain up to a point unquestioned. Nevertheless, the performative product is polysemic here and through this polysemy the stability and homogeneity of normative gender is questioned. Precisely because a text is irreducible (cf. Moore, 1986), mixed performances as texts practically establish a wrestling effect with reference to gender, and subsequently in relation to the very experience of identity as they acknowledge internal multiplicity and conflict.

To return to the original question of whether ambiguity can be a sufficient explanatory context, I would like to claim that performative theory is as much about ambiguity as it is about the reiteration of cultural ideals. Its primary usefulness, at least for the purposes of this book, is not its orientation to resistance, but its focus on practice. Still, as Cowan argues, 'eliciting symbols and meanings must be followed by asking whose interests they serve and how they come to be embraced by the community at large' (1990: 91). It is probably because the protagonists of this book are very well aware of power relations that they choose to employ ambiguity not only as a 'poetic goal', but as their 'only hope for self-preservation' (Battaglia, 1999: 117). Ambiguity has often been considered solely in terms of what it implies for a theory of the subject. As such it has been regarded as a notion that heavily relies on individual agency, and subsequently questioned on the basis of the conviction that 'a subject is never at one with her consciousness' (Moore, 1999: 166). Gender performativity, however, as I have already noted, does not belong solely in the sphere of consciousness. Ambiguity then must be seen not only as a strategic performance of resistance but also, and perhaps primarily, as a political habitat of alternative and conflicting sexualities, subjectivities, gender discourses.

The performative utterances around which this book revolves are conflicting not only in relation to their effect but also with reference to their very existence. The women of the *parea* live in conflict; they embody it at the very time they strive for a unified ideology of difference. In this sense, I claim that the present work is not simply about alternative sexualities, but primarily about alternative *textualities* – that is, about conflicting readings of existing cultural texts, and about the reflexive capacity of the social actor 'to use a particular cultural text to produce a specific orientation towards a given ideology' (Moore, 1986: 97) in an inconsistent manner. My use of the terms 'conflicting' and 'inconsistent' is critical here as it refers to the simultaneous acknowledgement and rejection of cultural norms by the women of the group. Through contradictory and intertextual performances the subjects of this book institute a rift between their own readings and the readings of the others, as well as within their own readings. As will be demonstrated, they resignify performative stereotypes effecting the production of multiple (and conflicting) texts that interact within a seemingly single performance. These textual interactions form the basis for the articulation of experience as social, intersubjective and embodied (cf. Moore, 1994: 3). Most importantly though, exploring these gendered performances is about the relationship between the individual and the social not as 'cultural antinomies' but as 'homologues of one another' (Strathern, 1988: 12, 13). The individual 'person' here proves to be 'a site at which its own interactions with others are registered' (ibid.: 132).

Thus, probably the burning question of this work is not simply gender, but identity and its conceptualisation not as a destiny but as the outcome of interaction (Weeks, 1987; Strathern, 1988: 127–8). It is clear that identity cannot be about 'categorical groupings' (Moore, 1994: 2), but about relations and the power of performance as a cultural process of 'objectification and embodiment' (cf. Johnson, 1997: 19). As di Leonardo and Lancaster argue, 'everyone occupies various categories at once' (1997: 67) and all these positions cannot be but provisional (Moore, 1994: 2), the outcome of a 'series of performative identifications' (ibid.: 124). The identification of the self with an 'other' (cf. de Lauretis, 1994) is thus embedded in the enunciation of an embodied subjectivity. In turn, the ability for plural and conflicting identifications and the acknowledgement of the fact that the body itself is 'socially marked in more than one way' means that identity is not unequivocal (di Leonardo and Lancaster, 1997: 67). Hybrid identities are produced through multiple identifications (Kirkham and Attfield, 1996: 213), 'through the occupation of a series of subject positions' that are sometimes conflicting, inconsistent, or 'mutually contradictory' (Moore, 1994: 4). It is perhaps in this very multiplicity, which does not deny the self her sense of coherence, that the creativity of the subject and its capacity to produce original 'figurations' (McNay, 2000: 20; Braidotti, 2002: 13) can be found.

Through the different chapters of this work, women will appear who hold multiple and conflicting sexualities; subjects who are, to use Strathern's term 'partible entities' (1988: 324). It is Carolina who dances all night with the girls and mourns her separation from her partner Fillipa, while at dawn she kisses her husband goodbye on the cheek and prepares orange juice for her teenage son. It is Emily who occasionally wears her Sunday clothes and escorts her mother to church, and at other times, in her jeans, sweats on the dance floor for the sake of a woman who hurts her. The protagonists of this book are women who literally embody conflict. Performative ambiguity is for them a means to articulate plurality and achieve opacity. In their struggle to remain non-locatable and thus at once safe and effective, they engage in a process of 'self-ambiguation' (Battaglia, 1999: 128). In certain respects, Strathern's theorisation of the Melanesian person can be used as a useful explanatory framework for the predicament of my informants. 'The condition of multiple construction, the person composed of diverse relations, also makes the person a partible entity . . . an agent can dispose of parts or act as a part' (Strathern, 1988: 324). Gender can thus be seen as a 'dimension' of the embodied experience of the individual who according to Strathern is 'a source of action' (1988: 57). The multiply constituted agent might not be the cause of action, but she is the one who acts 'because of relationships', and as such her identity is always relational and her position inherently multiple (Strathern, 1988: 273). The women of the *parea* live at the intersection point of differing and contrasting relationships; they are simultaneously mothers, daughters, lovers of women, wives of men. As a result, they have to learn how to manage opposing identities and often incompatible performances. Sometimes they perform for themselves and sometimes for others, being caught in a perpetual spiral of resisting and verifying – consciously or unconsciously – cultural ideas, normative idioms and most importantly the power relations that sustain them.

3

FLIRTING WITH THE 'OTHER'

Ritualistic incorporation in the realm of the *parea*

I saw her suddenly: and I thought 'God, she is so beautiful'. I remember her in the dim light, warm and radiant and graceful, so alive. I was lost, abandoned in the sparkle of her eyes, gone. It was only a moment: a moment that lasted for so long. I wanted to embrace her, to close her in my arms tightly, in a desperate attempt to freeze time, to snatch the moment.

In the above passage, Zoi, an established member of the company, explains how she felt when she saw Athena, then aged seventeen, for the first time. Athena had no relationship with the group and thus Zoi decided to introduce her to the girls' affective community before they engaged in an erotic relationship. Like Athena, the vast majority of the women who belong to the *parea* today are initiated members. According to what I was told during my early meetings with the group, this practice – more or less in the form that is found today – can be traced back to the late 1980s. I devoted considerable time and effort in my attempt to clarify how and why the girls began initiating others as opposed to merely relating to them. The older members of the *parea* insisted that everything happened by chance. As Rosita put it once: 'it all started as flirting and then became more elaborate. Finally it took the form of a custom.' Most of the current members, however, agree that initiation is meant to ensure that the women who will finally become part of the group will respect the community's claims to privacy.

As a friendship group, the *parea* bears many similarities to the male drinking parties described by Papataxiarchis who focused on 'emotional alliances' between men on the Greek Aegean island of Lesbos (1991: 156). The friendships he observed flourish in the local coffee-shops, and like the *parea* are based on drinking and eating commensality being at once sites for the articulation of gendered emotions and 'alternative to kinship bases of personhood' (Papataxiarchis, 1991: 158). In both ethnographic contexts, recruitment is based on personal choice, while alcohol consumption and dance seem to be the means for establishing strong emotional partnerships. *Kerasma* (treating somebody to a drink), a common practice in male friendships and the *parea* alike, ensures the egalitarian character of the companionship (Papataxiarchis, 1991: 158). In turn, while in Papataxiarchis' ethnographic example inclusion is directed by 'fellow-feeling' (*sympatheia*) (Loizos and Papataxiarchis, 1991a: 18), in the *parea* the girls choose to initiate others on the basis of erotic attraction.

Being an invented ritual, initiation to the *parea* is not always the same. Depending on the people involved and the circumstances, the manner changes varying from what could be regarded as merely 'intensive flirting' to practices that resemble a *rite de passage*. When a girl chooses to incorporate a new member she may begin the process of initiation by herself and involve the rest of the *parea* at a later stage, not involve them at all, or include the group as part of the initiation. The girls do not initiate every woman they flirt with, but every initiation process is simultaneously a process of flirting. In turn, flirting with people who bear no relation to the company is extremely complicated due to the fact that nearly all these women have a, so-called, heterosexual orientation. Apart from two girls who had some homoerotic experiences before they met with the group, in all other instances, including those that I witnessed, the initiated were never before involved in a same-sex intimate encounter. The goal of the ritual is thus two-fold: on the one hand a sexual and emotional relationship has to be established, and on the other the new partner has to be successfully incorporated into the collectivity. I have not yet witnessed any initiation that failed and thus I am in no position to tell under which circumstances it does. However, it is worth noting that sometimes the sexual and emotional involvement precedes and at other times, comes well after the affiliation of the initiate into the group. In the latter case the person who is to be initiated, at least during the first stages of the 'operation', is usually left with the impression that she is being approached as a friend and not with sexual intentions.

Flirting with 'the other', and then introducing her into the life of the *parea*, is in many respects a *rite de passage* and as such it conforms to Van Gennep's classic model. One can identify in the ritualistic incorporation of a new girl into the group an initial and a final state as well as a liminal period in between the two (Van Gennep, 1960; Danforth, 1982; Leach, 1976; Skouteri-Didaskalou, 1991). The 'initial state' usually involves discreet flirting masked as friendliness and can last from a few hours to a few days. The 'rites of transition' that take place during what can be characterised as the 'liminal phase' may include physical suffering due to forced excessive consumption of alcohol, or emotional suffering in the form of upsetting or even humiliating the initiate. Finally, the 'rites of incorporation' consist of prominent performances of inclusion frequently enacted by the *parea* as a whole.

The transition from the state of the unrelated and possibly threatening 'other', to the state of the insider and close friend is an important moment both for the initiate and for the *parea*. Hence, a notable initiation is one that effects not a smooth but a memorable passage, although it is also true that a number of women have been incorporated into the group without experiencing any kind of physical or emotional stress. In any case, the semantic and not merely objective success of the ritual relies heavily on what Herzfeld has called 'effective performance' (1985: 47). For the most part, the initiator, and subsequently the *parea* (according to the degree of the group's involvement), resort to frequently flagrant acts in order to achieve 'the memorable'. Their performance thus often swings from aesthetic loftiness to caricature but, owing to the girls' ability to orchestrate it stylistically, in the end they always succeed in creating the impression of an exciting transcendence. Through a series of memorable initiations, the *parea* (that is the initiators themselves) meditate on the poetics of the skilful performer. Herzfeld has shown how the youths from the Cretan village of Glendi learn how to be true Glendiot men through raiding and daring the most 'outrageous diversions' in order to achieve aesthetically pleasing memories (1985: 46). Similarly, the girls of my *parea*, in the course of every new initiation, rediscover the border between originality and meaninglessness, the threshold that separates the connoisseur from the ignorant and the ineffective.

Although ritualistic *passage* is not ethnographically unaccounted for in the cultural context of Greece, it has been mainly considered within the framework of either baptism, wedding or death (cf. Stewart, 1991; Skouteri-Didaskalou, 1991; Danforth, 1982; Seremetakis, 1991; Panourgia, 1995). In turn, the notion of *parea*, as a non-conjugal form of relatedness, has not escaped the ethnographic lens either (cf. Papataxiarchis, 1992; Loizos and Papataxiarchis, 1991a; Cowan, 1990, Zinovieff, 1991; Kennedy, 1986). However, the strategies of recruitment and inclusion in friendship groups occupy a rather marginal position in Greek ethnography. Initiation as a practice has been mentioned by Herzfeld (1985) in relation to young Glendiots and raiding, while Iossifides (1991, 1992) accounted for the nun's incorporation into the new family of the convent. In turn, Papataxiarchis has addressed the politics of *sympatheia* (fellow-feeling) as a basis for recruitment into male circles of friends, mentioning that the coffee-shop (*kafeneio*) is itself the context within which adolescent males, by their gradual inclusion into the drinking parties, achieve the status of adult members (1992). Nevertheless, ritualistic incorporation in a group as a context for the enactment of gendered performances is still in many respects an underdeveloped theme.

The ethnography included in this chapter suggests that initiation is a process of mutual change. By becoming part of the group the initiated enters the realm of gender syncretism, while the *parea* affirm their solidarity and performative flair anew. The initiated girl, much like a nun who enters an Orthodox convent (Iossifides, 1991, 1992), is confronted with a new 'family', acquires new 'kinship ties'[1] and learns how to appropriate a different semiological web in relation to gender and identity. Alcohol, food and substances such as hashish and bodily fluids form the symbolic foundations of new forms of relatedness performatively reaffirmed by the *parea* every night. Becoming part of the group, as when one becomes part of the 'Christian Community' through baptism, affects not only membership but also, and most importantly, identity. As has been noted by Bloch and Guggenheim (1981), and discussed by Rushton (1992), baptism primarily (and beyond Christianity) deals with the cultural self and the construction of identity. Rushton in particular, claims that the baby as the 'product of the mother is incomplete' (1992: 153); the process of realization and accomplishment of personhood takes place in a 'different, purely social and ideological environment' (ibid.). The *parea* treats the initiated person as precisely such, namely as a yet incomplete being that has to serve an apprenticeship and learn to deal not only with her desires and emotions but also with her very identity and gendered self. Initiation can be then regarded as 'a second birth', in the sense that Bloch and Guggenheim (1981) and Stewart (1991) describe baptism. However, this symbolic death and rebirth is not seen by the girls as accomplished instantaneously (as in the case of baptism) but as a procedure that takes time, effort and, sometimes, ordeal. Alcohol, instead of the baptismal water, is in this case the purifying substance and a prominent symbol of passage similar to fire (Danforth, 1989: 6) which bears cathartic and transformative qualities. It is the superior burning 'spirit', both in its literal and symbolic sense, that always plays a protagonistic role in the *parea*'s expressive performances.

In the pages that follow I will present two different initiations in order to highlight the fact that each instance of incorporation into the group pertains to different performative fields. In this manner, the first rite refers to 'poses of defiant masculinity'[2] while the second pertains to performative authenticity. As I have already stressed, initiation is a two way process; more than testing the initiated, what is being tested in the rite is the performative skill of the initiator.

About Chrisa and Maria

Chrisa enters the picture

Chrisa was a regular customer at *Harama*. Nineteen years old, slim, tall and brunette, she was studying at the local university. She discovered *Harama* when her fellow students chose the place for one of their evening dances.[3] Since then she started frequenting the club, in the beginning with company and later alone. She was usually sitting at the bar drinking slowly, enjoying the music, whispering the lyrics of the songs and sometimes moving her body according to the rhythm. Chrisa was always well-dressed following the custom of the Kallipoliots who consider a night at *Harama*, or any other place with live music, 'a night out'. At first, nobody paid any special attention to her. The girls of the *parea* were at the time too busy with Maria's separation, and Sotiris, the barman, was on bad terms with Thomas, the owner of the place, who was demanding to know how many shots were being served 'on the house' every night.[4] Sotiris was over-treating customers with free shots because he intended to start his own business the following year and he wanted to be very pleasant to the customers in order to 'build a good reputation in the market' (*onoma stin piatsa*). Hence, Chrisa visited the bar for about a month before she was noticed.

That Thursday night, the *parea*'s spirits were high because of Katerina's arrival. Katerina, an old member of the *parea*, had been working for the past 8 months as a civil servant in another town and she had come for a short visit. Almost everybody was present at *Harama* to welcome her. All the seats around the bar were occupied by the girls and the only person there who was not a member was Chrisa. She was sitting in the corner wearing a long black dress, a very elegant one, and high heels. Her makeup was almost invisible, her short hair very well set back with plenty of gel and she was not wearing any jewellery except for a ring on the last finger of her right hand. Sotiris was the only person who occasionally spoke to her.

Around 1.30 in the morning, and after the fourth round of shots, the *parea* started dancing in front of the bar. Katerina was the first to perform a *zeimbekiko*, and some of us formed a semi-circle around her.[5] We were all crouching over one knee, clapping for Katerina, wishing her a long life (*na zisis*) and throwing flowers. Flowers were also coming from Sotiris, who particularly admired Katerina's flair and was very happy to see her again after some time. Katerina was dancing ecstatically around a glass put on the floor in front of her.[6] Her *zeimbekiko* was particularly appreciated by the girls due to her complex and spectacular embellishments and especially because she somehow never seemed to repeat herself.

As with Cowan's informants (1990: 194), the girls expect the exceptional dancer, the *meraklu* (female 'master'), to be confident and original, to improvise continuously, to dance vivaciously, but more importantly to show *pathos* (passion). Passion is probably the most significant attribute of the dancer and the one that differentiates amateurs from skilled performers; dancing with passion means 'dancing the song' instead of simply performing the dance. This suggests that all *zeimkekika* (solo dances) should not be danced in the same fashion. A different posture has to be assumed for a *rembetiko*, another for a *laiko*, whereas a political song requires a distinct performance.[7] The people of Sohos studied by Cowan and my *parea* value some of the same qualities in relation to dance, but the girls do not demand from women a greater constraint and modesty than the male dancers as the Sohoians do (1990: 194). On the contrary, the *parea* mostly values *levendia* (dash, upstandingness, ability to fight, manfulness [*sic*][8]) which translates into the occupation of a large space during a *zeimbekiko*, or into provocative embellishments in *tsifte-teli*. Katerina, demonstrating *levendia*, was dancing that night with her arms extended all the time, and as a result of being quite tall, she indeed occupied all the space around the bar. Sotiris continued to throw flowers as a dedicated admirer of her skill and towards the end of the song passed her a shot of vodka 'for the thirst'.

Katerina drank the vodka and attempted to throw the last drops on the floor 'for the prosperity of the house' as she was dancing; throwing the last drops of a *kerasma* (treat) on the floor as a symbolic offering to the hospitable place that accommodates the girls is an old custom of the *parea*. However, that night the drops never reached the wooden floor, because Katerina threw them in the course of executing a last acrobatic embellishment. As a result the alcohol sprinkled Chrisa's face, taking her by surprise. She wiped her cheek with her palm while all the girls started apologising for the incident. To substantiate the apologies, Katerina ordered shots for everybody including Chrisa.

We continued dancing and chatting for another half an hour or so until everybody needed a break. The girls gathered around Katerina, sitting on the bar stools, and started updating her with the latest news of the *parea*. After finishing the first round of gossip, or 'edifying dialogue' as my informants call it (*enimerotikos dialogos*), Katerina asked who Chrisa was. Nobody knew her name at the time, Aphrodite however had seen her before and guessed that she was after Sotiris (the barman). Katerina commented briefly on the stranger's body and eyes, and the discussion turned slowly to Maria's recent separation from Klairi (both girls of the *parea*). We were updating Katerina, filling the picture with every last possible detail of the event, such as the kind of trousers and boots Klairi was wearing on the fatal night of the separation, which song she danced to and how she gave back to Maria the ring symbolising their relationship. Maria started feeling very emotional with the discussion and decided to interrupt it: 'It is time for joy' she shouted and stood up ready to dance a *zeimbekiko*.

While Maria was performing her *kapsoura* (infatuation, obsession) with her ex-partner in a heavy *zeimbekiko*, I started chatting with Chrisa, mostly in order to apologise again for the accident with the vodka. As I found out after some 10 minutes of discussion, she actually fancied Sotiris but the latter did not seem to respond well to her attempts to flirt with him. They had introduced themselves, and chatted a little, Sotiris had bought her a couple of drinks 'but nothing exciting' as she said (*tipote to syntaraktiko*). However, she was quick to add, Sotiris was still encouraging her and she was holding out hope. I admitted that Sotiris was a very handsome man when Aphrodite interrupted our discussion dragging me by the sleeve. She wanted me to dance to a particular song, partly because she knew it was my favourite, and partly because she thought that Katerina, as a guest, deserved everybody's exclusive attention that night. I complied and started dancing my favourite *zeimbekiko*. The girls were crouching on one knee, clapping for me as I was leading my steps around the glass taking special care not to touch it. The last thing I wanted to disclose was that I had difficulties with the glass. Trying to perform solo in front of a demanding audience, having drunk some five shots of vodka and a few other drinks was not easy, so I kept focusing on my task missing the details around me. When the last notes of the song were heard, I took a deep breath and performed the last embellishment. It was already time for another shot.

The girls consume moderate quantities of their favourite drinks, two or three each night, while the heavy consumption of alcohol usually takes the form of shots.[9] One girl after the other orders rounds of shots treating the whole company. The peculiarity of the shots, in comparison to other drinks, is that they are usually consumed communally and as Papataxiarchis (1992) has noted in the case of male commensality, all the participants in it are regarded as equals. In the same manner, when the girls of the *parea* share a round of shots they stress the egalitarian basis of their companionship and precisely because the alcoholic drink is consumed simultaneously by every member, the competitive nature of the activity is not as distinguishable as it would be in the coffee-shop (cf. Papataxiarchis, 1992: 226). The codes of drinking within the group do not impose restrictions upon the *kerasma* (treat) and unlike the coffee-shop there is no relation between drinking commensality and the hierarchical structures that operate outside the world of the *parea*.[10] Vodka in my case, as *raki* (a strong transparent spirit originating from grape skins) in the case of Papataxiarchis (1992: 162), remains strictly a symbol of emotional partnership.

Initiation for the sake of Maria

The day after we met Chrisa, we gathered at *Harama* again. Katerina was still in town but she had gone to see Thekla, her ex-partner in a long-lasting and recently finished relationship. It was one day before the full moon of October and *Harama* was full of people. When the spotlights went on they revealed a small but quite representative sample of Kallipoliot society: families with their children playing on the floor before the entertainment begins, young couples enjoying their Saturday night out and teenagers short of money, leaning against the walls, enjoying their first and probably last drink of the night. The recorded music stopped and Lillian, a member of the group and a singer at *Harama*, started the night's festivities as usual. The *parea* gathered around the bar and began singing along with Lillian as the latter turned around and greeted us with a smile. Maro's eye caught Chrisa sitting on her regular stool at the corner of the bar and commented laughingly: 'Did she sleep here?' I offered them the information I had gathered the previous night about her. Maria asserted that the girl looked beautiful and we all returned to our singing.

Later on, I asked Aphrodite whether or not I should mention to Sotiris something about Chrisa who was so patiently waiting for him every night at the bar. Aphrodite urged me to stop dwelling upon it because 'this is Sotiris' style. He likes no-one. The only thing that turns him on is giving hope to the girls so that they gather around his bar.' Aphrodite continued with a lecture on the psychology of barmen. According to her, there were three kinds of them: there was first Sotiris' kind, that is, the people who do this job because 'it helps their self-esteem'. Then, there are people who like to communicate with others and compose according to Aphrodite the 'true race of barmen/women'. The last kind consists of 'unimaginative' people who do the job just for the money.

Aphrodite used a metaphor: 'They sell drinks as someone would sell stockings. You will spot them immediately.' As I was listening to Aphrodite's lecture, my eye caught Maria who was chatting with Chrisa. I elbowed Aphrodite and pointed out the two girls to her. 'Sotiris is a nice guy, but Maria is better', she was quick to comment (*kalos o Sotiris, ki i Maria kalyteri*).

That night was Chrisa's time to dance and drink. She was performing endless belly-dances with Maria while the *parea* were throwing flowers. Sotiris was throwing flowers as well, as usual. Chrisa, however, believing that finally she had caught his eye, seemed delighted and kept dancing for about half an hour continuously. Maria was accompanying her without putting in a lot of effort, staying calm and self-composed, smiling and sipping her drink from time to time, while the girls were lighting her cigarettes when needed. Although Chrisa was quite a tall girl, Maria was clearly taller, slim with short dark curly hair. She was wearing a black shirt, black jean trousers and a silver belt with a matte finish, which was her only accessory. She was gracefully escorting Chrisa, yet without looking at her. In the background two little girls about 10 or 11 years old were dancing the same belly-dance on the edge of the dance floor looking at their mothers who clapped for them, being extremely amused by the spectacle. Their dance was a lot less refined than that of Maria and Chrisa, and their long white cotton socks, ending in black shiny shoes seemed somewhat unsuitable for the place. They were, however, enjoying the belly-dance as much as the adults, if not more.

Most rites of initiation in the *parea* start and end with a dance. Dance as a site of both performance and experience (Cowan, 1990: 4; cf. Sax, 2002: 5) is used by the girls as a field of exploration and creative enactment of gender ideas. As Cowan argues, in the dancing realm the actor both performs and experiences herself as a gendered subject (ibid.). The postures of femininity and even sensuality are carefully crafted in dance events from very early on, as the case of the two little girls demonstrates supporting McNay's – echoing Bourdieu (1990: 73) – claim that: 'bodily dispositions are not simply inscribed or mechanically learnt but lived as a form of "practical mimesis"' (2000: 39).

The importance of the dance for the *parea* extends even further, to the reflexive use of the body and the semiology of dance itself. The girls through dance are able to perform either femininity or masculinity or a masculine femininity, according to the circumstances. Although nowadays, at least in urban settings, the different dances have lost most of their gender-specific value, the semiotics of the body in relation to different rhythms still exist. Thus, women can dance a passionate and exaggerated *zeimbekiko* (solo) without being criticised, or misunderstood[11] and men usually accompany the *tsifte-teli* (belly-dance). However, the *tsifte-teli* still bears the connotations of a female dance in comparison to the *zeimbekiko* which is regarded as a male rhythm.

The first dance of Maria and Chrisa was a *tsifte-teli*. Maria, however, was not performing femininity but indifference. Calm and confident, assuming an androgynous posture of power, Maria was seemingly accompanying Chrisa when actually she was merely evaluating the latter's sexually laden performance. The dance, semiotically invested with sexual nuances, was transformed into a power game, which Maria was playing for herself and for the *parea*. Chrisa, although physically present, was semantically absent and so were the rest of the Kallipoliots who found themselves at *Harama* that night. As Faubion has spotted, women in Greece are perceived as 'phallically inactive' (1993: 221); Maria's and Chrisa's dance was aesthetically pleasing but certainly not politically or ethically dangerous. In the eyes of the non-initiated celebrants, their performance was as frivolous and inconsequential as the dance of the two 10-year-old girls with shiny shoes. So long as they are not directly associated with the category lesbian, women in Greece, may 'play' with each other but their acts still 'remain politically normal' (Faubion, 1993: 221).

The next day, Aphrodite, Maro and I were the first to arrive at the *parea*'s favourite tavern.[12] We had an early night the day before, that is we left *Harama* at around 3.00, so it was expected that most of the girls would show up at the restaurant. The waiter welcomed us with four cold beers and some special meze (selected food that accompanies the drink), and said the stereotypical: 'Good day. How are our[13] girls doing today?' (*pos einai ta koritsia mas simera*) only to receive the stereotypical answer from Maro: 'Not bad, but we will be better after consuming something.' I tried to bring the discussion back to the previous night, commenting on the fact that after some half an hour dancing with Chrisa, Maria finished her drink and disappeared. Maro said that she did well because, after all, nobody knew who Chrisa was, 'save that she only has eyes for Sotiris'. Aphrodite agreed with Maro, underlining the fact that Maria was just coming out of a relationship so she had better to be careful. She had just finished speaking when the chug of Maria's newly acquired Harley Davidson-type motorbike was heard from down the road. Maria was wearing a white shirt with sleeves rolled up, blue jeans and boots, while a scarf was protecting her neck from the cool air. She shut down the engine in front of the tavern, walked steadily into the place and sat on a chair next to Maro, lighting a cigarette. She served herself some beer, took a tiny sip from the glass and announced suddenly: 'I told her that I would be here', implying Chrisa, 'but now I am not so sure about it anymore. I do not think I have the strength for new adventures. Klairi [her ex-girlfriend] called today again.' The atmosphere was somewhat charged when Katerina arrived with Thekla, but we all continued talking and drinking, and Maria's statement seemed to pass unnoticed or at least uncommented upon. She had broken up with her girlfriend, Klairi, recently and it was indeed surprising that she had decided to start a relationship so quickly. I did not fail to observe that her glass was the first to be refilled by Aphrodite and Maro. This was a way to demonstrate their support to her and to let her know that she was the real centre of attention. Maria silently accepted the offer.

The 'ritual of the tavern' as the girls themselves call their midday gatherings has a distinct significance for the *parea. Harama* is unquestionably their natural habitat and the place where most of the life of the group unfolds. However, these midday gatherings and the coffee-parties[14] – examples of which I will offer later on in this chapter – are the sites where the group can explore the latest developments in its life. The bar operates mostly as a scene where things happen. The restaurants, coffee-shops and houses are places where the *parea* can reflect on the previous night's performances. Madianou-Gefou (1992) describes a similar site of all-male gatherings, this time not the coffe-shop (*kafeneio*) but the *katoy* (basement). In the basements of their houses, Mesogeia men transcend the confinements of everyday life, become sentimental and open their souls to their friends while sharing generous amounts of home-made wine (ibid.: 120). Similarly, the girls in these gatherings perform intimacy (cf. Herzfeld, 1985: 207) and share their pains and *kapsoures* (infatuations). Food and drink commensality facilitates the creation of further bonds between the members of the group always on an egalitarian basis. In this particular instance, however, the tavern (and later on the bar) will be transformed into arenas for contest. Chrisa's ability to drink will be tested and found wanting, whereas Maria's capacity to survive a broken relationship and embark on a new adventure will be celebrated.

As expected, Chrisa showed up at the tavern around 4.00 in the afternoon. She was casually but carefully dressed and very discreetly made-up. She greeted us and sat next to Maria. After saying how much she had enjoyed herself the previous night, she started talking about her university, how she discovered *Harama*, and of course Sotiris. The girls however were not listening to her. Slowly and in a very discreet manner everybody started talking to each other, ignoring Chrisa who ended up speaking only to Maria. Had I not been with the girls before I would have failed to understand their attitude. Usually the *parea* welcomes the company of everybody, they are very sociable and friendly, they arrange to meet all sorts of people, they go on excursions with them and generally do not give the impression of a members only club. In this case, however, the girls' attitude was part of the initiation rite: their friendship and acceptance was presented as a trophy to be acquired after sufficient testing, apprenticeship and even suffering.

Aphrodite continued refilling Maria's glass, and Maria started filling Chrisa's regularly until the latter got drunk. Although beer is not such a strong drink Chrisa was apparently not used to it at all. At first, she started laughing loudly and in the end she was crying while the *parea* continued ignoring her. Maria was sitting there with her body straight, her hands relaxed and her head slightly turned towards Chrisa but without fully looking at her. She was smiling from time to time, drinking and smoking. At some point when Chrisa started getting too drunk, Maria stood up and said to her: 'Come on, I will drop you home.' Chrisa attempted to get up off the chair without success. It was only then that the girls showed some interest. 'Drop her home and fix her a coffee. She is in a deplorable state' (*ehei ta halia tis*), Carolina suggested, not hiding her contempt. Maria offered Chrisa an arm, she took her out of the tavern and put her on the motorbike. She fastened Chrisa's hands in front of her to make sure that she would not fall off and started the engine. To be on the safe side, Maria was holding the fastened wrists, thus driving the huge motorbike with one hand. They soon disappeared in a cloud of dust and exhaust fumes.

During her initiation, Chrisa was about to be tested in different performative fields, and as one would expect, drinking and dancing were two of the most important ones. The girls appreciate alcohol and the accomplished drinker. The overwhelming qualities of alcohol, as a substance and a spirit (in its symbolic sense) can only be venerated by the master, the *potis* (habitual drinker). As is true for dance (Cowan, 1990), alcohol can be characterised as an ambiguous substance (Madianou-Gefou, 1992). Both are at once enjoyable and dangerous depending on the circumstances and who is defining the hermeneutics of the performance. Thus, a person – and especially a woman – who dances can be misunderstood (cf. Cowan, 1990: 21), and a person who drinks can become unsociable (Driessen, 1992: 74), while at the same time a good dancer is praised and a capable drinker thought to be good company. With special reference to alcohol, as Driessen (1992) notes, Andalusian men are expected to drink socially and to drink a lot without getting drunk. According to the *parea*, commensal drinking constitutes one of the pillars of their solidarity, whereas intoxication is not only regarded as unsocial but also as a poor performance and consequently as empty of meaning (cf. Herzfeld, 1985: 47–8). Every member of the group is expected to drink and at the same time to be able to stay in control of her performative skills. This comes in direct opposition to the belief – widespread in Greece – that women are not able to handle alcohol and they should therefore avoid drinking (Cowan, 1991: 67). Getting drunk could ruin a woman's self-presentation and might potentially lead to her being misunderstood[15] (ibid.: 206). In the context of the *parea*, a woman drinking liberally while demonstrating an ability to hold her liquor effects a masculine ethos and at the same time a 'successful presentation' of the self (cf. Herzfeld, 1985: 10). Alcohol consumption is hence treated by the girls as another site for the enactment of gendered performances.

What happened after Maria and Chrisa left the tavern was narrated to us by Maria at Vivi's house over coffee at 6.00 in the morning the following day. Maria drove Chrisa home with some difficulty, since the drunk girl was unable to give her directions. Fortunately, she did not have a roommate – quite unusual for a university student – thus Maria left her on a couch and found her way to the kitchen where she made some coffee. After the coffee Chrisa was better but still drunk and weak, so Maria put her to bed and left taking the house keys with her. She returned several hours later to find Chrisa awake with a terrible hangover. When Chrisa asked why she had taken the keys Maria answered: 'because this is what I thought I should do. I had to be able to check on you.' When I asked Maria why she took the keys (the excuse she offered to Chrisa did not seem convincing enough), she told me: 'to shock her'. Apparently, they drank some coffee in Chrisa's house and then Maria told her that she was going to *Harama* and asked Chrisa to join her. The girl complained about her physical state, which was indeed bad, but Maria insisted: 'the fresh air will do you good. Come'. Maria continued her narration with all the details of Chrisa's preparation for the outing. How she chose her dress, how Maria chose another dress and how in the end Chrisa wore the dress chosen by Maria, how she put makeup on and set her hair under Maria's gaze.

When Chrisa, accompanied by Maria, entered the club that night she occupied her usual seat at the bar, only this time a bit closer to where we were sitting. She started talking to me about how sick she was a few hours before, and how she was feeling better at present when Aphrodite approached us slowly. She ordered a tequila with lemon and put it in front of Chrisa who attempted to refuse the offer explaining that she was just recovering from the afternoon's hangover, and she politely thanked Aphrodite for remembering her favourite drink. The latter ignored the compliment about her good memory and induced Chrisa to drink because 'it was a treat and she should not refuse'. Chrisa accepted the offer.

Aphrodite and myself were the only people to talk to Chrisa that night. The rest of the girls exchanged a few words with her when circumstances demanded but nothing more. Nevertheless, all of us and especially Maria prompted her to dance not just to *tsiftetelia*, but also to *zeimbekika* (solo performances). Still, nobody bothered to form the customary circle around her when she was dancing, and even Maria was clapping for her standing and not crouching as she should have been. To make matters worse, Katerina put a glass on the floor and a lit cigarette on the edge of it to make Chrisa's task even more difficult. This was clearly an act of challenge to the dancer's abilities and skill with obvious connotations. It was as if Katerina had said to her: 'You are too drunk and too inexperienced to do it, so step back.' After some genuine attempts not to burn herself, Chrisa realised her inability to manage and left the dance unfinished. Maria continued it and after some rounds, just before the cigarette burned out and fell into the glass, she bent, put it in her lips and took a big puff while dancing. This time all the bodies were crouching in tribute to Maria's skill and experience.

Chrisa drank a lot that night. As soon as she emptied her glass this was instantly refilled. I asked Maro if the girl would be able to stand so much alcohol. 'She will end up in hospital' I commented, but Maro replied jokingly: 'Don't worry, my aunt is doing her shift tonight. [Maro's aunt was working in the public hospital as a nurse.] She will take care of her!' Fortunately, Chrisa did not need medical care. After the entertainment had finished, Maria took her home where she put her to bed and joined us at Lillian's house for morning coffee. It was already 5.30 in the morning.

A few days passed, and Maria's behaviour towards Chrisa, who followed the *parea* every night and sometimes during the day, remained the same. She continued giving her a hard time, pushing her to drink too much, challenging her dancing skills, appearing at her house at odd hours, imposing on her stylistic changes and disparaging her continuously, especially when the latter was getting really drunk. The *parea* was enjoying the spectacle, and each one of the girls played her role in this unusual process of flirtation. They embarrassed Chrisa at every opportunity by using some of the means described above, and took every chance to make her feel inadequate. I vividly remember a time when Carolina ordered shots, and just before Chrisa drunk hers she took the glass away saying: 'You've had enough. You are already drunk.' Then, there were other instances of exclusion such as when Eirini asked the girls laughingly: 'Should we treat Chrisa to a drink?', only to answer herself loudly: 'No, she will embarrass us once more by getting drunk.' One night Chrisa succeeded in staying relatively sober but instead of affirmation she received a new challenge: Fillippa decided to go home in Carolina's car and asked the girls: 'Does anybody feel like driving my car home or shall I leave it here locked?' Chrisa volunteered, only to receive Fillippa's rejection. The latter 'did not consider it a good idea' and preferred to leave the car locked at a place where parking was prohibited during the day rather than entrusting it to Chrisa's hands.

A week later, Maria decided to take a trip to Athens without informing Chrisa, who came to *Harama* expecting to find her there as usual. When she discovered that Maria was out of town she asked the girls 'where did she go?', but nobody seemed willing to tell her either where Maria had gone or when she would be coming back. At some point Martha ordered a round of shots for everybody but Chrisa. The girls wanted to drink to Maria's health since she was absent and allegedly she would not be coming back soon. When Chrisa realised she was excluded again she stood in front of the bar addressing herself to Sotiris and spoke out: 'Prepare another round. Ten shots for the girls because I miss Maria too and don't bother to include yourself.' The girls accepted the offer, formed a circle around Chrisa and drank the shots all together. After that Chrisa decided to dance. She put a glass on the floor by herself, a burning cigarette on it and said loudly: 'For Maria, even though she forgot some people who love her.' The girls clapped for her, still without crouching, but congratulated her tenderly after the dance. Finally, her behaviour was beginning to meet their standards. She had been for the first time rebellious, assertive and non-compliant and the girls decided to give her the affirmation she deserved. For the rest of the night the *parea* was dancing and drinking conspicuously, including Chrisa in their festivities. When the evening came to an end, Maro and Bea volunteered to drive her home before we all gathered at Vivi's place for coffee.

By the time that Vivi served the coffee the first light of the day was already appearing. That dawn I heard many triumphant stories as the girls started remembering how they first met the *parea*. Papataxiarchis has noted that men love to narrate stories, which have an emotional significance and focus on male achievement (1991: 174). Likewise, the rite of initiation ensures that every girl has at least one moving story to tell about her personal accomplishments. Throughout that coffee session the *parea* as a whole were constantly affirming their solidarity as they narrated their common history by telling their individual stories: 'We became friends again as Chrisa started becoming a friend. To her health' said Carolina as she was sipping her coffee.

From that night, Chrisa came to *Harama* regularly and joined almost all the gatherings of the *parea* since the girls were showing her that she was welcome. Nevertheless, she was still unaware of the fact that most women in the group were couples and nobody was willing to reveal that to her, at least not in so many words. No one was hiding their affection for the other and Chrisa saw instances of great intimacy, however, as I have noted earlier, intimacy between girls in the Greek context often fails to convey a clear sexual message.

Several days later Maria suddenly reappeared in *Harama* and Chrisa who had been constantly looking at the door for the past eight days, was the first to see her. She ran towards Maria and gave her a big hug but the latter headed directly to the bar and touching Martha's shoulder asked: 'How are things going?' Martha nodded: 'Well' and offered Maria a seat while Sotiris prepared her favourite drink. Maria started sipping it, looking everybody straight in the eye. As Herzfeld has noted, the word used in Greek to denote gesture is *noima* that also stands for meaning (1991: 96). Maria was non-verbally seeking to find out, not only whether the initiation was accomplished, but most importantly whether the performance of the rite succeeded in having *meaning*. Twelve pairs of eyes gave her the same answer 'yes'.

For the rest of the night Chrisa's face was radiant and the rest of the *parea* were looking at her with a light smile on their faces and a twinkle in their eyes. The spotlights were flashing, Lillian was singing, the customers were enjoying themselves and there, in the midst of flowers and half-empty bottles of whisky, Sotiris saw his ex-admirer disappearing into Maria's arms. Unknowingly perhaps, he smiled too. Aphrodite ordered a drink. The night was still young.

An act with meaning: restoring Maria's damaged masculinity

'Glendiot men engage in a constant struggle to gain a precarious and transitory advantage over each other. Each performance is an incident in that struggle and the success or failure of each performance marks its progress' (Herzfeld, 1985: 11). What Herzfeld so eloquently describes in the above passage encapsulates the everyday life of the girls, with a slight difference: competitive performance in the *parea* concentrates on the self rather than being directed towards someone else. Chrisa's initiation is a representative example of how the girls are involved in a continuous contest, not against each other, but over the limits of their *own* performative abilities. This particular case of incorporation dealt less with the actual strategies of inclusion and more with Maria's need to prove her *eghoismos* (self-regard). Maria – as was stated earlier – had recently broken up with her partner and her separation, one of the most stressful experiences I witnessed with the *parea*, had left her emotionally and performatively weak. For quite some time after her ex-partner left, Maria was suffering without being able to transcend her agony or transform it into a meaningful performance. Her self-regard was wounded and although the *parea* was very supportive Maria refused to accept that she was still in love with her ex-girlfriend. Chrisa's initiation was thus a celebration of Maria's self-hood, a proof that she was too tough to admit defeat.

The main motif of Chrisa's ritualistic incorporation into the group was erotic desire masked as indifference. The flirtation was dispassionate and more painful than pleasant, while Maria seized every opportunity to manifest – mostly to herself – that she could remain confidently in control. Maria's exhibition of indifference reached its culmination with her absence from the last stage of the initiation. In the framework of her *eghoismos* (self-regard), she allowed the *parea* to finish what she has started, conspicuously turning away and thus demonstrating that she did not even care to witness Chrisa's integration into the group.

The initiation was successful, that is, it had meaning; but as Herzfeld argues, meaning is to be found primarily in the relationship between text and context (1985: 207). The context in this case was not Chrisa's inclusion *per se*, but Maria's painful last separation. By means of this initiation Maria succeeded in producing again after a long time, a stylistic enactment of pride by proving that she could still win the contest with herself, that she remained able to transform pain into strength, weakness into stamina and passion into indifference. Chrisa, on the other hand, was never told what was at stake. Until she was finally affiliated to the group she was oblivious to the fact that Maria was sexually attracted to her. She simply existed in order to facilitate a performance fashioned to restore Maria's damaged masculinity. Nevertheless, Chrisa soon realised that the peculiar girl who lured her into a seemingly incomprehensible contest of drinking and dancing 'to be friends'[16] was not actually interested in her friendship at all.

One night, after the initiation was over, Chrisa and Maria came to *Harama* together. The sophisticated ring on Chrisa's last finger, that I had noticed when I first saw her sitting at the corner of the bar, had given place to a small plain silver one. Maria was wearing an identical ring on her right hand.[17] They walked into the bar tightly embracing each other and announced their erotic relationship to the *parea*, that celebrated with the new couple by drinking endless shots of yellow tequila. None of the girls was saying much but they were clearly feeling emotional. Towards the end of the night, Lillian and Thekla (members of the group and singers in *Harama*), dedicated to the *parea* a song which the girls sang with all their strength tightly holding each other:

and we are still alive
on the stage
like a rock group.
Whether or not the stage will hold us
the clapping will tell.

Interlude

The second initiation to be presented was a more prominent one than Chrisa's, in the sense that it pertained to desire and flirt-related performative excellence (cf. Herzfeld, 1985). Maria's self-esteem as a member of the *parea*, which formed the basis of the previous initiation, undoubtedly produced a distinct ritual, however, what a rite of incorporation usually deals with in the context of the group are the techniques of flirting. The girls very often establish partnerships with each other and, although courtship in these cases is more elaborate, wooing a person who does not belong to the community, and initiating her into the company, is always considered a challenge that nearly every member of the group has to face on behalf of the collectivity. Faithful to my original claim, I insist that initiation in the *parea* – and the realm of homoerotic relations – is seen as a contest to be won primarily by the initiator, since according to the girls, the disciple can only be as good as her master.

Due to the fact that flirting with 'the other' plays a key role in this second initiation I intend to incorporate into my discussion Zinovieff's ethnographic case of *kamaki*. 'Kamaki', or the phrase 'to make kamaki' (*kano kamaki*) describes the actions of a Greek man who pursues a (usually foreign) woman with the sole intention of having sex (Zinovieff, 1991: 203). *Kamaki* literally means 'harpoon' but it metaphorically applies to situations of erotic seduction. Zinovieff (1991, 1992) translates *kamaki*, very aptly in my opinion, as 'hunting' and the men who habitually make *kamaki* as hunters.[18] None the less, as will be demonstrated, my *parea* uses the term 'kamaki', with connotations somewhat different from the meaning that Zinovieff's informants ascribe to the word. The primary difference stems from the girls' distinct performance of what Herzfeld (1985), Papataxiarchis (1991, 1992) and other ethnographers describe as 'agonistic masculinity'. As I have noted before, the women of the *parea* engage in conspicuous exhibitions of their performative abilities, however, their *agonas* (struggle) is directed more towards the self and less towards the other members of the group. In the context of erotic seduction, what motivates the girls beyond the act itself is how the act is performed (cf. Herzfeld, 1985). As a result, sex with a woman is regarded as something that theoretically everybody can achieve. What the girls regard as meaningful performance is making an initiate feel the same kind of passion and desire that the initiator experiences. Thus 'kamaki', or flirtation (*flirt*) as my informants more often call it, does not end at the moment of the actual sexual encounter but rather when the initiated person is thought to have developed strong feelings for her initiator. In the ethnographic case that follows, Maro, an established member of the group, flirts and incorporates into the *parea* Bea, an engaged woman who had just returned to her home town to prepare for her forthcoming wedding. The relationship that Maro and Bea established as a result of the latter's initiation, was one of the most passionate erotic relations that I had encountered during my stay with the *parea*.

About Bea and Maro

'I want this woman'

When I first met Bea she was in her late twenties, looking for a job. Her professional qualification was a B.Sc. in gymnastics. She was slim, tall, with dark hair and blue eyes. She had just arrived in Kallipolis, her home town, after finishing her studies in Athens where she had also been working as an instructor in a rather smart health club for three years earning a good salary. She was engaged to Nikos, who was also from Kallipolis and who had also studied gymnastics in Athens. Since her graduation, Bea had been investing her money in a house she was building in Kallipolis that was intended to accommodate the couple after they married. For his part, Nikos sold a piece of land he had inherited in order to start a new business, a health club, where both of them could work. While Nikos was setting up the club, Bea was looking for a job as an instructor, so that she could become 'acquainted with the Kallipoliot clientele' (*na kerdisei pelateia*).

Bea came one Thursday night to *Harama* with a cousin of hers, who had just split up from her boyfriend, for a drink, and since there were only the two of them they sat at the bar just next to us. The first to spot Bea was Maro. She pointed at her and said loudly: 'I want this woman' (*auti ti gynaika ti thelo*). My spontaneous reaction was to make fun of her comment: 'And how are you going to get her?' I said, being at the time unfamiliar with the girls' skills and mastery in seduction. While the *parea* began observing Bea and commenting on her appearance, Maro smiled at me and replied: 'Give me a week.' Much to my astonishment, I saw her waving at the barman from whom she ordered a round of four shots: for Bea and her cousin, for herself and for him. Sotiris prepared the shots, and he put them in front of the girls who accepted the offer with an affirmative smile. Maro approached them. 'It is a pity to be so sad on a spring night' she said to the girl who, as we found out later, was Bea's cousin. The cousin said something about men who manage to break women's hearts, and Maro replied: 'Bottoms up. Tomorrow is a new day. Let's drink to tomorrow.' They drank the shots, and Maro returned to us, behaving for the rest of the night as if the two girls did not exist.

When Bea and her cousin prepared to leave *Harama*, Maro followed them and discovered where Bea lived. The following day, she waited on her motorbike outside Bea's house until the latter came out, and as she was approaching her car, Maro nearly hit her with the motorbike having set it up it in such a way that it seemed totally Bea's fault. She was on the motorbike waiting, with the engine running, so that when Bea prepared to cross the road she did not see any vehicle coming. It thus appeared as if she were careless, and she had not checked properly. Maro fell off on purpose, supposedly in her attempt not to hit 'the careless girl', and told the terrified Bea: 'Oh my God, you almost killed me.' When Maro took the helmet off they discovered that they knew each other from the previous night, and Bea asked her if she wanted to be taken to the hospital. Maro replied that a coffee would suffice and they went back into Bea's house. They started talking and as soon as Maro discovered Bea's profession and her need to work, she promised that she would talk to her boss about it. Maro was a physiotherapist in one of the most popular health clubs of the town. She took Bea's telephone number, talked to her boss, who was actually an extremely good friend of hers and an occasional lover, and Bea found a job the following day. Maro became thus a friend and a colleague, and 3 days later they went out together to celebrate. Up to that point, Bea was, predictably, totally unaware of Maro's sexual intentions.

As Bea told us later, Maro was marvellous on their first girls-only night out. She was very carefully dressed and she had a special way of creating a festive atmosphere. Apparently they drank a lot and they had a very good time, with Maro prompting Bea to dance and escorting her in endless *tsifte-telia* (belly-dances) and heavy *zeimbekika* (solo performances). In the end, they both went to Bea's home with the excuse that Maro had forgotten the key of her own house and it was too late to ring the bell. (Maro was actually living with her parents while Bea was living alone.) Bea told us that they made love that first night and it was not until the following morning that she fully conceptualised the situation, as previously the possibility had not even crossed her mind. This is how Bea described her feelings to me:

> The next morning I remember thinking that when I first met Maro I was afraid that with her elegance and sex appeal she could be a possible threat to my relationship with Nikos [her fiancé]. I remember myself thinking that Maro was the last woman I could suspect of having preferences for anything but a man.

Bea claimed that making love with Maro, that first night, was one of the most marvellous things that had ever happened to her:

> It is not that I had an unsatisfactory sexual relationship with Nikos. Not at all. But this was different. This was everything that I had dreamt of. I think that actually it was everything a woman ever dreams of.

I want her to come looking for me

If Bea was the hunted woman in a *kamaki* situation, the story would have ended somewhere here. According to Zinovieff (1991, 1992), the goal of a conventional Greek hunter is quick sex. As she has noted, the *kamakia* rarely establish relationships with the women they hunt and the reason these men put forward is that they automatically lose any respect for the sexually conquered woman who 'becomes equal to a prostitute and therefore worthless and without challenge'[19] (ibid. 1991: 210). The girls of the *parea* on the other hand have a completely different ethos *vis-à-vis* hunting and sex. They consider hunting meaningless if a serious *kapsoura* (infatuation) does not lie behind it. A girl might express her *kapsoura*, or not (like Maria in the first case), but at all times a serious emotional involvement has to exist.

The quality of the performance, in turn, is not judged by the accomplishment of the sexual encounter itself although the latter has to be, by general agreement, of exceptional standard. Like the Cretan men described by Herzfeld, the girls 'do not rest on their laurels, but continue to earn them' (1985: 47). In this context a meaningful flirtation is one that succeeds in turning the hunted woman into a hunter, and Bea's initiation was not thought to have been completed until the latter demonstrated her desire for and need to be with Maro. Before then, Maro had not even introduced Bea formally to the *parea*. They were spending time alone, she was helping her at work, she was flirting with her intensely, but she was also deliberately passing one or two days without seeing her. She was calling Bea, sometimes at 3.00 in the morning, was arranging romantic meetings with her by mail and they were going out quite often but she did not introduce her to any of the other girls, with the exception of Aphrodite.

Approximately three weeks later, Maro disappeared. She said to Bea that she was not feeling very well and that she was staying at home. She did not go to work for two successive days during which she avoided any communication, while Bea had specific instructions not to call at Maro's place because Maro's mother was nosey. Of course, Maro was not sick although she was indeed staying at home. Anticipating what Bea would do, she instructed us that in case she appeared at *Harama* we should not send her away, but be kind to her and keep her there until the evening ended. She also instructed us to notify her if this happened and to escort Bea home when it was time to leave.

Indeed, at the end of the third day, Bea came to *Harama* in search of Maro. I remember her walking into the place looking at the bar and approaching us slowly. Aphrodite was the only person she knew, so after excusing herself she asked her if she had seen Maro. Aphrodite replied that Maro had stayed home because she was not feeling particularly sociable these days and she invited Bea to stay for a drink. One shot led to another and after a couple of hours Bea got really drunk and started crying. She was obviously upset and confused and, as she told us later, afraid that Maro had changed her mind and started avoiding her. Bea's trouble – apart from her emotional suffering – was that she did not know anything about the *parea* and thus she did not dare share her feelings with a group of virtually unknown women. All she could do for some time was cry in the arms of Aphrodite who finally offered to take her home. I went along in order to drive Bea's car, and as soon as I reached her house I saw Maro waiting outside the door on her motorbike. She took Bea in her arms and they went inside, while Aphrodite and I were trying to find a taxi back to *Harama*. As I was informed later, Maro's timely appearance outside the house was the result of a telephone call by Martha, who informed her that Bea was being driven home. Soon after that night the two girls established a stormy relationship full of intense emotions and infinite flirting, while Bea's relationship with Nikos, her fiancé, was the subject of discussion in endless coffee gatherings, some of which will be presented in a more detailed ethnographic account later. For the moment, however, I would like to return to Bea's first contact with the *parea* and its ethnographic importance in relation to the concept and practices of erotic seduction.

The girls, like the men who practice *kamaki*, often use lies and tricks in order to approach a woman, and later, in order to achieve their goal (cf. Zinovieff, 1992). Nevertheless, as I have noted, in the case of the Greek hunters the goal is sex (ibid.) whereas in the *parea* the ultimate aim is the emotional involvement of the initiated. In the case of Bea, the critical moment when her initiation ended victoriously was when she went to *Harama* actively seeking Maro, in other words when she responded to hunting by exhibiting a motivation for hunting herself.

In order for the girls to achieve and ensure a manifestation of passion by the person with whom they have flirted, they improvise, or use some commonly shared methods. In both the cases of Bea and Chrisa the technique of evading to make the other person feel lovesick or to evoke feelings of insecurity is a device that the girls employ frequently especially with uninitiated partners. Although improvisation is greatly valued within the group, repeating a successful technique in an effective way only highlights performative excellence for, according to the girls, there are no successful techniques, only potent performers. Thus, similarly to what Herzfeld has noted about the Glendiot's tendency to enjoy well-tried tales (1985: 141), authorship in these cases does not count. Cowan (1990) and Herzfeld (1985), but also other ethnographers such as Danforth (1982) and Seremetakis (1991), have observed that an act, a dance embellishment, a tale, or a lament, and in my case a flirting technique, never has a fixed meaning. Meaning is always relative to the performer who has room for improvisation even in instances of repetition.

Most initiations in the community explore and negotiate masculinity and femininity as well as the relationship between gender identity and erotic attraction. In the context of the *parea*, flirting with women who profess a heterosexual identity is more often than not about the girls' own *eghoismos* (self-regard).[20] The conceptualization of *eghoismos* as a masculine idiom (cf. Herzfeld, 1985), is in turn central to the ethnographic exposition of these particular performances when examined together with the girls' unthreatening femininity. For it might be a masculine *eghoismos* that motivates a girl to actually chase a (heterosexual) woman, but it is femininity that permits her to approach this woman, associate with her and finally sleep in her bed. Every member of the group who wants to prove herself through successfully luring a (heterosexual) stranger into an erotic relationship has thus to rely on the belief, prevalent in the cultural context of Greece, that physical proximity between females is rarely seen as having explicit sexual connotations. Had Maro been a man, Bea – especially being an engaged woman – would probably not accept a drink at the bar, an invitation for a night out and most certainly she would not have consented to sharing a bed with her. Seen in this light, initiation is apparently a site for the renegotiation of gender ideals. More than being a mixed performance, incorporation into the group aims at exploring not only masculine and feminine performatives but also sentiments and the very poetics of selfhood (cf. Herzfeld, 1985; Dubisch, 1995: 206). Femininity, as an embodied quality and at the same time as a deinstitutionalised idiom, becomes thus the means of attracting other women, of celebrating difference, the singularity and complexity of the subject (cf. Braidotti, 2002: 11) as well as of destabilising the boundaries between homosexuality and heterosexuality (Corber and Valocchi, 2003: 2–3). What Braidotti (2002: 11–12) argues in her book *Metamorphosis* captures eloquently the politics and poetics of self-hood in the context of most initiations in the *parea*:

> One of the aims of feminist practice is to overthrow the pejorative, oppressive connotations that are built not only into the notion of difference, but also into the dialectics of Self and Other. The transmutation of values could lead to a reassertion of the positivity of difference by enabling a collective re-appraisal of the singularity of each subject in their complexity. In other words the subject of feminism is not Woman as the complementary and specular other of man but rather a complex and multi-layered embodied subject who has taken her distance from the institution of femininity . . . She, in fact, may no longer be a she, but the subject of quite another story: a subject in process . . . who has already undergone an essential metamorphosis.

At every initiation and also on other occasions, the girls reclaim qualities and feelings conventionally thought to be masculine and at the same time attempt to redefine femininity and sexuality. Confirming oneself through sexual/erotic conquest becomes a pivotal aspect of the girls' identities while associating with a woman is revealed to be far from sexually safe. As such female sexuality is not necessarily tied to a heterosexual model while the exclusively masculine tenor of *eghoismos* is challenged.

Recruiting new members into the *parea*, apart from being an excellent means for questioning conventional beliefs about sex, gender, sexuality and self-realisation (cf. Corber and Valocchi, 2003: 1–3), is also vital for the survival and growth of the community. Initiation is an important rite of passage for every girl who has to succeed at some point in establishing a relationship with a woman outside the group. In this respect, flirting with the other pertains to multiple performative and symbolic levels. It is a testing of skills for the girls, frequently an emotional and physical ordeal for the initiate and a mark of advancement for the group as a whole. Thus, on the pretext of restoring some hurt masculinity, in the course of proving one's aesthetic flair and abilities to charm, or for some other personal and usually highly contextual reason, the *parea* frequently drafts in new members. Either because they had really mastered the artistry of seduction, or because they were actually adept in identifying who was prone to respond positively to their invitation, the girls never failed in initiating new members. It is partly for that reason that the community remains alive and develops stronger and more extensive roots in Kallipoliot society. For every new girl brings with her, apart from her self, her creativity and inspiration, new links and resources that allow the group to function not only as a site for the enactment of gender performances, but also as a support network that frequently provides its members with the very means necessary to lead a different kind of life.

Conclusion

This chapter has focused on the rites and the politics of incorporation into the *parea*. I have approached initiation to the group through two distinct ethnographic cases in order to show that each ritual can take the form of a social drama (cf. Turner, 1974) that aims to negotiate particular tensions through performance. Most initiations are accomplished for the sake of the agonistic self who – as part of a collectivity – always tries to gain an advantage over itself, and they can be seen as fields for the negotiation of masculinity and femininity. Flirting with the other is then mostly about the self that 'undergoes elaborate objectification' (Faubion, 1993: 163) in the course of establishing an alternative 'poetics' of genderhood (cf. Herzfeld, 1985), or as Braidotti would call it an alternative 'figuration' (2002).

The *parea* places great emphasis on authentic performances and distinct initiations. Notions of 'spiritual community', 'rebirth', images of 'passage', 'purification', 'pain' are appropriated in order to enrich the women's repertoire with new rhetorical strategies. Their main objective is always the active production of meaning (Herzfeld, 1985), a process that is interwoven with the fashioning of a particular gender subjectivity. The case of the girls testifies to what Herzfeld has called *disemia* (1987). The *parea*, a symbolic community on the margins of a greater collectivity, assertively and aggressively refuses marginalisation and the 'problematic dualisms of normal/excluded marginal/central' (McNay, 2000: 18) by resorting to authenticity as a means of celebrating agency and creativity (ibid.: 118). The invented ritual of hunting for new people who add themselves to the group is thus an act of conspicuous self-assertion on behalf of the *parea* as a whole.

Dance, as a site of gendered experience (Cowan, 1990), and the effeminised female bodies of the girls constitute key signs in every process of initiation. Especially within the context of flirtation, the girls through dance enact masculine femininities by merging the two performatives into one in such a way that the meaning is not only dependent on the performer, but also on the way the audience chooses to respond. Since, in the Greek context, as Faubion (1993) has also observed, the expression of intimacy between women remains within the realm of propriety, the girls emphasise their female attributes in order to evoke sensuality in such a manner that dance becomes a metaphor for sexuality itself. In the course of dancing the body is thus transformed into a sexual sign whose content the girls attempt to manipulate while keeping its form intact. The Kallipoliot audience who enjoy themselves in the same space as the *parea* recognise the sign's form, but they fail to decode its content. Through the appropriation of culturally specific ideas, feelings and representations of the female body, the girls can flirt with, and even reach the bed of the hunted women and finally make love with them, while they continue to feel unthreatened and safe. Each and every instance of initiation then becomes a contest in performative ambiguity and inventiveness where the initiator has to prove her skill in passing undetected all the way to its conclusion. This is, of course, the first stage. Like a Cretan raiding (Herzfeld, 1985), where successfully stealing an animal is only half the task, a sexual encounter is, for the members of the *parea*, only the beginning.

The second stage of the contest – and this is where my *parea* differs from the classic male hunter described by Zinovieff (1991) – deals with the emotional involvement of the initiated. The effective initiator has to invoke within the other person feelings as strong as those that she herself has. In Herzfeld's ethnography, Cretan men steal to be friends (1985). In my case, the girls initiate in order to be partners in a relationship where passion and desire play the most important role. The initiation is complete only when the hunted is transformed into a hunter. Then the performance of the initiator is said to have *meaning*.

Each and every incorporation of a new member into the group, and subsequently every auspicious enactment of *eghoismos*, relies heavily on the successful production of performative ambiguity that relates not only to gender identity but also, and perhaps most importantly, to the survival and growth of the *parea*. The community lives literally on the margins of meaning. The women of the group succeed in accomplishing their project by exploiting the subsidiary as well as the primary definitions of different forms of social action in their constant attempt to formulate an alternative discourse on gender and personhood (cf. Alsop *et al.*, 2002: 103). They are women who engage in public and assertive performances of self-regard and same-sex erotic desire from standpoints invested with less power than those of the Cretan men (cf. Herzfeld, 1985), or the hunters of foreign women (cf. Zinovieff, 1991). The indeterminate and unspecified connotations of their performances allow them to achieve their objective, and flourish in the midst of a modernised albeit still provincial Greek town.

4

RELATIONSHIPS

It can be said that relationships are important fields for the intersubjective realisation of identity in so far as they render the self part of a greater socio-cultural framework. As du Boulay has noted in relation to the Greek village of Ambeli, the individual 'looks to the community . . . for his final *raison d'être*' (1974: 13). According to her, 'the family is seen to exist in the context of the community' and it is to the community that the individual 'looks to confirm his identity' (du Boulay, 1974: 13). Likewise, every woman who belongs to the *parea* ratifies her identity *vis-à-vis* the community through a series of erotic relationships and the establishment of intimate friendships.[1]

The girls enact friendship and erotic love in such a way that they both become interwoven illustrations of the strong emotional basis upon which the group is formed. Aphrodite introduced me to the *parea* with these words: 'Never forget that we are an affective community (*synaisthimatiki koinotita*).' It was not long before I realised that in this affective community different ways of relating fostered each other in a complementary fashion, constituting the expression of sentiment as a site for the enactment of alternative representations of the self (cf. Abu Lughod, 1986: 34).

The *parea* does not stand in opposition to any conventional form of relatedness, be it biogenetic kinship or marriage.[2] Both friendship that takes the form of so-called 'fictive kinship' (cf. Weston, 1991/1997: 117) and erotic love are realised in the group in such a way that not only do they not clash with one another, but they also permit the community's co-existence with the greater culture that surrounds it. It would be thus safe to support Weston's claim that gay families are not '*replacements*' but 'chronological successors to, the families in which individuals came to adulthood' (1991/1997: 116, original emphasis). In the case of the *parea*, the women remain organised around the principle of emotional self-sufficiency. Love, affection and ritualised erotic union are thus expressed in a manner that promotes non-conventional idioms of intimacy and identity (cf. Nardi, 1992; Weston, 1991/1997).

In order to explore the rich web of relationships sustained by the girls and reflect upon their importance, I will divide this chapter into two large sections. The first is concerned with the notion of friendship as performed by the *parea*, while the second examines the erotic relationships developed within the group. Throughout the chapter, I treat friendship and erotic union as particular *contexts*, 'spheres of activity in which ideas of gender can be identified' (Loizos and Papataxiarchis, 1991a: 4) and which correspond to the distinctive notions of relatedness and gender identity that the girls promote.

The idiosyncratic structures of kinship

Friendship is probably the most salient form of 'relatedness' in the *parea*. It permeates all spheres of the girls' activities and it is conceived to be the primal expression of emotional connection. In fact, the ethnography that follows suggests that friendship within the group is a versatile, all-encompassing notion around which the girls have developed their own idiosyncratic version of kinship. Every member of the group has her best friend – her buddy (*kolliti*) – who performs friendship as well as several other roles characteristic of consanguineal relationships. The friends-as-family pattern is actually found in many studies of gay communities (cf. Green, 1997: 115; Nardi, 1992; Weston, 1991/1997). It has been noted that 'fictive kinship' and close friendships in general are forms of alternative relatedness to the heterosexual family (Green, 1997: 115) that may operate as sources of social, economic and political support for gay people (Nardi, 1992: 117; Weston, 1991/1997: 115).

Choosing the term 'fictive' in order to describe relationships formed by choice is not intended to indicate the authenticity or primacy of biogenetic kinship. While the family is embedded in the western individual's social and symbolic existence, contemporary families do not always fulfil the needs of their members (cf. Collier *et al.*, 1997: 80). At least in provincial Greece this is particularly true if one's needs entail accepting and sanctioning a homoerotic lifestyle. Friendship in the *parea* is an idiom that often accomplishes roles typically performed by consanguineal kinship and ought to be treated not as a substitute that stands in opposition to, but rather as a continuance of institutionalised, biological family (cf. Weston, 1991/1997). In her detailed study of gay families, Weston adopts the terms 'families we chose', or 'families by choice' expressing however a slight reservation since '[c]hoice is an individualistic and, if you will, bourgeois notion that focuses on the subjective power of an "I" to formulate relationships to people and things, untrammeled by wordly constraints' (1991/1997: 110). I believe that both the terms 'fictive' and 'families by choice' are appropriate to describe such forms of relatedness. Because the notion of 'fictive kinship' has been employed in ethnographic accounts of spiritual kinship in traditional settings, its reclaiming in this particular instance denotes my wish to abolish the boundaries between conventional/alternative, gay/straight, homosexual/heterosexual and to treat relatedness as a multivalent context with historicity and cultural depth. In turn, the very word 'fictive' – in its semantic association with 'inventive' and 'imaginary' – could perhaps suggest creativity and choice. The self can 'imagine', 'choose' and create forms of relatedness, not as a sovereign 'I' who is the author of her experience, but rather as a subject 'with an originary capacity for figuration' (McNay, 2000: 28; cf Braidotti, 2002: 3), who is 'actively engaged in the interpretation of experience and therefore in a process of self-formation' (McNay, 2000: 76). It is precisely this creativity expressed in the context of chosen kinship – but also in all other contexts where the self is realised – that denies the inevitability of social order (ibid.: 29) revealing the hollowness of identity idioms. The latter are not hollow in the sense that they are empty of meaning but rather in that they are incomplete, permeable and imprecise capable of being filled with many dissimilar meanings at different points in time or even concurrently (Theodossopoulos, submitted; cf. Scott, 1988: 49; Alsop *et al.*, 2002: 2).

In the *parea*'s case, soon after a person is initiated into the community, one of the girls approaches her and becomes her best friend. The match is usually random, although sometimes age or particular circumstances become significant. For instance, it might happen that a girl's best friend leaves the town to work somewhere else, or to study. The buddy who is left behind might establish a novel close friendship with a new individual who joins the *parea*. This close friendship is generally an egalitarian, stable, reciprocal relationship that presupposes a commitment. Best friends behave towards each other as if they were kin and because the relationship is based on affinity its non-material and egalitarian basis might change according to the circumstances (cf. Rezende, 1999; Abrahams, 1999). Being a buddy (*kolliti*) – as the girls call their best friend – implies shouldering the responsibility to care for and provide your friend with all the emotional and practical support required. This is not to say that the rest of the *parea* remain detached. However, the best friend is the one who feels the direct consequences of whatever happens in her buddy's life. Likewise, a girl might give money to her buddy, whereas the rest of the *parea* will just lend her money and expect to be repaid at some point, while in some instances a woman might be required financially to support her best friend for long periods of time. In general, the buddies are expected to share everything and attend to the emotional and physical well-being of their best friends at all times.

Best friends occasionally have sex with each other, but they never establish a purely sexual relationship. Papataxiarchis has observed in the context of male friendships based on drinking commensality that, 'you cannot go with the wife or the sister of the man [i.e. your friend] with whom you drink every night' (1991: 168).[3]

Likewise, in my case, the best friend cannot sleep with her buddy's partner, and most of the time, entering a relationship with the ex-partner of a friend is also avoided until considerable time has passed after their separation.

The girls frequently use the word *oikogenia* (family) in order to refer to their best friends. The buddy is often called sister, or even mother by her friend[4] and sometimes the girls refer to the friends of their partners as mother-in-law. The best friends of the partners are supposed to co-operate, pool their resources and extend their care and loyalty to the partners of their friends. In the case of Papataxiarchis' male 'friends of the heart', men's partners are regarded as threatening to men's friendships (1991). Conversely, the girls do not see close friendships as standing in opposition to partnerships but as idioms that facilitate one's sexual and emotional life by being a separate and intimate psychological space. Since many sexual relationships are established between members of the group, every girl is a potential partner, and thus, according to them, every girl cannot be an intimate friend. As Lia said to me:

> One's buddy is one's family. In this way relationships within the group are more balanced. It is through this role that one can see the *parea* as a social space. It is only due to these friendships that we remain erotic beings. Otherwise we would all have been just friends.

Friendship, as established and practised by the girls, encompasses both conventional ideas about friendship and 'fictive' kinship and, as such, it extends to almost all spheres of emotional affinity. Probably the closest ethnographic relative to my *parea* are the male friendship groups recounted by Papataxiarchis (1991, 1992). His informants, like the girls, establish non-hierarchical, highly emotional alliances with an overemphasised sentimental function and a devalued instrumental one (Papataxiarchis, 1991: 161, 1992). Nevertheless, in Papataxiarchis' case, friendship stands as an anti-structure with reference to kinship (ibid.: 156), whereas in the case of the *parea*, friendship and the alternative kinship that the girls form cannot be clearly differentiated (cf. Bell and Coleman, 1999: 6). Reed-Danahay has observed that in Lavialle friendships and kin-based relations often overlap, while in Texas 'friendship is used to express a relationship of kinship' (1999: 152). Although Reed-Danahay refers here to biological kinship, whereas in the *parea* friendship stands for 'kinship we choose' relations, it is still safe to argue that in some cases it is indeed difficult to separate these two idioms of affinity. With reference to the girls, it is also important to note that the 'kinship lines' they have developed are governed strictly by the politics of fellow-feeling thus encouraging an alternative model of nurturance altogether (cf. Collier *et al.*, 1997: 77). This kind of relatedness based on personal choice but nevertheless constructed upon familial metaphors, is comparable to the case of the convent as recounted by Iossifides (1991, 1992). In the convent, the nuns consider each other sisters and their selves as married to Christ (ibid.). These female renunciators, who have denied all blood ties upon entering the convent, 'adopt the familiar idiom of kinship in order to actively transcend it' (Loizos and Papataxiarchis, 1991b: 232). The *parea* engage in a very similar process, with the exception that the girls do not exclude the body and sexuality from the equation. In Iossifides's case, the objective is the accomplishment of spirituality which is achieved through the repudiation of desire (Loizos and Papataxiarchis, 1991b: 232), while the *parea* aim at establishing strong emotional affiliations that reify both sexual desire and the body.

I will proceed with the ethnographic case of four women, all members of the group. The incidents described took place several years before I met with the community, but they became legendary since the girls frequently indulge in the pleasures of story-telling. As Herzfeld (1985) and Papataxiarchis (1991) have noted, men's talk usually focuses on male achievements thus constituting 'the fashioning of the male self, a shared experience by male friends' (Papataxiarchis, 1991: 174). Weston has also observed that apart from sentiment and emotion that play a central role in gay families by choice, 'the narrative encapsulation of a shared past' is a significant feature (1991/1997: 115). Likewise, the girls of the *parea* love recounting the achievements of individual members, as part of the shared history of the group. What is usually the main theme of these stories is not the male self, but the multiply-constituted person who stretches in all directions in her struggle to simultaneously perform more than one subjectivity.

Athena, Chara, Zoi and Lia: the chronicle of an effective diversion

Athena's buddy for years was Chara. They were friends before they met with the *parea* and they were both initiated simultaneously by two other girls, Zoi and Lia, who happened to be buddies as well. Soon after Athena and Chara were initiated (they were both 17-year-old schoolgirls at the time), Athena's mother discovered some erotic letters signed by her daughter's partner, Zoi, and started pressuring her to reveal who Zoi was and what exactly was going on between them. Furthermore, knowing that Chara was Athena's best school friend, she got in touch with Chara's mother and they started interrogating Athena together in order to find out if Chara was also involved in these stories. The implications of the *parea*'s exposure would have been extremely serious, especially since the two girls were underage. Legally, there was nothing the two mothers could do, however, a disclosure would seriously threaten the group's existence in the closed environment of Kallipolis.

Athena refused to give any information to her mother or to the mother of her best friend.[5] In fact, after the four girls discussed the situation they came up with the following plan: Chara and Lia (the two partners) kept a low profile for some time whereas Athena and Zoi (the other couple) left Kallipolis and went to Athens. There, Zoi who was studying Classics, helped her partner Athena to finish school and participate in the Panhellenic exams in order to enter university. After a strenuous preparation period, Athena got a place in the department of archaeology while Chara (Athena's buddy) who was left back home with her partner Lia (Zoi's buddy) was also successful, and soon after the exams they all reunited in Athens. When Athena's family realised that their daughter had done so well in her exams they decided to reconcile themselves with her and Zoi who was of so much help during that difficult time.[6] Athena told me that, after her successful exams her mother no longer believed that she and Zoi were having a sexual relationship. Reflecting upon those years Athena recounted:

> In her mind [implying her mother] such a relationship could only result in some catastrophe such as drug addiction or something similar. In my mother's conceptual schema a 'lesbian' like Zoi could never help me to get into university. After my success, she inferred that a boyfriend was behind that letter, and he was signing as Zoi so that nobody could find out who he really was. She still believes that. I told her the truth at the time but she never believed me.

Zoi's family was not able to send her much money in the first place and Zoi had to attend university as well as work, and help Athena with the preparation for the exams. Throughout this period, Lia, Zoi's buddy, was working at two jobs in order to send money to her friend to support herself and Athena. Chara on the other hand, Athena's buddy, was sending them clothes, books and notes from her own private teachers. As the exams approached, Lia went to Athens and stayed with her best friend and her partner. She was cooking and caring for the house while at the same time she took on a night job as a bartender so that they could all financially sustain themselves. This is how Athena spoke about that time:

> The exams were approaching and I was awfully stressed. Zoi was coaching me well, but I was still weak in ancient Greek. I remember the day that Lia arrived. It was mid-May, less than a month before the exams. We were working for hours on the big kitchen table with Zoi, while Lia was squeezing oranges for us. I do not think that I have ever drunk so much orange juice in my life! The way Lia supported her best friend, and subsequently me, shows how family is anybody you love and trust. I have separated with Zoi for some time now. But Lia was and will always be to me like a second mother. She was a mother to me when I most needed one. My biological mother knew only how to criticise and intrude in my life. She never supported me in the way the best friend of my partner did.[7]

As Dubisch (1991) has argued, women's relationships *vis-à-vis* the Greek social system remain largely undertheorised. A general bias towards male relationships developed in the public sphere, as opposed to female relationships which are seen as part of the domestic realm, can be observed throughout the corpus of Greek ethnography (ibid.: 34). The ethnographic case I have presented above supports and questions at the same time the argument that this male-centred view is largely a result of the data themself (cf. Loizos and Papataxiarchis,

1991a; Dubisch, 1991). The kind of relationship between mother and daughter, for instance, traditionally seen as permeated by the metaphor of honour and shame where shame (*dropi*) is transferred through the mother to the daughter, is evidently present in my ethnographic case. Athena's biological mother (as she herself calls her) is acting precisely within the frame customarily noted by various ethnographers. On the other hand, the story of the four girls illustrates precisely, as Dubisch has argued, that women's relationships are not natural ties 'bounded by natural feelings' (1991: 39). The alternative mother–daughter relation observed above is not simply the consequence of natural affection, but rather a constructed type of kinship which belongs *strictu sensu* neither to the domestic (ibid.: 40) nor the public realm revealing the potentiality of the spaces in-between conventional taxonomical schemata. The emotional connection developed between Athena and her 'fictive' mother-in-law, to speak in conventional terms, is experienced in terms of a collectively fashioned idiom that exists as a continuance and a corrective of natural kinship. What these girls are involved in – and subsequently all the girls of the *parea* – is a strategic recreation of kinship ties which aims at the negotiation of the notion of kinship itself. In a way this is not unique. As Just claimed, based on the observation that his informants 'politely ignored' some affinal connections (1991: 132), even conventional kinship and affinity are open to conscious manipulation: the value of kinship 'can be added when and where it is necessary' (ibid.: 131). In a somewhat similar manner, my *parea*, by attaching the quality of kinship to friendship, disconnect an inherently social metaphor from its naturalistic context.

Dunne, who has worked with lesbian couples, investigating women's professional and domestic lives, argues that the relationship between public and private is intricately related to the institutionalised character of sexual and emotional expressions (1997: 226–8). Heterosexuality, she argues, 'rests on dual processes of differentiation and hierarchisation' (1997: 228), thus obscuring the overlapping nature of public and private worlds (ibid.). Thinking anew about one's sexuality often encourages a different way of conceptualising one's social existence (ibid.: 186), while the more egalitarian basis of lesbian partnerships often accelerates women's professional and educational advancement[8] (Dunne, 1997: 228). What is probably even more important with reference to my ethnographic analysis is that homoerotic experiences are often found to be linked with feelings of empowerment (ibid.: 21, 231), evident in the case of my four informants. The connection between homoerotic experience and feelings of empowerment, however, is not intended here to serve as an instance of what McNay calls 'naïve accounts of the transformatory potential of libidinal practices' (2000: 155–6). In addition to being a context for the construction of alternative gender narratives, the *parea*, often through a culturally specific idiom of friendship, provides the girls with a support network and a discourse that enables them to question a number of social or personal ideas, beliefs and constraints. Change – partial transformation – of gender ideas and relations is certainly achieved in a 'gradual and complex fashion' (ibid.: 156) in relation to the 'inherent historicity of social practices' (McNay, 2000: 13). The case of the four women of the *parea* supports McNay's claim that 'possible transformations within gender identity are uneven and non-synchronous phenomena' that pertain both to stereotypical and alternative notions of femininity, friendship and relatedness and are thus impossible to be captured by conventional dualisms of public/private, central/marginal, hetero/homocentric (2000: 27).

Indeed, with reference to same-sex asexual relationships in the Greek context, Loizos and Papataxiarchis have noted that remarkably influential friendships – either among men or women – are developed in contexts where the actors share a common predicament (1991a: 22). It is true that the relationship between the best friends enables the girls to organise their defiance against a restrictive notion of gender normalised into distinct spheres of experience. However, I would also like to stress that the intensity of the emotional relationship is not always related to the subjective position of the actors. The ethnographic case that follows shows that the emotional bonding created between the members of the *parea* is often internal to the relationship and originates from the relationship *per se* rather than revolving around the shared sexual identity of the agents involved.[9]

Nora and Angela

Nora is one of the oldest members of the *parea*. She is a married woman in her mid-thirties with two daughters and has been working for the last ten years as a journalist. Her best friend, Stella, left for France some four years ago and, since then, Nora has established a new close friendship with Angela. Angela, in her early twenties, was born in Germany where her family still resides. She came to Greece for a summer holiday with the intention to return to Germany, but she met with the *parea* and changed her plans. The decision to stay, according to her, was partly based on the fact that she did not want to abandon her newly acquired best friend. Recounting that time, Angela told me:

'I was introduced into the parea *by Lina. It was early June and I came for a summer vacation to Greece. My Greek was rather poor, limited to the kind of vocabulary a family uses: you know, the "pass me the sugar" type of thing. However, I was having a great time for ten days until I met Lina. She approached me, she flirted with me and so forth. I got the hint from the very first moment and this surprised her a bit. So as you can imagine, the "initiation" was skipped. I got to know most of the girls and I liked them. It had not happened to me to fall for a woman before, but Lina was a really special case. I had a terrific time during the summer, I loved the atmosphere of the* parea. *Anyway, I acquired a mate as well . . . Everybody does in this company. We became close with Nora very quickly. Although I was very young at the time and at a very different stage of my life, I felt strongly for her. She was clearly the best friend I ever had, and in all*

probability the best mate I could ever have. When the summer finished I suddenly realised that I had to abandon a great romance and an intense friendship at the same time. I dealt with the first. I separated with Lina under a huge emotional load, but when the time came to leave Nora behind I just couldn't. So I made my decision. I did not want to go back to Germany. "Sod it", I said, I'll stay here with my friend [Nora]. *She meant more to me than all the other people back in Berlin and . . . here I am!'*

Angela's narrative exemplifies precisely what Kennedy has observed with reference to women's friendships in Crete, namely that these relations have 'significantly more psychological depth than many of women's other interpersonal bonds' (1986: 131). The women of Hatzi – Kennedy's field site – reported that their friendships were often as strong or stronger than their relations with their husbands and kin, and commented on 'how beautiful their lives were with their friends' (ibid.: 130). Similarly, although Angela and Nora did not exactly share the heavy burdens of a Cretan woman's life, they developed an emotional bond that compares to and often 'surpasses kinship ties' (Kennedy, 1986: 121). The women of Hatzi had to deal with a strenuous 'androcentric' environment permeated by 'jealousy, hostility and gossip' (ibid.: 123). A best friend they could trust was for them, not surprisingly, a precious relation. Conversely, the women of the *parea*, although they share the common fear of exposure and at the same time a collective experience of difference, frequently appear to value their friendships independently of the external environment. In the specific example of Angela and Nora, the decision of Angela to stay in Kallipolis was certainly not cost-effective. Her life would have been much easier had she left. Angela, and other girls of the group who are young, single and economically independent, always have the option of residing in another town or city where their movements would be significantly less restricted. However, many of them choose to remain part of this affective community and to jealously maintain their friendships. As Emily, a lawyer in her early thirties, once said to me: 'It would be easier to live my life somewhere else. But, wherever I go, without my friends, without my *parea*, I will feel kinless, without a homeland [*apatris*]. So I choose to be here amongst my family.'

Close friendship is a familiar notion in Greek ethnography. The girls offer another example of intense emotional bonds developed and maintained away from the jurisdiction of institutionalised kinship, which none the less contain kinship in an alternative form. It would be extremely difficult and analytically pointless to attempt a classification of the ethnographic case of the *parea*. Whether one calls what these women have developed 'alternative kinship' or 'alternative friendship' makes, I think, no real difference. The girls engage in a collective process of constructing strong emotional ties as creative, autonomous and at the same time culturally constructed agents. Inherent in this process, is in turn, the blurring of traditional boundaries in a conspicuous mixing of allegedly distinct forms of relatedness. 'The conscious playing with ambiguity, uncertainty and ambivalence which friendship affords' (Rapport,

1999: 115) becomes the context for the construction of relations between people who are not bound by biogenetic kinship ties, but nevertheless through living together develop connections similar to the ones observed between relatives (cf. Schneider and Smith, 1978: 42; Abu Lughod, 1986: 62).

The group as an affective community, and more specifically the concept of the best friend, are certainly not unique examples of contexts where alternative idioms of relatedness and personhood are constructed. As Bell and Coleman have argued 'networks of intimacy, frequently unrelated to kinship ties constitute key arenas of social interaction and identity formation' (1999: 5). Furthermore, the corpus of Greek ethnography has numerous other examples to offer. First, the spiritual kinship built through baptism, which as Herzfeld (1992) argues, is an influential part of the social organisation. The convent (Iossifides, 1991), male and female friendships and so forth are but a few of the different 'transformational contexts' in Greece at present (Loizos and Papataxiarchis, 1991). What is significant with reference to the *parea*'s process of reconstructing familiar cultural idioms is that they clearly aim towards multiplicity rather than towards an undifferentiated identity. Their affective community does not constitute solely an anti-structure to kinship (as for instance in Papataxiarchis', 1991, or Kennedy's, 1991, cases), or to the secular world (cf. Iossifides, 1991, 1992). Friendship in the *parea* is a framework where kinship, gender, identity and locality are creatively and simultaneously redefined.

The girls 'play' with more than one metaphor at the same time in an attempt to deconstruct and reassemble them in different ways. Friendship, kinship, emotions become in the *parea* what Herzfeld suggested for gender roles: 'facets of a more general rhetoric of concealment and display' (1986: 219). Friendship is the only legitimate homosexual relation sanctioned by Greek culture. It is not surprising then, that the girls chose to imbue it with such a rich meaning. Seen in this light, the fusion and transformation of familiar cultural constructs is part of the general politic of concealment and display that the girls strategically employ in order to exist convivially with the greater culture that surrounds them.

Falling in love; tying the knot: flirtation and relationships in the *parea*

The women of the *parea* devote much time and energy to flirting and establishing relationships with each other. *Harama*, their favourite haunt, is transformed every night into a scene where the girls, through drinking and dancing, literally stage their erotic selves. My introduction to this sexual and emotional world relied on observation and on taking active part in conversations, since the *parea*'s commentary on 'things that happen' proved, sometimes, to be more useful than witnessing the happenings themselves. Who is with whom, why and for how long, how are they getting on, when was the last time they had a fight and why, are subjects of a collective meta-commentary regularly practised by the girls, that provided me with insights I would never have gained just by observing them. I was there every night, at the same place following the *parea*'s rhythms. Yet, the picture I was constructing was poor, flat and wordy in comparison to the complex, colourful and concise illustrations that the girls were producing. In time, I learned how to listen as well as how to observe.

The girls assert that they foster an alternative sexuality. However, what is alternative about their erotic lives goes beyond homosexual praxis to the construction of an erotic idiom that emphasises pleasure *per se*. As Loizos and Papataxiarchis (1991a) have noted, in the Greek context men and women's sexualities are intrinsically related to conjugality and procreation. Even in the case of pre-marital sex, which is nowadays an established part of erotic behaviour in Greece, many women appear to treat sex within the schema of conception: 'what makes sex natural, pleasurable and desirable is that it leaves the door to conception open' (Loizos and Papataxiarchis, 1991b: 225). A sample of the ethnographic accounts of female sexuality in Greece fully supports the authors' claim. Handman observed that Pournariot women treated sexual encounters within wedlock as a necessary evil for procreation (1983: 122). Hirschon accounted for the opinions of the Yerania women who talk of sexual intercourse as the evil act (1978: 68), and regarded love itself as a catastrophic and undesirable emotion (1989: 114).[10] Sex and courtship in Greek ethnography seem to be inseparable from procreation and frequently from the domestic model itself and are depicted as governed by the rules of chastity and naturalisation.[11] The woman who actively seeks to enjoy herself, even in the context of the café, constitutes the dangerous and undesirable metaphor of the female who does not – as she ought to – repudiate (sexual) pleasure (Cowan, 1991: 197).

It is true that the model of female sexuality in Greece has grown out of the 'shame–chastity–reproduction–marriage' syndrome and revolves nowadays increasingly around pleasure and satisfaction. As the socio-eonomic circumstances change, erotic relationships are conceptualised nowadays in terms of romantic love and voluntary commitment as opposed to honour and 'settling' (*apokatastasi*) that predominated in the past (cf. Collier, 1997: 68). However, the desirable cross-sex relation in the Greek context still remains largely one that is – or has the potential to be – stable, symbolically related to partnership if not marriage and as a result not completely disengaged from reproduction[12] (cf. Argyrou, 1996: 90–2). In this framework, the girls undoubtedly promote an alternative model of sexuality since, in the *parea*, sexual expression is organised solely around pleasure and is completely disengaged both from reproduction and the idea of stability. Relationships are established consciously on an ephemeral basis, and excitement is the only criterion of a fulfilling love life. In many respects the girls enact Gidden's concept of 'pure relationship',[13] that is:

> a situation where a social relation is entered into for its own sake, for what can be derived by each person from a sustained association with another and which is continued insofar as it is thought by both partners to deliver enough satisfactions for each individual to stay within it.
> (1992: 58)

Through flirting and the establishment of short-lived relationships, the *parea* promotes a different notion of female sexuality that blurs the boundaries between self and other, and questions nature and the distinction between masculinity and femininity (cf. Munt, 1998: 43). In the ethnography that follows, the girls exhibit, through instances of effective performance and semiotic appropriation of familiar signs, a seemingly conventional but nevertheless distinct erotic behaviour. The first part of this section is devoted to flirtation, the *parea*'s all-time classic occupation, while the second is devoted to the ritualised establishment of erotic relationships.

Love is in the air

The girls adore flirting and love the spectacle of someone flirting. They can spot it immediately and usually simultaneously, or even prior to the person concerned. For them, life without flirtation is dry and boring and thus they are always ready to transmit or receive the magic waves of courtship. The *parea* treats eroticism as a communicative skill *par excellence* and a matter of ambience. As Lillian once characteristically said: 'If love is not in the air it is nowhere' [meaning if people do not flirt with each other then passion is absent]. So everybody makes sure that the *parea*'s air at least, is full of love.

Since flirting is such an important enterprise it is not surprising that the girls practise it in a thousand and one different ways. Amongst them, who is going to flirt in the most innovative fashion is an all-time classic competition. Flirting with a person outside the *parea* (that is, initiating a new girl) is for the girls one of the most exciting and refreshing spectacles of 'agonistic' masculinity (cf. Zinovieff, 1992; Herzfeld, 1985). However, flirting within the *parea* never loses its glamour because it calls for even more complex and subtle exhibitions of performative excellence. I therefore chose to open my ethnographic presentation of the girls' flirting techniques with the following instance of courtship in order to demonstrate the intricate forms that flirtation can take among the girls.

It is Friday, 10.00 in the evening and Georgia's house is full of people. Aphrodite, Maro, Martha, Giota, Klairi, Fillipa, Lia, Emily, Athena, Elena and myself are trying to find a place in front of one of the house's mirrors. The same is happening in Vivi's house with another bunch of girls preparing themselves for the night. We all like this little ritual, although we only do it twice a month or so. The wardrobes are wide open and on the floor there are bags and small suitcases full of clothes, shoes, makeup bottles, lipsticks and hair dryers everywhere.[14] *In a corner of the bathroom, Giota is applying mascara to Martha whilst shouting at her to stand still, or she would end up like a clown. Martha is laughing and instead of obeying her would-be beautician she slaps Lia's bottom in a playful manner. Maro is bringing us coffee from the kitchen, balancing delicately on incredibly high heels, while Georgia stretches her leg provocatively on my knee with the excuse of arranging her stockings. I manage to say something flattering about this remarkably long and slim leg that makes its delighted owner smile self-approvingly. Aphrodite comes for some help with her hair and Klairi who is sitting next to me on the couch starts spreading a handful of gel on it. Giota is now painting her nails and Athena is prompting her to stop doing that because it is 'proven that nail polish is cancerous when it comes in contact with the interior of your body'. Giota remains silent while Klairi remarks innocently: 'Athena has stopped biting her nails for all I know, long ago'. Aphrodite looks at me to make sure that I got the hint.*

The scene just described had three main protagonists: Giota, Athena and Klairi. Giota and Athena had a short affair that ended two months before. After their separation and, up to that night, Giota had not appeared interested in initiating a new relationship, not even a short affair, whereas Athena already had a new partner. Her comment towards Giota about the interior of the body (connoting the vagina) was thus a sharp reminder of her prolonged singleness. It was almost as if she was saying to her: 'you choose to stay alone just because you haven't got over me yet'. It was just then that Klairi took the chance to send a double message. First, an ironic hint towards Athena: 'your word-game failed to make sense' and, second, a clue to Giota: 'I care for you and I do not intend you to stay single for long.' After that night, Giota and Klairi were flirting intensely for two weeks. The above instance was the start of a stormy relationship that lasted for more than eight months.

Flirtation, as a genuine case of the poetics of erotic interaction is based on surprise, originality and creativity (cf. Herzfeld, 1985: 16). In the case that follows, Carolina offers an example of flirting ingenuity based on the element of surprise. The courting is aimed at Fillipa, Carolina's girlfriend for the last three years:

The sound of Lillian's voice singing one of our favourite songs is soothing. The place is full of smoke and young people standing with their backs against the wall. Harama is a theatre, now more than ever. It is almost as if everybody is holding their breath. Lillian's voice a cappella is the only sound. A young girl steps onto the dance floor. She offers Lillian a bouquet of red carnations. Lillian is flattered and embarrassed. She keeps her eyes on the floor. The door opens and somebody breaks the silence. It is a man holding a big bunch of red tulips. He approaches Sotiris, the barman. It is disturbing, we want to listen to the song. The man walks slowly towards Fillipa. He gives her the flowers and disappears. The girls look puzzled. Fillipa is reading a card. She takes her coat. She is already gone. Nobody asks where to, she will tell us everything tomorrow.

That night Carolina was supposed to be on a business trip in Athens with her husband, but due to something unexpected she ended up going alone. The flowers that arrived at Harama for her partner Fillipa were accompanied by a card that, as we found out later, read laconically: '*There is a taxi outside. I'll be waiting. I love you deeply. Carolina.'* Fillipa entered the taxi that had specific instructions to drive her to an expensive hotel in Athens where Carolina had reserved a special room, and was waiting for Fillipa so that they could have breakfast together. What was even more surprising was that Carolina had arranged a four-day trip to Milan for the two of them. Soon after breakfast they flew together to Italy.

Carolina's flirting initiative was treated by the *parea* very positively. It was considered to be sophisticated courting not only because it was based on surprise but mostly due to the fact that its ultimate success relied upon Fillipa's attitude. Carolina staged a romance that could not have been realised had Fillipa not entered the taxi, or if she had second thoughts about the destination, or even if she had been hesitant to alter her work arrangements. What Carolina did, according to the girls, was a delicate 'touch-up' on a long-lasting relationship. 'It was elegant, it had the touch of the first-time-in-love' as Elena said, or 'It was cinematic, and at the same time effective in reminding Fillipa that she should always remain spontaneous and erotic' as Martha put it.

As I have already mentioned, flirtation is for the girls a highly cultivated communicative skill, an erotic conversation where body language, dancing and consumption habits are all part of the *parea*'s expressive mode. The example that follows demonstrates precisely how the girls treat dance both as performance and experience (Cowan, 1990). The protagonists are Zina and Elia, an older and a relatively new member of the group. Zina was part of the *parea* long before I was introduced into it. She had been living for some time in Thessaloniki where she was studying law. Through her student years she kept in touch with the girls and often came to Kallipolis to 'go wild' with 'her mates'. However, for the previous ten months her visits had been rare. Apparently she had an extremely difficult time due to her involvement in the drug culture of the city. As soon as she graduated, Zina returned to Kallipolis and to the *parea* because, as she said, this was 'the only way for her to be cured'. Once back, her adaptation to 'the old ways' was a matter of days. I soon realised that she was a beloved friend of the older members who kept organising special parties at *Harama* to welcome and relax her. The girls created a very family-like atmosphere and placed Zina at the centre of attention and affection. We soon learned her tastes, her previous relationships, we witnessed all the ups and downs of her 'illness' and we updated her on every single thing that happened while she was absent, so that the time gap was filled from both sides. The instance recounted below marked Zina's final reincorporation into the group and the conclusion of her 'adventures':[15]

It's Thursday and Harama *is not full yet. Thomas, the owner, said that there were not many reservations that night. He didn't seem upset however. 'We will party today girls', he announced in a playful manner. Lillian and Thekla, the singers, and members of the* parea, *opened the night with Zina's favourite song. Sotiris, the barman, will have to work hard tonight with all the shots and the special treatments that each one of us is ordering for Zina. I cannot but observe her from where I sit. She is beautiful, or at least she is a 'type'. She looks small though and tired, something that shows in her face. Nevertheless, she is energetic, she laughs all the time and she seems anxious to talk with everybody . . .*

Half of the songs tonight are devoted to 'Zina and the girls'. The customers must be at a loss, reckoning that it must be somebody's birthday. Zina is escorted by Elia to the dance floor. They dance a tsifteteli [belly-dance] *that proves to everybody that Zina hasn't lost her touch. They manipulate each other's bodies beautifully and they look one another straight in the eyes. The rhythm changes into a zeimbekiko* [solo performance] *and Elia crouches first. She wants Zina to dance the solo, which she performs really well. Elia waves at the waiter. He comes and throws at Zina's feet dozens of flowers. They are not cut, as usual, but whole with their stems. Elia waves at Martha who goes onto the dance floor with two tequila shots. Elia and Zina drink them 'bottoms up' as the latter is dancing.*

The above description of Elia and Zina dancing is only one of the many examples of manipulating the meaning of traditional celebratory practices. Apart from the dance itself, it is worth stressing the use of flowers as a flirting device. Flowers are conventionally thrown to dancers and singers as a means of honouring their abilities. They can also be employed in conventional courting behaviour, while they frequently become the field of antagonism usually between male celebrants (i.e. whose 'table'[16] throws more flowers to the members of their company who dance, or to the singers). The flowers thrown in all the above cases are cut high near the head, so that they can be tossed from a distance. Elia, however, ordered the flowers with their stems in an attempt to give to the gesture an additional distinct meaning from the one it already had. She was seemingly throwing flowers to a good dancer, but in reality, she was *offering* them to Zina. By slightly altering the form of the flowers used, she changed the meaning of the gesture in a way that nobody but the *parea* realised. The girls enjoyed this flirting technique because although it lacked in complexity and surprise, it was still spontaneous, original, and most importantly, public. For even the most sophisticated flirtation when done in private is considered by the community to be performatively weak. The *parea* evaluates courting behaviour in terms of performance, while in turn, a stylised performance in the context of the group draws its strength from its audience. Hence, the strongest possible flirting should ideally combine complexity, originality and surprise, and be preferably realised in front of a mixed audience (i.e. in front of the *parea* and unrelated people) succeeding thus in pertaining to more than one sphere of meaning (cf. Herzfeld, 1985).

In this sense, dance is one of the *parea*'s favourite contexts for flirtation. For it is public and enables the girls to exploit the ambiguity of familiar body postures in order to display their eroticism to each other and to conceal it from the rest of the celebrants who happen to be present at *Harama*. The women of the *parea*, acknowledging that meaning does not 'lie in the body' but on the 'codes used for reading the body' (cf. Cowan, 1990: 25), take advantage of the neutralising effect of two female bodies dancing sensually. In the eyes of the Kallipoliots, the sensuality evoked by these bodies can only be directed outwards, that is, towards the male audience and not inwards (i.e. at the female dance-partner). In this manner, the girls engage in a process of simultaneous decontextualisation and recontextualisation of the dance. They convert the event into a compelling spectacle while, at the same time, shielded by this seemingly safe same-sex context, they employ elaborate dancing techniques in order to flirt with each other.

In this process of recontextualisation, the semiotics of the dance change, the male/female dichotomy collapses and the body comes to embody a syncretic and non-hierarchical experience of gender. The significance of such instances of semantic ambiguity is then not simply the result of a collective, intellectual 'fetishization of symbolic indeterminacy' (McNay, 2000: 155) but relates to a conceptualisation of gender as 'a lived set of embodied potentialities' (ibid.: 25). As Butler suggests, the construction of embodied gendered selves is to be viewed as 'a temporal process' (1993: 10) while the indeterminacy of embodiment and performance (cf. McNay, 2000: 33) pertains to both the destabilisation and the crystallisation of gender norms (cf. Butler, 1993). The women of my *parea* use the dance both as a language and as a meta-language. As Cowan argues, the dance-postures that the performers assume, foster and often challenge gender ideas and relations (1990: 24). Likewise, through dance, the girls formulate an alternative praxis and at the same time articulate political (non-verbal) statements about the concept and the experience of gender, albeit by means of the same stereotypes they wish to challenge[17] which are, as a result, further reified. In every such ambiguous performance gender ideals are at once overthrown and reinscribed upon the body highlighting the 'human capacity for simultaneously incorporating and transcending the very variables . . . which structure it' (Braidotti, 2002: 21).

Apart from dance, alcohol consumption is another site of non-verbal erotic communication. The different qualities of alcoholic spirits, such as strength and colour, constitute metaphors for distinct emotions. Again in this case the symbolism is familiar, but so idiomatically reproduced by the *parea* that those who do not share the girls' codes cannot translate them. The specific context of *Harama* makes alcohol consumption an even more tangled practice, for it is a space where everybody, irrespectively of their gender or other considerations, is entitled to drink and free to choose from a variety of spirits. In this modernised nightspot which is frequented by relatively younger people, women in general are not regarded as marginal to the production of *kefi* (high spirits)[18] (cf. Papagaroufali, 1992: 49). The relatively flexible atmosphere of *Harama* enables the girls to practise drinking in a subversive manner and therefore to question conventional ideas about alcohol consumption and femininity (cf. Papagaroufali, 1992; Cowan, 1990: 65–7).

Papagaroufali (1992) gives an account of women who transform a traditionally male space, a *kafeneio* (coffee house), into their meeting place and strategically engage in convivial drinking as a means of negotiating dominant discourses on gender and power. The position of women in celebratory contexts is conventionally governed by the rules of modesty and restraint since drunkenness, loss of control, and release of sensuality are considered dangerous for the reputation of the household (Cowan, 1990; Papagaroufali, 1992; and also Driessen, 1992, for Andalusia). Through the establishment of the 'Women's Coffeehouse', Papagaroufali's informants inverted the traditional dynamics by refusing to allow people, and especially men, to survey their drinking behaviour (1992: 59). Instead, the women became the hosts and the insiders and therefore those who watched the visitors of their social space (ibid.).

In my case, the politics of subversion take a more subtle form. The *parea* chooses a place where all celebrants have equal access to the consumption of alcohol and, by following the codes of male stamina, they manipulate the sign of female modesty. They drink vast quantities of alcohol but they remain in control thus exhibiting a conventionally male quality (cf. Madianou-Gefou, 1992) which can nevertheless pass as female modesty.[19] In other words, they reconcile through performance what is traditionally treated as a pair of irreconcilable opposites, achieving a sophisticated diffusion of boundaries. In this manner, alcohol consumption in the realm of the *parea* constitutes a metaphor for the celebration of the syncretic self, who focuses on internal multiplicity in an attempt to transgress structural oppositions rather than simply invert them.

With reference to flirtation, alcohol is, as I noted, a key substance of the *parea*'s erotic conversations. In the case that follows, courting is realised by means of dance and consumption, always in the mixed scene at *Harama*, and indispensably from the general politics of concealment and display (Herzfeld, 1987). The protagonists of this example are three girls named Eve, Elena and Agnes. Elena and Agnes, both in their early twenties, were a couple but lately they were not getting on so well. The main reason for that was Elena's flirtatious encounters with Eve, a relatively new member of the *parea*, that provoked Agnes' jealousy. Eve was 17 years old at the time and recently separated from Martha, the girl who initiated her.

Elena is treating us to the fifth round of shots tonight. She came to Harama *alone, since she and Agnes, her partner, had a row earlier in the afternoon at the tavern. Agnes is terribly jealous of Eve to the point that she only came to the tavern because she knew that Eve was working and was not going to be there. The rest of the girls slightly disapprove of Agnes' hostility towards Eve, and Tania, her best-friend, prompts Agnes to 'take the situation into her own hands' and stop directing her emotions towards the girl. 'Eve is free to do whatever she wants', Tania said to Agnes at one point. 'You want her?* [implying Elena] *Get her back. You can't? Let her go. Eve is only taking her chances.'*[20] *Agnes, however, would not change her mind. When Eve arrived unexpectedly at the tavern, 'because her work had finished earlier', Agnes left the place furious, after saying to Elena, her partner: 'Do whatever you want with her. I don't give a damn.'*

Later that night Elena came to Harama *alone and she was happily and freely flirting with Eve. I was more than sure that her relationship with Agnes was soon going to end, but Aphrodite had a different opinion: 'The new is beautiful, but the old is always better',*[21] *she said to me. Although I understood what she meant, I couldn't quite relate the proverb to the situation and I was too preoccupied, like the others, with the spectacle of Elena and Eve dancing. I did not give Aphrodite's words any more thought at the time. I just observed Eve sensually moving her body. 'Her youth is blossoming. This is why I fell for her', Martha commented, and I fully sympathised with her. She and Eve had separated just a month ago, but Martha seemed to have gotten over it completely and she was now enjoying the sight of Eve flirting on the dance floor with someone else.*

In the midst of the spectacle, the door opened, shedding some light on the place and Agnes appeared. Her unexpected entrance promised everyone a night full of incident. Agnes took a seat at the bar and started chatting with Sotiris, the barman. When her partner Elena and Eve left the dance floor and came over to us, Agnes was behaving indifferently to their mutual flirting. She appeared too preoccupied with a round of shots she decided to treat us with, and she was explaining to Sotiris what exactly she wanted him to do. The first round arrived and they were ordinary shots of vodka. The second round though, took us completely by surprise. The shots were plain water. Agnes laughed. 'It served you right', she said looking persistently at Elena. We expected the next shot to be vodka or at least water. But no, we were wrong, the next shot was pure alcohol[22] *that burnt our stomachs. Agnes grasped Elena by the waist and looked her straight in the eyes saying: 'What's the matter? Was that one too strong for you?' Five minutes later, they were kissing passionately in the lounge. It was then that I remembered Aphrodite's words: 'the old is better', or at least more experienced, I whispered to myself . . .*

Agnes confirmed Aphrodite's speculation by demonstrating to everyone that her skills in erotic communication were superior and far more sophisticated than those of Eve: 'The difference between me and the 17 year old you are flirting with, is as big as the difference between water and pure alcohol.' This is what Agnes metaphorically but explicitly said to her partner Elena. According to Klairi, a girl of the *parea*, had Eve been more experienced, she could have shown that her flirting skills were equally cultivated. However, Eve did not do that, so Agnes was proclaimed the winner in this courting contest. Through the discussions I had with some of the girls about this incident, it became apparent that somehow everyone believed that Agnes and Elena's relationship was not threatened by Eve. Their conviction was based on the knowledge the girls had of Agnes and her talent to flirt and charm people. When I asked Martha, Eve's former partner, 'whom she had been betting on', Martha said to me that she had not believed for a moment that Eve could prevail upon Agnes:

> and not because she is younger than her. Eve's weak point is not her youth, but her primitiveness. She is acting without thinking. She can charm anybody with her physical appearance, but when it comes to creativity and inventiveness, when it comes to originality, she falls short of one's expectations. But don't fool yourself. She is a quick

> learner. In a couple of years you won't recognise her [meaning she will improve dramatically].

I have discussed extensively with the girls their beliefs about flirtation, and particularly whether they considered flirting to be a talent or a skill. There was a general agreement that flirting is a skill. 'People learn how to flirt better when they practise it', as Emily said. According to the women of the *parea*, proficiency in flirting does not correspond to one's age, but certainly reflects one's lifestyle:

> You can find older people that do not know how to flirt and you can find adolescents that master it . . . The more you flirt, the more you learn, the more **innovative** [*efeuretikos*] and **original** [*authentikos*] you become. It's like sex. The less you practise it, the more you are prone to lose the touch, Lillian maintained [original emphasis].

The use of alcohol as a means of erotic communication is certainly not exclusive to the *parea*. Papagaroufali (1992) gives an account of young women who take the initiative when courting men at Athenian bars. Alcohol consumption becomes in this case a context and a 'medium for purely sexual communication' (ibid.: 64–5). Likewise, for the girls of the *parea*, alcoholic spirits serve also as metaphors on the basis of which a non-verbal dialogue is realised. The effectiveness of flirting in such cases relies heavily on the originality and wit so to speak of the metaphor. What is important for my informants, in addition to the pleasure of conquest (cf. Papagaroufali, 1992: 65), is the gratification they feel in accomplishing an effective performance that triggers an enthusiastic response. In other words, although the practice itself is similar, the motives of the women of the *parea* and those of Papagaroufali's informants are not identical. In her case, the women use alcoholic drinking as means to 'reverse and thus violate established roles' (ibid.: 65–6), whereas in the framework of the group alcohol consumption becomes a 'language' that enables the women to articulate and enrich complex erotic utterances. The *parea* manipulates established ideas about gender, not so much through direct reversal and violation as through mixing male and female elements into a multi-gendered performance. The *kamaki* (erotic hunt) practised by the girls is organised around a different ideology from the one promoted either in Papagaroufali's instance (1992) or, for example, in Zinovieff's case (1991). The latter's informants, the men who hunt foreign women, in search for often a single sexual encounter, claim that an educated hunter is useless: 'You don't screw with books', they assert (Zinovieff, 1991: 208, 1992).

For the *parea*, on the other hand, intellect is regarded as superior to physical characteristics. According to my informants, it is creativity that constitutes sophisticated flirting, and the ability to express oneself symbolically and to construct new webs of signification. Similarly to my argument with reference to the forms that relatedness takes within the *parea*, and the claim I put forward earlier in relation to the 'resignification' of dance events, I believe that flirting is a context where 'originary capacity for figuration' is demonstrated (McNay, 2000: 21). Semantic dislocation – a feature of the *parea*'s collective ethos *par excellence* – is more than a discursive or practical game of resistance and subversion. It is a site for the realisation of agency as the creative 'capacity to institute new or unanticipated modes of behaviour' (ibid.) which, nevertheless, are historically and culturally charged thus yielding to 'cultural, institutional and instersubjective constraints' (McNay, 2000: 23). What is then valued most by the girls is not only a politic of resistance but also *creativity* and semiotic *originality* manifested in flirting as the ability to communicate the same message: 'I want you to want me as much as I want you, and I intend to show that in public', in a slightly different and unexpected manner each time.

The girl's courting behaviour is literally balanced between cultural stereotype and authenticity (cf. Faubion, 1993). The transformation of shared cultural codes, such as dance and consumption, into a private/public dialect fostered by the group as a whole, forms the basis for meaningful performances and yet ones that do not openly provoke the heterosexual ethos of the town. The public realisation of the sensual sexual self is the ultimate goal for the girls *vis-à-vis* flirtation. The latter consists of the articulation of an assertive public statement of desire, but it is a performance that acquires meaning only if reciprocated by an equally assertive public statement. In this context the 'personal is political', but the women of my group display by concealment and thus employ and reify the very cultural idioms they wish to transcend. In all these erotic dialogues, the *parea* are constructing an idiosyncratic gay identity, one that is 'established in the glance of others and exchanged by the looks' (Munt, 1998: 31) and the postures, one that is consumed, danced, reflected upon and enacted in a discursive and embodied fashion. None the less, the girls do not only fall in love, but they also 'tie the knot', albeit temporarily. The next section is then about the *parea*'s ritualised 'weddings'.

The wedding

> *Mana hekeis mi sou tzi, an da mila mi poulsis.*
> *Mana na paou, na ino horas.*
>
> [Mother you put me on the scales you sold me like a bunch of apples.
> Mother now I'll go and become the property of strangers][23]

We are all gathered as usually around the bar. We pretend to enjoy the music, but everybody is anxious to find out what happened with Maria and Michaella. Every now and then some girl is looking at the door just to check if anyone is coming. Tania orders a round of shots and just before we drink them she asks: 'OK Bet. Are we going to have a wedding or not?' The girls are laughing. 'We will soon know, come on', Nana urged them to stop guessing. At some point the door opens. It is Maria and Michaella, together. They approach the bar. They are both wearing the same tiny pendant: a silver ligature of two M's. The new relationship will be celebrated for three whole days as is customary.

The establishment of a new erotic relationship is, for the *parea*, a highly ritualised instance. The girls are usually paired or in the process of flirting, and their erotic liaisons can last from anything between a month and three years. The average length of a relationship though is between six and eight months. Three-year relationships are relatively rare while a month-long relationship is equally uncommon. Short relationships, however, are proportionally more than those which last for more than a year. The pattern of short-term erotic relationships has been noted by other studies of gay communities as well (cf. Green, 1997: 116). Green has argued that long-lasting relationships were probably seen as anti-community by lesbian feminists, because although they 'did not involve men, the personal/private character of long term relationships threatened to remove the couple from the public/political sphere, to put them back in the home' (1997: 120). The *parea* does not regard relationships as being a danger to the community's political vigour, probably because activism is not part of the group's agenda in the first place. As I have noted before, the girls promote a concept of lover-relation that resembles Gidden's notion of the pure relationship in so far as they believe that people should 'sustain an association with one another' for as long as 'both partners get enough satisfaction' (1992: 58).

According to the *parea*, every relationship is a chance for 'seeing oneself through the eyes of others' and therefore an important opportunity for growth, change and reflection. In order to highlight the significance of a lover relationship, the girls always mark its start by a public ritual. It is worth noting that two girls can hang out together, sleep together, or flirt with each other for months without having a relationship or, at least, without regarding their affair as being a relationship. In order for two individuals to become a couple certain rituals have to be performed. The protagonists of the above example, Maria and Michaella, were in fact together for some three months. However, they had not decided whether they wanted to formalise their relationship and they were thus systematically avoiding, up to that night, calling their affair (*shesi*) a relationship (*desmos*).

The difference between an affair (*shesi*) and a formal relationship (*desmos*) is mainly one of ritualistic acknowledgement. The establishment of a relationship does not necessarily imply that the partners are more committed to each other, or that they have different responsibilities deriving from their union. Neither is a *desmos* necessarily more stable than a *shesi*. Both types of erotic relationship are regarded by the *parea* as experiences and last as long as they 'have something new to give', as Angela put it. 'In the beginning of any *kapsoura* (infatuation) people might fantasise that they will stay together forever. But every relationship is really another experience of the many you seek in life' (Maria). Nevertheless, every new relationship, although it does not necessarily imply structural changes in the lives of the partners, remains important for the construction of their individual narratives. The girls reflect on their personal histories in terms of their past relationships. The passage of time and the contextual changes in their lives are accounted for in terms of 'the time of Maria' (when I was with Maria) or 'after I separated with Chrisa'. Every new *desmos* is considered as a distinct cycle in the life of each girl and as a means of realising the self intersubjectively:

> Each formal relationship [*desmos*] is a process of self-reflection. You decide to see your self through the eyes, the body and the senses of the other. You **choose** to embark on this project, and this is what we celebrate: a conscious decision to start something that will end soon, but during which you will enrich yourself. It is a wedding [*gamos*]; the wedding of those different parts of your self that will be reflected in the multiple mirrors the other is going to hold in front of you.
>
> (Emily, original emphasis)

In a sense then, the girls' 'wedding' is a rite of passage, or actually one of the many rites they invent to mark their continual passage from one state to another. What is peculiar to the *parea* though, is that it is the actor who attempts to construct her own transformation by deciding that this and not another relationship will serve as a symbolic context for the enactment of self. In turn, all these decisions are performed and ritualistically celebrated in the mixed scene of *Harama*, through the familiar cultural metaphor of a 'wedding' thus substantiating Dubisch's claim that culture itself is negotiable (1986).

I will now proceed to account for the ritualistic acknowledgment of a relationship as invented and performed by the *parea*. One of the most important features of the 'wedding' is the materialisation of the rite into a symbol, the 'bond' or *desimo* as the girls call it. The bond consists of two identical objects that the partners carry or wear as tangible evidence of their union. As long as the bond exists the relationship is considered valid. The following ethnographic example demonstrates how a couple regarded themselves as being in a relaionship although they were physically and geographically separated for quite some time.

The parea *is extremely happy tonight because Kia is behind the bar. Sotiris, the old and beloved barman, has gone to work on an island for some three months and Kia, an established member of the* parea, *has taken his place. Although everybody misses Sotiris, it is good to have Kia in there. She is able to follow even faster than Sotiris all the different drinks that the girls order. Sotiris had learned the* parea*'s ways through practice and, as a result, he was always prone to make a crucial mistake in the preparation of the different drinks, whereas Kia knows exactly what to serve and when. The girls are happy though for another reason as well. They believe that some work will benefit Kia who is somehow 'down' these days. Her 'latest adventure', a Swedish girl, has gone back to her country and Kia misses her terribly. Rea has been away intermittently for the past* *two years but Kia was still wearing the 'bond', a watch on her right hand, and so was Rea. Their relationship can at best be described as inactive but it was regarded as extant and legitimate by everyone.*

The bond is taken off only when the girls decide to separate formally. Its presence signifies that the partners still remain in the conceptual realm of the relationship irrespective of any other affairs and sexual/emotional encounters they might have. In the example of Kia and Rea, the two girls were actually leading entirely different lives, but they still refused to end their – purely platonic by this time – relationship that had started three years ago.

It has been a month now since Kia began working in the bar. Harama *is full almost every night despite the hot weather. Most of the indoors clubs close for the summer but* Harama*'s customers seem to be content with the air-conditioning and the voices of Lillian and Thekla. It is 1.00, the festivity is at its peak, and the* parea *is gathered around the bar celebrating Kia's birthday. Around 1.30 Rea suddenly appeared out of nowhere. She is working in Athens so we do not see much of her. The girls kiss and hug Rea, as does Kia who then prepares a round of shots for the welcome. Rea finishes the drink and leaves a box on the bar. We can all see that she is still wearing her bond, a watch on the right wrist. As her hand is leaving the box and Kia's hand is moving towards it, the two identical watches meet and I cannot but think that these bonds are just representations, souvenirs of something that ceased to be alive long ago. Kia is holding the beautiful black box which is wrapped in a velvet silvery ribbon. She opens it and there inside lie two identical lighters. They are made of silver and each one of them has crafted upon it the image of a small watch. Rea looked at Kia and said with a tender voice: 'I thought that our watches are getting old, so I wanted to renew our bond. But somehow I felt that these two watches still deserved to be there.' That was, I suppose, Rea's way of wishing happy birthday.*

Rea stayed with us for the rest of the night and left for Athens the following day with one of the two lighters in her pocket. The other one remained with Kia.

The bond embodies and conceptually marks the decision of two girls to remain not only in a particular relationship, but also in a particular symbolic life cycle. The importance of this material object, however, is not confined to the denotation of an interpersonal choice. For the bonds, even when they stop signifying a relationship, are still worn by the girls or carried around as accessories. As such they are part of a collective history, tangible evidence of the group's past, non-discursive narratives that symbolically strengthen the cohesion of the girls' affective community and recall its past. In a sense, they are 'memories cast'[24] in silver, gold and wood, pieces of material culture that symbolise the *parea*'s collective consciousness as well as the individual stories of its members.

Every new relationship, apart from being manifested in the bonds, needs to be performed and celebrated for approximately three days. During this period the whole *parea*, or at least the members that are in town at the time and those that have no other pressing arrangements, are present. The only shots that are served during the 'wedding celebrations' are tequila, since this particular spirit is believed by the girls to be the drink of passion. For three nights the people present, and especially the couple, dance continuously, while around 5.00 in the morning those women who are still there gather in somebody's place for coffee. During the day some women might also meet for lunch in a tavern conspicuously to celebrate their own exceptional unions over some wine or beer. These celebrations mark the beginning of a new era, not only for the partners involved, but also for the group as a whole. 'Through commensality [*metheksi*] you achieve active participation [*energi symmetoxi*] in your friends' lives. You change with them' as Giorgia has put it.

Often towards the end of the ritualistic celebrations of a new relationship, the girls sing as loud as they can their favourite song – a song they gave me as a present when I first left Kallipolis, 'so that I remember the *parea*'s ambience:[25]

As long as our bodies can endure, as long as there is something in our fridge, we will be living the love of our life, and when we pass away, it will transform.	Oso antehei akoma to sarkio mas ki oso yparhei kati sto psygeio mas erota zois emeis tha zisoume ki otan tha svisoume tha metallahtei.
. . . In a new car, we will be hanging around so that the neighbourhood can listen to our singing	S' ena kainourgio IX tha trigyrname na mas akouei I geitonia pou tragoudame
And since I am not tired yet of sharing with you the last twenty years, with a song like this let your emotions of eternal love be fluid.	Ki afou den eho kourastei mazi sou na eho moirastei eikosi hronia m' ena tragoudi san ki auto vale sto aisthima reusto gia agapi aionia.

In the beginning of this section I accounted for the difference that exists between the dominant model of gender and sexuality and the one that the girls promote. Indeed, the *parea* has developed a unique idiom based on desire, pleasure and the principle of personal realisation in the midst of a wider Kallipoliot/Greek framework that promotes stability and the ideal of family rather than self-advancement (Dubisch, 1986; Salamone and Stanton, 1986). The girls, both through their courting behaviour and their idiosyncratic erotic unions, foster a sexuality that emphasises pleasure and engage in a poetics of genderhood (cf. Herzfeld, 1985) that revolves around gender syncretism instead of duality. I maintain that the *parea*, rather than being a unique ethnographic instance in its context, is only another expression of intra-cultural variation, one of the many different and contrasting frameworks for the enactment of the gendered self.

As Loizos eloquently put it, not only is there no single notion of gender 'in that abstraction called Greek culture', but also from one 'context', 'domain', 'discourse' to another one can identify multiple and frequently conflicting ways of accomplishing gender and sexuality (1994: 78). Whether the focus is on the *parea*, the convent (Iossifides, 1991, 1992), Herzfeld's example of the women who transform submission into subversion (1991a), the girls of Sohos who try to articulate a different notion of femininity (Cowan, 1991, 1992), or the Maniat women who have the 'last word' through mourning (Seremetakis, 1991), gender is 'plural rather than single' and 'divergent rather than convergent' (Loizos, 1994: 76). In this manner, the *parea* is only another instance of the differences within (Moore, 1994; Braidotti, 2002) the Greek context rather than a unique case in an otherwise homogenous cultural framework.

The girls are the first who support this view both verbally and through praxis. Their symbiosis and sharing the same literal and cultural space with the inhabitants of this provincial town is a political statement. The *parea* engages in the process of gender 'constructivism' (cf. Faubion, 1993) in such a fashion that they do not separate themselves from the rest of the Kallipoliots, suggesting that homosexuality is not simply about difference. Instead, it is an experience that cannot be separated from its context (Green, 1997), and one that 'can tell us a great deal about women's experiences in general' (Dunne, 1997: 227; cf. Corber and Valocchi, 2003) as well as about their differences and particularities.

The erotic conversations of the *parea* are performative, often non-verbal utterances based on the ambiguity of dance and consumption as sites of social action (Cowan, 1990: 5). They are fragmented conversations that emphasise the use of metaphor and alternative semiotics for the production of meaning. The girls have their codes, their own distinct *langue*, which is nevertheless voiced in the form of an ordinary *parole*. Eroticism and sexuality, then, often become the context within which the women of the *parea* compete over who will produce the most innovative, subtle, complex and unexpected paraphrases.

Epilogue

> *These are the substances that tie us: the plate {of food}*[26] *and the glass {of alcohol} we share. The sweat of the dance and the tears of the joy and pain*
>
> {Autes einai oi ousies pou mas enonoun: to piato kai to potiri pou moirazomaste, o ithrotas tou horou kai ta dakrua sti hara kai sti lypi}

This is what Thekla, an old member of the group, told me reflecting on one of the numerous instances of commensality within the *parea*. This chapter was concerned with the distinct shapes that relatedness takes within the community I studied. The girls consume that which ties them (cf. Iossifides, 1991, 1992), or rather, through consumption and performance they articulate emotions and construct ties of affinity. Affective kinship in the form of the best friend and symbolic marriage, as enacted in the cases of ritualised erotic union, are allegories by which the girls promote alternative gender concepts and relations governed by the politics of pleasure and syncretism.

Relatedness, as an engendered idiom, is for the *parea* stripped of natural or naturalised vestments and understood solely in terms of a shared experience. Desire remains the only authentic feeling that the girls worship acknowledging, nevertheless, its ephemeral quality. Through the perpetual de- and reconstruction of emotions and symbols, the girls generate their collective narrative(s) of gender in a symbiotic fashion. They thus attempt to blur the boundaries both between several different genres of expression (verbal, 'consumptive', bodily and so forth), and between allegedly inviolate gender distinctions.

5

SEPARATION

It is Thursday, around two o'clock in the morning and Harama *is not full. We are waiting for Thekla and Lillian*[1] *to finish the song so we can have the seventh round of shots all together. I am waiting for Maro and Bea who are late tonight. They usually come early on Thursdays. Martha is showing me two boys dancing. 'Look at them. Aren't they gorgeous? I think I know one of them . . .' I cannot share her excitement. My mind is on Maro, my best-friend. She and Bea have been having problems lately – it seems that their relationship is about to end. I am nervous. 'So where is she?', Martha is elbowing me harder and harder. 'Who?', I manage to reply in the end. 'Maro. Where is she?' My answer, a rather dry 'I am not sure', does not satisfy her. 'Don't worry, she will come', Martha tries to reassure me.*

When Maro enters alone we all exchange glances. She walks extremely slowly, cautiously I would say, towards the bar. I give her my shot, a small glass full of vodka. She lights a cigarette and starts sipping the drink. We are all silent. Time passes slowly. 'Maro, say something', I whisper and she responds: 'We have finished.'

In the previous chapter, I have accounted for the establishment of erotic relationships in the *parea*. Here, I am focusing on themes relating to the conclusion of those relationships. The girls regard erotic liaisons as seasons in time – they start in order to end, and they end in order to give way to new experiences (cf. Giddens, 1992: 85). As happens with the decision to initiate a relationship, the resolution of every erotic union is acknowledged by the group as a whole. In my ethnographic account, I intend to draw a parallel between separation as ritualistically enacted by the *parea*, and the literature on death rituals as these are performed in most areas of Greece. In the same manner that the girls collectively celebrate the start of an erotic relationship, they indulge in a period of shared grief when a relationship ends. Although I acknowledge that death and separation are distinct spheres of sentiment, a theoretical comparison between the two forms of ritualised grief is, I believe, fruitful in untangling the importance of pain as a contextual emotion for the construction of individual and collective narratives and as a 'statement about a person's relationship with the world' (Lutz and White, 1986: 421).

My decision to look at the similarities between the ethnographic accounts of death rituals in Greece and separation, as realised by the girls, relates not only to some obvious performative resemblance, but also to the fact that separation from an erotic partner, as a context for the expression of grief, has so far escaped the ethnographic lens of Greek specialists. The subjective experience of pain due to being separated from a person has been examined in relation to either death, marriage, or the departure for foreign and distant lands (*xenitia*).[2] As Danforth argues, *xenitia* and marriage are powerful metaphors for the experience of death since they too involve the strain of a painful separation (1982: 33, 90–5). In turn, the analogy between death and separation is acknowledged throughout the literature on death rituals in Greece (Danforth, 1982; Seremetakis, 1991; Panourgia, 1995). None the less, as opposed to the cases of marriage and *xenitia*, the separation involved in death is experienced as permanent (Panourgia, 1995). This is why I do not attempt to parallel the emotions involved in death and those involved in separation from an erotic partner but, instead, I treat the rituals through which these emotions are expressed as a theoretical metaphor for the exploration of the way the girls stage their performance of pain.

In this chapter, I approach collective mourning as a context for the construction of gender identity through the aesthetics of pain (cf. Seremetakis, 1991: 3). It has been argued that pain and suffering are some of the many cultural materials that Greek women employ for the 'presentation of self in performances that we might term the poetics of womanhood' (Dubisch, 1995: 212). The performance of pain and grief is achieved by the girls by means of literal and non-literal forms of expression. Narrative, as a technique for inducing pain (Caraveli, 1986), and the consumption of alcohol and hashish, as substances that facilitate the creation of a highly emotional condition, are two of the main expressive routes of the *parea*. Physically exhausting dance, narration and consumption are means of both performing and transgressing pain, but also of creating and disseminating the *parea*'s discourses on gender and identity.

Through separation, the girls celebrate the ephemeral as the quality around which their erotic expression revolves. The end of every relationship is simultaneously the conclusion of an era in a girl's life, and the beginning of a new cycle that will bring new experiences and excitement. In this manner, whereas the mortuary rituals attempt, according to Danforth, to mediate between life and death, ritualistic separation in the *parea* mediates between two different cycles in life, and is completely disengaged from the notion of destiny. It is a staged drama (cf. Panourgia, 1995: 104) orchestrated by the girls as a way of asserting their choice to live not by the rules of stability, but by the ideal of temporality.

Seremetakis (1991) introduces the concept of ritualisation as an attempt to acknowledge the spatio-temporal flexibility of death rites in Mani. Although in my case, the ritualistic enactment of separation is a bounded experience with reference to space and time, I also witnessed the resolution of a relationship as encompassing complex and heterogeneous narratives, touching upon more than one sphere of meaning and praxis. Hence, I treat separation as the culmination of a collective performance that draws upon certain cultural metaphors, and not merely as a performative instance.

In the case of the *parea*, the metaphor of pain cannot be disengaged from the metaphor of agonistic masculinity proclaimed in the cases of flirtation, for they are both (cf. Loizos and Papataxiarchis, 1991a) 'transformational contexts' for the enactment of the gendered self and the collective construction of the *parea*'s discourse.

The end

The parea treats separation as part of an invented ceremony without the performance of which resolution of a relationship cannot be realised. Consequently, for a relationship to be considered as dissolved the following has to happen: first, the bonds have to be displaced. The bonds are two identical material objects worn or carried by the partners that symbolise their union.[3] The displacement of the bonds usually happens privately. However, one of the partners usually announces it to the rest of the group. In the opening passage, I described precisely the scene where Maro enters *Harama* alone in order to inform the *parea* that she has separated from Bea.[4] The removal of the bonds signals the irreversible dissolution of the relationship and the start of the second stage of separation, that is the mourning period or *penthos* as the girls call it.

The mourning periods I witnessed lasted for approximately three days during which the ex-partners did not see each other. The *parea* was divided in two and each subgroup stayed with the respective girl most of the time.[5] Who would spend time with whom depends in turn on the various affiliations the women have. For instance, I was told that it is customary for the woman who has initiated one of the girls who separates to be part of her support group. Current partners, however, as a general rule, try not to be in the same subgroup, since one is supposed to participate both physically and emotionally in the process. In turn, by keeping herself away from the person that she cares for, she demonstrates her active identification with the separated woman. The girls also tend to support the best friends of ex-partners since these people were, as Nana explained to me, 'at some point part of the immediate family' (*e, pos, kapia stigmi imastan oikogeneia*). Finally, if a girl is new to the group and no other considerations exist, her choice may be random. In all the cases of separation that I witnessed, there was an almost perfect balance with reference to the number of the people constituting each subgroup which is, up to a point, the result of conscious manipulation on the part of the girls. In the event of the separation of a new member, for example, who has not yet built any acquaintanceships in the *parea*, many women, ignoring their individual ties, join her support group which usually ends up being larger than the one of her ex-partner.

Each support group is composed of different women each time. Depending on their engagements and circumstances they stay with the separated girl for about three days, in the course of which vast quantities of alcohol (especially Jack Daniels) are consumed mainly by the protagonist who, during the night dances only *zeimbekiko* (solo performance), frequently to the point of physical exhaustion. Jack Daniels is regarded as the appropriate drink for the ritual because it is dark and strong and, according to the girls, analogous to the darkness and intensity of their emotions. Likewise, *zeimbekiko* is the only dance performed for it is regarded as the dance which can express pain and feelings of loss (cf. Cowan, 1990), as opposed to *tsifteteli* which is a joyful and flirtatious rhythm. My ethnographic description will explore these three days of shared mourning through the dissolution of several relationships. Although a general pattern is identifiable, each case has its own distinctive elements that carve it into the collective memory of the group, for the conceptual death of a relationship, just as the physical death of a person (cf. Panourgia, 1995: 202), can be a route to authenticity.

After describing how Maro entered *Harama* without wearing her bond, I will now proceed with Elli and the first night of her separation from Giota. Elli and Giota had been together for more than eight months.

We have already drunk the second round of shots and I can feel the effect of the strong Jack Daniels. As the spotlights illuminated Elli, for a moment I noticed her lower neck. The cross [her bond] *although absent was still there, a small white area on her skin contrasting with her deep tan. Several other girls had followed Dina to Giota's place. They will go to another bar with her today and tomorrow and the day after, and to another tavern, and to another coffee shop. It is almost as if the whole* parea *is separating and it feels strange. Lena and four other women are escorting Elli to the dance floor. Thekla is singing a heavy* zeimbekiko *for Elli, and the girls form a semi-circle around her and crouch on one knee as is customary while she dances. The song is a political one, composed for Cyprus I think, but the lyrics seem to suit the circumstances: 'They have cut me, they have separated me in two . . . And you are like a drop of blood on my lips and like the wind in my fingers.' Elli is dancing to this and the next song and the one after. She is exhausted, I can see it from where I stand. And yet she is still dancing. It is my turn to go and escort her as some of the girls have to rest. I go towards the dance floor with a shot of Jack Daniels. Elli is drinking it without stopping to rest. I crouch as well. I start clapping. I can see from here that her sweat is dripping to the floor. Soon another shot comes and another. Her face is still. Her eyes shut and her arms wide open. From time to time she glances at the ceiling, just for a second and then the eyes close again. Lillian is coming towards us. She sits on the edge of the dance floor and sings from there. She and Elli had a relationship once. Finally, we take Elli back to the bar. Sotiris the barman is offering her a glass of water. Instead, she drinks another shot as she is resting her back against the wall. Soon she dance again.*

The scene just described is indicative of what usually happens during a separation, frequently from 12.00 at night until 5.00 in the morning, although it is true that older members of the group and those who have experienced a number of such events frequently tend to engage in lighter versions of the ritual. Danforth (1982) and Seremetakis (1991) note that in the event of the death of a person, at least the close family and relatives stay together and mourn over the corpse overnight.[6] Likewise, the women of the *parea* demonstrate their support to the separated girl by making sure that some of them are by her side most of the time, sharing part of the physical exhaustion due to dancing and the excessive consumption of alcohol. In both the contexts of death and separation, the expression of sympathy takes the form of physical presence. Pain as well as joy, irrespective of their intensity, are emotions to be shared and they need an audience in order to be properly enacted (Dubisch, 1995: 216).

In most separations, Thekla and Lillian, who work as professional singers at *Harama*, slightly change the programme to include more *zeimbekika* (solo performances) and especially songs, the lyrics of which relate to separation or estrangement. In this way the songs become lament-texts that enable the amplification of grief and ensure the emotional participation of the whole support group (cf. Seremetakis, 1991; Caraveli, 1986). In turn, through the repetition of these songs in various separations, the girls accomplish an archetypical metaphor of sorrow. Panourgia notes that people might use the appropriate context of a funeral to cry for other dead relatives besides the one buried (1995: 124–5, 156). Similarly, Lillian in this instance watches Elli, her ex-partner, dancing her separation with another girl. Through the present she can perhaps recreate the past, for she knows that probably Elli was once dancing in the same fashion, to the same songs, in order to express her grief for the end of their relationship. The rest of the girls who support Elli in this emotional and physical ordeal have also danced more or less to the same songs in the past and felt similar emotions, and they can thus relate very closely to what is being enacted before their eyes. In this manner, the ceremonialisation of separation can be seen as one of the many techniques the girls use to stage a collective performative of pain.

I will now proceed to Anthoula's separation from Olymbia. Anthoula and Olymbia had been together for approximately six months before the former decided that it was time for the relationship to end. I happened to be in Anthoula's support group, since her best friend Martha once had a long relationship with my best friend Maro. After dancing and drinking for several hours, we left the bar to go to Anthoula's place for coffee.

Martha is preparing coffees for everybody. Most of us are quite drunk, but Anthoula seems worse than everybody else. She is extremely thin and alcohol affects her quickly. She is exhausted from the continuous dancing and she has lost her strength completely, so Martha had to carry her upstairs. She is now sitting on the floor, resting her back against the wall. When the coffee was brought she couldn't even lift the cup to her lips. Martha had to give it to her little by little.

After a while, Anthoula starts talking about her, about Olymbia, about their relationship – only the good moments, such as the time they started flirting and their weekends together. She talks slowly and we listen. Nobody is in a hurry. For a couple of days we will all recount this relationship. We will follow it from the start to the finish, recreating it, reconstructing it in our minds; but only the good moments, the moments of happiness, excitement and passion.

It is 8.00 and those ones left have finally decided to sleep; most of us where we were sitting, the two best friends, Anthoula and Martha in the bed. I could hear Anthoula crying until I too fell asleep.

Reconstructing a relationship's good moments is an indispensable part of separation as enacted by the *parea*. Nobody talks about the fights, or the split itself, no questions are asked and no analysis is made. Separation is precisely the context within which the partners are free to recreate their relationship, and finally to make it part of the *parea*'s history the way they want it to be remembered. The girls become authors of their past as they render it anew during their conversations with their dead relationships (Danforth, 1982; Seremetakis, 1991). In turn, the process of rewriting individual histories cannot be but a collective one. As Caraveli (1986) notes, lamenting needs a performer and an audience, for it is the audience who legitimises the performer's claims to truth by playing the role of the witness (Seremetakis, 1991; cf. Ricoeur, 1991: 153; McNay, 2000: 98).

Throughout the three days of the separation process the *parea* eat only small quantities of food and there is generally the assumption that bodily desires are subjugated to the intense emotions of sorrow that the girls feel (cf. Panourgia, 1995: 117). Their commensality strongly resembles the commemorial dinner customarily shared after the burial by the family and close relatives of the dead in Greece (Seremetakis, 1991; Panourgia, 1995). Seremetakis (1991) accounts for the extension of kinship ties, through collective participation in mourning and the metaphoric use of kinship terms, and describes how the mortuary ceremony is transformed through performance 'into an affective collectivity' (ibid.: 88). In my case, the women of the *parea* construct and intensify their relationships through participation in the grief of the separated person, and by 'bonding in pain' they establish a 'sisterhood in pain' (Caraveli, 1986: 178, 181). By sharing the same substances and emotions, the girls reaffirm their ties and fuse the boundaries between individual and collective narratives (Dubisch, 1995: 214). Both the *parea*'s past and the individual life histories are constructed through moments of sharing. In the passage that follows the girls accompany Maria to a tavern and listen to her narration carefully. Maria has just separated from Klairi, her partner for the last 11 months.

The table is big enough to accommodate fifteen people. We order just four different plates of food that will go in the centre and all of us will eat bits and pieces from every plate and we will drink plenty of wine. Maria is sitting at the head of the table and next to her, on her right, is her best friend Maro. We start nibbling slowly, silently in the beginning. Soon Maria starts talking again. She talks about a poem, their poem and then about ***their*** *song. She talks about that day, the first of May, when they went together to the countryside alone and Klairi smelled the newly born grass. She was laughing and she was beautiful . . . The images of the countryside started merging with Maria's face . . . The tavern that the other girls went to is only ten minutes from here,* *but if I go to see what is happening I will upset everybody. Martha is with them. She will tell me afterwards. . . .*

The period of collective mourning is consciously transformed by the girls into a 'dead time', a time where day has little difference from night and when the heads of those who manage to attend most of the event rarely clear. The group – or at least those who can be present throughout the process – repeats the cycle of eating and drinking for what is sometimes a good 72 hours. The newly separated girls are at the centre of everyone's attention along with their best friends while the rest of the women are all around them. More alcohol lies upon the yet undigested alcohol of the previous night, and the commemorial of the relationship is only briefly interrupted by sleep.

For all the girls I have talked with, the process of separation was difficult. Not only because all of the *erotas* (erotic feelings) has to be expunged, but also because the mourning period is simultaneously a time of realisation that a new *erotas*, more intense and perhaps more exciting, is yet to come. Once the grief and pain are properly exorcised, a woman is considered ready to pursue another relationship, to flirt again, to be friends with the person she was sleeping with a week ago. More difficult (always, according to the girls) is the realisation that the recent lover is entitled to do the same, that is, to flirt with someone else and pursue another relationship. It is for these reasons that the women of the *parea* find the mourning period cathartic and helpful: 'After some days of focusing on a relationship, crying, getting drunk, talking, there is not much left. By the end of the third day, you start looking forward to making a new start' as Lillian said to me.

I should also mention at this point that a relationship ends when some passion still remains. The girls walk out of an erotic union when they still feel capable of loving each other. Therefore, a relationship does not exactly die, it is terminated. Unlike physical death where to die young is regarded as a great misfortune and somehow as an inversion of the order of things (Panourgia, 1995; Seremetakis, 1991; Danforth, 1982), for the girls a relationship *has* to die 'young and beautiful'.

> The relationship needs to be mourned when people can still mourn it properly. Mourning means grief and grief presupposes love. If a relationship is worn out how can one feel grief? The relationship has to die when it is still young and beautiful, and be mourned collectively [*omadika*] and intensively. What will be left after all this pain is a pure scent of love, and compassion and friendship for the person with whom you used to share a part of your life. There is no other feeling that hurts. Only appreciation.
>
> (Elena)

The end, part two: some more instances of collective mourning

I escort Maro to the dance floor together with six other girls. I am the first to crouch to the floor and I will be the last to get up. The other women alternate when they feel tired, but the best friend rarely leaves the circle.[7] *Since a girl has enough strength to be there and dance, it is considered shaming for her best friend to be tired of kneeling or clapping. Maro has ordered a specific song to start her second night with: 'I am an eagle without wings, without love and joy.' It is a slow, heavy* zeimbekiko *and she performs it beautifully despite the fact that we have already drunk five rounds of Jack Daniels. She continues dancing for more than 15 minutes. The first signs of exhaustion appear. She is breathing with difficulty and her hair is already wet on her face. Nikos, the singer, waves to the band to slow down the rhythm of the next song. I change my clapping accordingly to facilitate her. By the time she finishes, she makes a sign with her hand – 'a quicker one'. Some more shots come and we drink them without interrupting the dance. Maro drinks two in a row and puts an empty glass in front of her. This will make her movement even more difficult as she will have to watch her steps in order not to touch the glass . . .*

Dance and the body become, especially in the case of separation, important contexts for the enactment of pain and its transgression. Enduring the physical exhaustion is a matter of pride among the girls. Through challenging their physical limits they engage in the production of even more engrossing and compelling performances not only of grief, but also of masculine *eghoismos*. Cowan (1990) refers to the *mangas*, the person who dances *zeimbekiko* (the solo dance that the girls perform pre-eminently during their separations): as the consciously anti-social masculine persona, who smokes hashish and 'repudiates the values of both the peasant communities and the urban middle-class' (ibid.: 174). For the 'acutely self conscious' *zeimbekiko* (male) dancer 'women exist only as obsessions', although he is paradoxically in a permanent state of 'torture [from] love and anxiety' (Cowan, 1990: 180). The conflicting image of the *mangas* who simultaneously suffers for and disclaims the object of his passion is the one enacted by the girls during the endless *zeimbekika* they dance. Their bodies thus become expressive mediums of pain and personal loss (Dubisch, 1995: 214, 217) as well as defiance, while the self is presented as both wounded by and larger than pain. In the course of suffering the girls literally embody the conflicting emotions that arise from their conscious decision to follow an ephemeral erotic lifestyle.

Similar to the Maniat mourners of Seremetakis who through self-inflicted violence transform their bodies into a text of disorder (1991: 73–4), the girls, by means of exhaustive dancing transform their bodies into texts of pain and conflict. *Ponos* (pain) as enacted by the *parea* is thus not unrelated to a culturally specific 'poetics of womanhood' that emphasises suffering[8] as an important part of female subjectivity (Dubisch, 1995). At the same time the embodied narrative of separation in the *parea* is greatly inspired by the model of an obstinate, vigorous self mostly associated with a masculine *eghoismos* (Herzfeld,

1985). Hence, drawing on familiar motifs traditionally associated with femininity or masculinity, the girls construct their own idiosyncratic and gender-syncretic politics of pain. Uncontrollable emotions, together with physical stamina and the blurring of consciousness, paradoxically accompanied by a conspicuous sharpness in movement and precision in the dissemination of information, form the persona of the separated. A persona that is neither explicitly male nor female, and which combines the signs of pain and indifference, vulnerability and toughness, expressiveness and concision in stylistically accelerated performances:

We have finally reached home after a difficult night. Maria threw herself on to the couch and soon we all had our coffees. Maria was silent. She was silent for what seemed like hours. Finally she started crying and then talking about her relationship with Kelly. Having followed the whole event, I'm tired, my head is spinning and I am barely able to follow what Maria is saying. Her speech is inarticulate, fragmented. It is like a child's speech, full of images, one succeeding the other with no obvious connection between them and yet I feel as if I was there. Through this fragmented talk she literally showed me – she did not narrate – she ***showed*** *me her past. And then she stopped. She stayed silent for some time and finally started crying again. Her best friend Maro is holding her tight. We all approach them. We hold one another and stay embraced while Maria falls asleep on our bodies.*

The role of the best friend and consequently of the whole support group is to be an audience who listens and legitimises the girl's verbal and non-verbal narrative. The friends sustain the centre of a drama that is staged and performed for the sake of one person and simultaneously they ensure, through participation, the transition of their friend from the realm of pain back to the everyday reality of the *parea*. With reference to the group as a whole, separation is undoubtedly a context where the girls perform bonding through pain (cf. Caraveli, 1980, 1986). Suffering becomes thus 'a basis for women's identification with other women' (Dubisch, 1995: 214) while the narrative produced is not about some personal, or natural emotion, but relates to a politically invested process (Braidotti, 2002: 22) of shared (female) experience (Dubisch, 1995: 213, 214).

Danforth (1982) and Panourgia (1995) note that death rituals are usually occasions for the public exhibition of the solidarity of family and close friends. Although from experience, I do not disagree with Panourgia who implies that this solidarity is only a facade and that death brings first and foremost discordance and conflict in the family (1995: 71–2), in the case of the *parea*, the girls employ pain to actively reaffirm their affective ties. In this sense, separation is another 'transformational context' (Loizos and Papataxiarchis, 1991a) for the construction and sustenance of alternative relationships.

I will conclude my ethnographic account with two scenes relating Anthoula's separation from Olymbia: the first unfolds at the bar, while the second takes place at the communal table. In this particular case, Anthoula decided to spend her mourning period in another bar, while Olymbia went to Harama:

Anthoula has been dancing for some time now. I am sitting on the bar watching her and the girls. With me are Aphrodite and Eirini. We will soon go to the circle, but in the meantime we have ordered shots to carry to the dance floor. The waiter is surprised that we do not throw any flowers 'to the girl who has danced so much today'. We cannot explain to him that flowers are never thrown in such cases. 'We offer her shots', Aphrodite replies. 'She prefers them.'

Today is the last day we will eat together. Anthoula seems better and we made our first joke. In a sense it is like a long recovery process. The trip is already organised. The day after tomorrow we will all finally be in Athens together. Anthoula is eating with quite an appetite. Just a few hours, just another night and tomorrow we will all wake up in a better mood. 'We will have to go back to this bar again for a celebration this time', Anthoula said and it seemed as if she has read my mind.

On completion of this invented ritual, the girls usually organise a reconciliation trip to another town. During this trip, the split *parea* unites again and the ex-partners see each other for the first time since their separation and usually exchange their bonds and often other gifts as well. Afterwards, the *parea* goes to a night-spot to enjoy themselves. The transformation of an erotic relationship into one of friendship is accomplished in the case of Maro below during a visit to Athens.

The relationship has died. Long live the relationship. *Or* Let's be friends again

When we arrived in Athens the sun was rising. We went straight to Emily's house, an old property, but big enough to accommodate some twenty people. We sit around the big table in order to have some coffee. Maro and Bea are looking at each other. They are a little nervous but they try to behave casually. Soon, they are hugging each other and they smile. Maro gives Bea her bond, an earring, and receives Bea's identical one. The small earring in their left ear looks exactly the same as before. Then Maro offers her a present as well: a small music box. Bea opens it and listens to its music for quite some time. Her present is a tiny icon of the holy Mary holding the baby and kissing it. It is small silver icon, half the size of a hand with a small ring on top where it is supposed to be hung on the wall. 'Keep it with you. It will protect you on the motorbike', Bea says. 'I will keep it with me always', Maro replies and puts the icon in her key ring after kissing it. They hold hands. We leave the room. They deserve some time alone. . . .

Seremetakis claims that the exhumed bones of the deceased are 'tangible emotions'[9] (1991: 215–17) arguing that the common history of reciprocity in Inner Mani is written through 'historicised exchanges of feelings', and is inscribed on the physical environment (ibid.). Similarly, the girls, through the exchange of material objects invested with emotional significance, write in every single separation the 'last word' of their own narrative (cf. Seremetakis, 1991) and enrich the collective present of the *parea* with palpable objects that recount a shared past (cf. Sutton, 1998). They thus invest the other with signs of the self in a process of constructing intersubjectively the history of their affective community and making it ever-present through material artifacts. Rings, icons, small pendants, watches, pairs of identical objects worn or carried around for years after a relationship has finished silently construct the myth, the legend of their possessors. The newly introduced girl to the *parea* is confronted with a past full of great loves and passions that reminds one of the scenario of a *film noir*. The protagonists of this celebrated past and the material evidence all around her serve to bring a very tempting tale alive. As for the girls, immediately after a relationship has finished and for quite some time afterwards, they indulge in a process of rewriting history, beautifying and mythologising it.

Through stormy *kapsoures* (infatuations) and painful separations the women of the *parea* manage to stage their erotic and gendered selves contextually in an embodied as well as a narrative fashion. As Dubisch has argued 'women's own stories about themselves can be seen as another type of female performance', one that is not personal but resonates with greater idioms of experience and identity (1995: 212). The girls' stories locate them in the *parea* and are simultaneously about 'being a woman' (ibid.), being a woman with an alternative sexuality, as well as trying to be a strong voice from what seems at times to be the margins of power. Their rhetoric reconciles seemingly irreconcilable subjective positions and experiences, being at ones 'narratives of self-understanding and meta-narratives of femininity' (McNay, 2000: 98).

The *parea*'s strong inclination to recount and recite their experiences supports Braidotti's claim that narrativity is a 'binding force' and a source of 'significant figurations' (2002: 22). Likewise, McNay, exemplifying Ricoeur, makes quite an extensive reference to narrative as a feature of both individual and social identity (2000: 74–116). According to McNay, narrative offers a 'temporalised understanding of the self' (2000: 27), one which is not determining but generative of a self-identity that is neither the result of pure free will nor external imposition (ibid.: 85). Imbued with historicity and cultural meaning, narrative 'never takes place in isolation from pre-given ideological forms' (McNay, 2000: 98), which are reified through repetition thus strengthening a community's sense of origin and identity (ibid.: 97). At the same time, however, the uncontrollability of speech (cf. Butler, 1997b: 28) always entails the possibility of new and unexpected significations constituting the self a creative and dynamic entity whose unity is to be found in the very process of *becoming* (Braidotti, 2002: 22; cf. McNay, 2000).

In the case of separation in the *parea*, narrative as a culturally recognisable site of individual and collective identity-making pertains both to the creativity of the actor and the authoring of personal and shared history. Commemoration of the dead relationship is thus another context for the negotiation of gender ideas, social relations and the reworking of the tension between normative values and the desire of the actor to exist as a creative agent. Reciting only the relationship's good moments, for instance, both challenges the local stereotype of gay partnerships as being non-productive unions characterised by jealousy and rivalry, and contributes to the crystallisation of an idyllic and almost naturalised understanding of romantic love. At the same time, however, the indeterminacy of speech effects a non-strategic kind of self-transformation that is inspired by and inspires the collective imaginary of the group. The shared experience of being at once a Greek woman and a girl of the *parea* abolishes, through narrativity, the boundaries between self and other (heterosexual/ homosexual, central/marginal, traditional/alternative) precisely because the self and the other coincide, occupying in this case, the same physical and emotional place in the world.

A final instance of rewriting history through narrative is Lillian's story. Lillian, a member of the group and a singer at *Harama* explains to Stella, a new girl of the *parea* 'why she always wears a cross'. The cross happens to be an old bond and simultaneously the object through which the past is recreated and mythologised while notions of gender, identity and the self are exemplified:

> Why I always wear this cross? Ah, this is a big story. I first put it around my neck some three years ago and since then I never took it off. It means much. It connects me with somebody. Somebody that is far away now . . . No matter where I go or what I do, I touch its surface and it feels exactly like touching her body: so smooth . . . She was beautiful, the most beautiful woman you've ever seen. I used to look in her eyes and see myself and my great, great passion for her. She was the only woman about whom my best friend told me: this woman is going to tear you apart. But I didn't listen to her. I didn't listen to anybody. Nothing and nobody was important back then. I was holding her body every night and everything seemed so small, so unimportant. Once, I made her cry. I swear, I didn't mean it. So foolish of me! Just a couple of words . . . I was careless and I made her cry. She looked me straight in the eyes and told me 'I am going to leave.' I didn't believe her. How could she? But she did. And it was the first time that I could actually hear the sound of silence in me. Nothing. Void. Non-existence. I lost her and myself together. I was aimlessly drinking, dancing and even pretending that I did not care. I was pointlessly crying, trying desperately to put out the fire she had lit in me. It took me some time. It took her three days. It doesn't matter. It was my fault for I had been proven incapable of cherishing the little time we had together. I knew she would leave one day. I might have left her if that matters. But I was not ready for that. I wanted the fantasy to last for another day, another month, another second. It didn't. It ended right there. Abruptly. Some bad spirit came and swept everything away. I died. It was an instant death. I died and yet I could feel the pain. It was strong just like her and blue just like her eyes . . . I see this cross now and I remember. From time to time I can hold it and travel back and find the Lillian I was: younger, more beautiful

> maybe, and in love. Then it passed, as everything else. I felt other bodies. I saw myself through the eyes of others and felt again in love and separated and I saw my ex-partners crying for new loves. The cross is still here. Every night when I sing, the lights of the spots make it shine, and the other day, my girlfriend touched it as we were making love. It stays with me. We sleep together, and eat and lie under the sun in the summer. A small cross, that's all what it is. . . .
>
> (Lillian)

Separation is for the *parea* the context where the girls engage in a ritualised enactment of pain as well as in a collective meta-commentary of gender ideas and relations. Through the performance of pain, the women of the group construct their shared rhetoric of the ephemeral in an ongoing conversation with the past. Their biographical accounts, based on the commemoration and rehearsal of the past, are collective instances for achieving self-realisation both in a reflexive and in an unintentional manner. Each separation enables its protagonist to become the author, or rather the novelist of her own story and subsequently of the shared history of the group (Seremetakis, 1991). Already given and original ideas about emotions, sexuality and relations fuse in the same narrative and gradually become part of the *parea*'s myth(s).

In this process of textualisation, the actor through dance and consumption engages in a gender syncretic embodied performance that attempts to transgress familiar gender idioms by accommodating vulnerability and strength, by consuming and being consumed by pain. The girls assume the posture of the *mangas*, the strong and indifferent masculine persona which embraces passion and is tortured by it (Cowan, 1990), as the most genuine expression of emotional conflict. Through the metaphor of the *mangas*, they collectively meditate on gender syncretism, and mediate between the pain over something that ends and the joy for the new experience that will follow. The resolution of a relationship is thus yet another transformational context (Loizos and Papataxiarchis, 1991a) for the staging of the idiosyncratic self who is nevertheless firmly positioned in a specific social, cultural and gendered world. Conceptual death becomes a route to authenticity, a highly emotional avenue for the collective realisation of difference and simultaneously a narrative performance of shared experiences of Greekness, provinciality, womanhood and homoeroticism.

Every new separation is an opportunity, not for the *demonstration* of group solidarity (cf. Panourgia, 1995), but for the *performance* of bonding (Dubisch, 1995; Caraveli, 1986). The girls create and sustain their affective community through shared feelings, substances, material objects (Seremetakis, 1991), and through reciprocally being the audience for each other's 'effective' performances (cf. Herzfeld, 1985). Pain can be thus understood as a performative context that 'provides a language for the construction of self' (Seremetakis, 1991: 5). The girls' tales are clandestine narratives of a periphery, which might be denied the power to openly express itself, but none the less has a very distinct experience of empowerment and autonomy (cf. McNay, 2000: 5). Ritualised separation is then an ongoing storytelling of the actors about themselves (cf. Geertz, 1973) and a context for the realisation of the agent who when 'faced with complexity and difference [manages to respond] in unanticipated and innovative ways' (McNay, 2000: 5). Through the sharing of sentiments, but also by being part of the same insubordinate mythology, the women of the community collectively conceive of a concept of gender identity that strives to go beyond the traditional prescriptive discourses, thus composing a unique and distinct history of defiance.

6

CONTEXTUAL IDENTITIES

By explaining so far the *parea*'s performances in terms of a culturally specific poetics of personhood, I have repeatedly focused on those practices that connect the group to the specific socio-cultural context of Greece. As Moore argues, however, the acknowledgement of the existence of particular groups who hold alternative perspectives or adhere to less preponderant discourses within a specific cultural framework is not sometimes as central as the study of the influence those discourses have on individuals and groups (1994: 16). My intention here is therefore to show how particular women who happen to be members of the *parea* influence and are influenced by hegemonic discourses. At the same time, through presenting individual cases, I wish to highlight the multiplicity of gender models available in the particular social setting of provincial Kallipolis.

The different conceptions of selfhood that can be identified in Greece obviously pertain to gender, class, as well as certain spatio-temporal considerations. Different generations of cultural subjects, in different locations enjoy diverse degrees of accessibility to differing representations of the (gendered) self (cf. Cowan, 1990). As Cowan has argued, with reference to the narratives of young Sohoian girls, we need to see gender in Greece not as a single, homogenous and fixed narrative of complementarity but a context permeated with ambiguity where different – and often conflicting – discourses of gender co-exist (1992: 146). In turn, a given ethnographic account of inter-cultural difference cannot readily settle with a distinction between traditional and modern, younger and older or urban and rural. Such antinomies are undoubtedly artificial and do not fully convey the theoretical significance of the 'differences within' (Moore, 1994: 34; cf. Braidotti, 2002: 14), while at the same time they obscure the importance of context and temporality for to the construction and negotiation of gender identity and relations (cf. McNay, 2000: 27). The possibility of multiple and even conflicting identifications cannot be conceptualised outside the framework of multiple discourses that are 'appropriate only to specific contexts' (Moore, 1994: 34; cf. Loizos and Papataxiarchis, 1991a). The ethnography of this chapter attests precisely to the idea that the flexibility and 'inner dynamism' of the person (Wekker, 1999: 132) relates closely to the contextual quality of identity.

The appreciation of the practical/discursive and intersubjective character of the self (cf. Moore, 1994: 41) combined with the idea that there is 'no discursive meaning without interlocution and context' (Clifford, 1988: 41) point to the importance of contextuality for the development of the internally differentiated subject. The moment a discourse or practice turns into a distinct identifiable cultural idiom, it is separated from the specific 'performative situation' and becomes textualised, that is, it is no longer tied to particular actors but 'assumes a more or less stable relation to a context' (Clifford, 1988: 38–9). If we regard the self as 'textual', then surely, its 'various motifs, its compositional themes' are not only context specific (Faubion, 1993: 159), but also context dependent. In this sense, a change of context allows and even dictates the rise of a different subjectivity in so far as 'a single subject can no longer be equated with a single individual' (Moore, 1994: 55). Such a view of the person is not to be conflated with a notion of subjectivity as dispersed, dislocated, ahistorical and eternally trapped in the politics of oppression, exclusion and resistance (cf. MacNay, 2000: 1–6, 75–8). Conversely, the different contexts are sites imbued with historicity and cultural meaning, where the multiply constituted subject is realised in its *movement across* and *encompassing of* distinct social fields. It is precisely because the self is both synchronically and diachronically occupying multiple positions and is engaged in different relations struggling to meet distinct and at times conflicting expectations that we cannot speak of a homogenous, straightforward subjectivity. This is not to deny the unity of the self, but rather to argue for a dynamic sense of self-coherence found in the very process of moving, becoming, creating, acting and relating.

The protagonists of this chapter testify to intra-cultural and inter-contextual variation as they assume distinct subject positions relevant to different contexts (cf. Moore, 1994: 55). Moreover, in the framework of this constant shift, they demonstrate how their various contextual subjectivities are interconnected and articulated against a greater cultural project of 'a constructivist poesis' of a 'more agonistic vision of the self' who must always be original and unprecedented (Faubion, 1993: 183). The women in this chapter are all unique: a mother, unique in her pain or in her transcendence in accepting her daughter's sexuality, an archetypical wife, an authentic thinker. In their diversity, they are typical–atypical examples of a culture that praises conformity while, at the same time, it acclaims singularity, values distinction and demands from its subjects ever-powerful performances.

In the pages that follow, I will present and comment upon the narratives of five women of different ages and diverse socio-cultural backgrounds. They have all been part of the *parea* for at least five years and some of the older ones were among the first people to form and join the group. It is also worth noting that what is included in and what is excluded from the cases examined is subject to what the girls themselves decided to talk about.[1]

The case of Elena

Elena is 24 years old and she has been in the *parea* for more than five years. The occasion of her initiation to the group coincided with the death of her father. The fact that she became the provider for her household when she was only 19 years old is a salient theme in her narrative. Elena claims that she does not have any difficulty being simultaneously a member of the *parea* and the head of a family that still adheres to more traditional cultural norms. In the pages that follow she elaborates on the past and present circumstances of her life, while an ethnographic account of the interaction between the *parea* and Elena's family is also provided.

ELENA: *When my father died everything was collapsing around us; financially and emotionally. Basically we had no income other than a tiny pension. You see my father was working in two or three jobs and most of the money he was earning was 'black'* [i.e. not subject to taxation]. *This, however, meant that his pension scheme was insignificant. My mother was always a housewife. It was very difficult for her to find any job other than cleaning houses, or offices. As you've probably understood by now, my family was never rich, not even wealthy, but she was used to being the housewife* [*noikokyra*], *the mistress of her house* [*kyria sto spiti tis*]. *Can you imagine what a humiliation it would be for her to become a cleaning lady* [*katharistria*], *or a maid* [*ypiretria*] *all of a sudden? This was not an option back then, and still it is not and it will never be. Besides, how much could she earn? My two sisters were fifteen and fourteen; tender ages. They had to go to school, to be educated. We needed much more money than she could ever earn. I remember when I first met the girls* [*the parea*]. *It was less than two weeks after the death of my father. It was tough in the beginning but they all helped and especially Thekla. I was madly in love with her back then. It was my first relationship with a woman, the first time I was in love with a woman. Before her I had a boyfriend. But he was young. He couldn't relate to what happened to me. So that relationship faded away.*

At the time my father died, I was in my first year at the university, studying to become a nurse. I suspended my studies, came back to Kallipolis and found a job as a secretary. I was working all day but the money was not enough. Aphrodite [a member of the *parea*] *offered me this job at 'Petrol'* [a nightclub] *where she was the manageress. I remember earning in one night as much as I earned in the other job in three days. It was then with the help of the girls* [the *parea*] *that I came up with the idea of 'setting up' bars instead of working in them. It meant more money and more freedom. My own job! I wouldn't have succeeded if it were not for the* parea*'s help and their excellent networking. Normally you need to have a degree to do this job which is practically interior designing. But they knew so many people who owned bars and they introduced me and they gave me ideas in the beginning . . . So, I made it. Besides I always had an artistic inclination . . .* [laughter]. *Today my sisters are both at the university. Maraki* [tender nickname for the name Maria – literally little Maria] *is studying archaeology and Sofia law. I still work hard to support everybody,*[2] *but praise the Lord* [*doksa to Theo*] *financially we are secure.*

Elena's profession is 'setting up bars'. Most bars in Greece are renovated twice a year, while it is not unusual for a given club to move location every summer in order to attract more customers. Elena is appointed as an interior designer and she is famous in the town for establishing the most elegant and idiosyncratic spaces. At the time of my fieldwork she had probably the biggest and most stable clientele in Kallipolis.

Elena still lives at the family house where occasionally the girls of the *parea*, always presented as friends, gather for coffee. Elena's girlfriend, Katia, visits the house a lot more frequently. She has a very warm relationship with Elena's mother, Mrs Evangelia, who makes sure to cook Katia's favourite food and prepare her favourite preserved fruit. Katia on the other hand never forgets to bring Mrs Evangelia her treat: two bars of bitter chocolate as well as the occasional bouquet of flowers.

The first time I visited Elena's house I was accompanied by Maro, Martha and Zina and we were expecting more girls to come later. We were sitting in the living room for some quarter of an hour before Mrs Evangelia came in with *kerasma*, a tray full of coffees, preserved fruit and cold water.[3] She was smiling and seemed extremely happy we were there.

ELENA'S MOTHER: *Welcome to our house. Why don't you come more often? It is a pleasure for me to see my daughter's friends. You have to come one day for dinner. I cook well, or so they say. My child's friends are my friends too. I'd like you to know that. Oh, my girl! If it were not for my Elena who struggled alone we wouldn't have made it. I lost my husband five years ago. He left me with two children and Elena. How much I have suffered. . . .*

Mrs Evangelia continued by showing us the photos of her late husband praising his character and rehearsing all the good things he did when he was alive, followed by a detailed account of the troubles (*vassana*) and the anxiety (*stenahoria*) and pain (*ponos*) his death had brought. Addressing herself to me she said at some point:

'*You can't even imagine what troubles we had to go through after his death my child! I was left alone with two children and my poor Elena who was trying to make up for everything. I didn't know where to start and nobody was willing to help. Debts! People coming and asking me for money . . .*[4] *The only thing I cared about was my children. I was going to sleep every night and I was saying to God: God, look at a mother's pain. I have suffered to raise these children, I wanted to see them progress, to become something better than their mother. My Elena though, my worthy child . . . She came one day and told me: Mother don't be scared. I am here now. We will pull through . . .*'[5]

From time to time Mrs Evangelia sought the affirmation of Maro and Zina who had apparently heard the same stories before. As I found out later, Elena's mother was routinely going through the same narration every time a new person visited the house. This time it was my presence that triggered the colourful story-telling, which culminated in praise for Elena for bringing the family through. According to Zina, who knew Elena even before the latter joined the *parea*, Mrs Evangelia was extremely proud of her daughter's character and the way she had struggled[6] (*agonistike*) since the death of her father. She was also determined to let everybody know it and she did so by engaging in what Dubisch calls 'competitive suffering' (1995: 214). It has been argued that Greek women adopt the idiom of suffering through which they compose specific narratives of womanhood, trying to convey their experience of being women and mothers as well as the difficulties that such a life entails (Dubisch, 1995: 217–23). Through this culturally specific poetics of womanhood (ibid.), Elena's mother both communicated her feelings and testified to the difficulty of her daughter's social role, namely that of the struggling provider (Dubisch, 1995: 215–17).

With reference to suffering as a poetic and performative expression of Greek women, Dubisch notes that such a notion might be open to misreading due to the negative connotations of suffering itself (1995: 223): 'Some of the non-anthropologists were concerned about my model . . . That women adopted suffering seemed to them to imply the exploitation of women in Greek society' (Dubisch, 1995: 225). Irrespectively of the value-free approach that the ethnographer is entitled to have towards the culture she studies (ibid.: 224), I wish to argue that 'competitive suffering' as a poetic strategy for women is a powerful performance, enacted in a very similar fashion to the 'poetics of manhood' as depicted by Herzfeld (1985). In this particular instance, Mrs Evangelia was publicly composing the picture of the emotional as well as the practical hardship of a mother (and a daughter) in a few statements, which indeed succeeded in capturing her audience who could not resist the power of repetition (Herzfeld, 1985: 145). Her routine of engaging in a performance of suffering[7] highlighted 'what otherwise the actions would have to do for themselves: [it] presented the protagonist's improvisational skills in a favorable light' (Herzfeld, 1985: 141). That was the *simasia* (meaning) of her poetics that went beyond the Herzfeldian *eghoismos* (the 'canon of being different' and thus good at being a man):[8] a powerful, public expression of being **unique**, in the sense that each mother's pain is always unique in its severity (Dubisch, 1995: 214, 219) just as this particular daughter's bravery was unique in its determination. The performative of the suffering mother is thus no less public or powerful than that of the assertive man. In fact, one could argue that the uniqueness of a mother's pain – any mother's pain – involves an identification 'not only with other women but also with others who share women's experience of marginality' (Dubisch, 1995: 214), resonating thus with narratives greater than the actor herself.[9] Women – just as men – perform thus an idiosyncratic *eghoismos*, which although 'a *canon of being different*', 'can be only understood as a *social* category' (Herzfeld, 1985: 11, original emphasis). Being good at being a woman[10] is then an idiom of difference/uniqueness that is always performed

– similarly to the masculine *eghoismos*[11] – 'on behalf of a collectivity' (ibid.: 11). Seen in this light the performative of the suffering mother is not about 'individual, natural emotions' that belong to the private realm but a publicly enacted idiom that seeks to articulate and express a culturally specific female experience[12] (Dubisch, 1995: 213–15). With reference to Mrs Evangelia, the recounting of her pain (*ponos*), anxiety (*stenahoria*) and troubles (*vassana*) serve also to highlight her daughter's worth (*aksia*) in keeping the family together.

After reciting her troubles (*vassana*), Mrs Evangelia proceeded to show us the pictures of her other two daughters. She was proud of the fact that they were studying at the university and they would become scientists (*epistimones*), a concept which in Greece covers practically all fields and disciplines including social sciences, humanities and education (cf. Argyrou, 1996: 35). The university degrees that Elena's sisters would hopefully bring, make for Mrs Evangelia – as well as for the rest of the Kallipoliots – all the difference between mere financial security and social mobility, success and dignity (cf. Faubion, 1993: 59). Once again, Elena's mother mentioned the protagonistic role of Elena and how 'she sacrificed her education for that of her sisters'.[13]

Half an hour later, Katia, Elena's girlfriend, arrived at the house. She hugged Mrs Evangelia tightly and gave her two bars of her favourite chocolate. Elena's mother blushed. She was pleased with the chocolates but also slightly embarrassed because as she explained, she thought it rather childish to love chocolate that much. She was about to become emotional again, but instead she murmured, 'God bless you' to everybody and went to the kitchen 'in order not to be getting in your way'. Elena closed the door behind her and kissed Katia on the mouth.

The case of Elena is a success story of women. Mrs Evangelia, Elena, her two sisters, the *parea* (with its networking abilities) are all Greek women who operate in a complex cultural framework where conventional, alternative, modern and traditional ways of thinking and living are interwoven to produce a rich but still very familiar cultural amalgam. The death of a father is the beginning of this story and, at the same time, an event to be dealt with in the framework of various available discourses.

The family's immediate problem concerned the self-interest (*synferon*), or rather the welfare of a particular household rather than that of the individuals who comprise it (Theodossopoulos, 1997: 264, 1999). As Salamone and Stanton (1986: 99) and Hirschon (1989: 141) point out, the concept of the single individual and consequently of personal accomplishment are insufficient for understanding and explaining Greek culture. Hence when Elena's family found itself in a critical financial situation everybody's 'first and greatest loyalty . . . [was] to their immediate dependents' (Loizos, 1975: 290–1). This was dictated by a collective interpretation of *synferon* (self-interest) that aims to safeguard the household's prosperity and prestige (Theodossopoulos, 1999; du Boulay, 1974; Hirschon, 1989).

In this situation, someone had to work and, in the absence of a family business, somebody had to undertake wage labour. The fact that there was no man in the family, however, meant that a traditional approach to the gendered division of labour (Hirschon, 1989: 104) could not be applied. One of the two older women, either Elena or her mother, or both, had to become the provider(s). The choice of Elena over Mrs Evangelia, however, was clear in this case. Elena's mother belonged to a generation that treated women's work outside the home and family business as a violation of the traditional protocol whereby women had to work in the household and men to provide (Loizos, 1975: 54; Hirschon, 1989: 99–100). Furthermore, Mrs Evangelia was used to being the mistress of her home. Being forced to work as a cleaner or a maid, since she had no other qualifications, would be mostly unpleasant and demeaning for her (cf. Loizos, 1981: 178). As Hirschon very eloquently points out, when a woman is forced to work in a domestic job she is put in a 'subordinate position under another woman' who evaluates her abilities as a *noikokyra* (housewife–mistress of the home) (1989: 101–2). The centrality of the role of *noikokyra* (Hirschon, 1989; Salamone and Stanton, 1986) for a Greek woman of Mrs Evangelia's generation, explains why Elena was unwilling to let her mother undergo this emotional ordeal.

On the other hand, Elena grew up at a time when feminist ideas and alternative models of femininity were available (cf. Cowan, 1992), and thus she did not see the household as her exclusive place (Faubion, 1993: 174–6). She was 'the urban-educated' woman (ibid.) who had more qualifications and more resources, and she was hence deemed more fit to play the role of the provider. From that point all the cultural representations, characteristic of what was once understood as the conventional role of a man/father, were incorporated into Elena's modern narrative of the working woman. She tried to establish her own business rather than continue working for others (cf. Hirschon, 1989: 84–5), and she strived to ensure not only the financial stability, but also the social prestige of the household by financing and supporting her sisters' education (cf. Faubion, 1993: 59). The *parea*'s role in this story was important in the sense that it provided Elena with a supportive space and enough networking to complete her plans. In many ways, the group became for Elena an alternative family in so far as it provided her with 'an emotional and economic network' (Goddard, 1996: 179) that allowed her to fulfil the responsibilities she had undertaken *vis-à-vis* her biological family.

None the less, Elena's case cannot be said to be unique. Ethnographers of modern Greece have repeatedly testified to defiant female performances that constitute part of women's cultural power in Greece (Dubisch, 1995; Seremetakis, 1991: 238). The story of Elena affirms Dubisch's argument that gender constructs are often 'contextually interpreted and manipulated by both men and women' (1986: 28). Reviewing a wide array of recorded cases in the regional literature, Theodossopoulos mentions that due to 'male migration or other unforeseen circumstances' that forced husbands to pursue wage labour away from the community, women were often left to do most of the jobs traditionally assigned to men (1999: 616). One of his informants in Zakynthos says characteristically: 'In the past women used to do all the work. Old Mrs Popi managed to hold her household without her husband and she did well' (ibid.). Although the same informant claims that a 'woman cannot produce the same results as a man', she admits later that: 'when the men are away women can do everything' (ibid.). Similarly, Cowan refers to the case of Sofia, a widowed woman who shouldered alone the responsibilities of marrying her only child. On the night of the wedding when everything had gone well Sofia danced a radiant *zeimbekiko*, the solo dance that used to be performed by men (1990: 192–3).[14] An additional example is offered by Seremetakis, who also mentions the extensive engagement of Maniat women in what could be traditionally called male farming activities, that diffuses the gender divisions of social space conventionally observed in Greece (1991: 202). From the same book, among the numerous laments Maniat women perform over the dead body of a loved one, I singled out a particular verse composed for a woman's aunt: 'she struggled in life, because my uncle – out in the world I will say it – did not care on his part, he was earning lots of money, and was throwing it in the tavernas, with wine making friends and brothers' (Seremetakis, 1991: 209).

The actual cases of women who, due to various circumstances, have to assume the traditionally understood male role of the provider are undoubtedly many more than the documented ones in Greece. By establishing this, I wish to explore the theoretical consequences of women's engagement in male practices. One of the most central arguments in the present work is that 'the development of self-awareness is both discursively and practically produced' (Moore, 1994: 41). If practice is involved in the production of gendered subjectivity as much as discourse is (de Lauretis, 1997; Cowan, 1990; Moore, 1986; Butler, 1990, 1993, 1997a), then surely the displacement of gender idioms (Butler, 1990, 1993) that takes place every time a woman assumes a culturally perceived male role must have an effect, not only on her subjectivity, but also on the way she is perceived by others. None the less, the ethnographies of Greece do not fully validate this claim. With reference to the examples offered above, Theodossopoulos' informants state that '"if the man does not work or if the man does not work enough, there is no wealth in the household' (1999: 616), while the widow dancing *zeimbekiko* was almost 'misunderstood'[15] by her fellow Sohoians (Cowan, 1990: 197). Cowan notes that although Sohoian women often work both in and out of the home, they are only described by men as 'helping', because as an informant of hers stated, 'it is the man who has the responsibilities' (1990: 54). The belief that a woman's primary allegiance is to her household – irrespective of whether she might be contributing to it financially in addition to her role as a wife and mother – has been noted by many ethnographers of Greece (Cowan, 1990: 54; Hirschon, 1989: 100;[16] Faubion, 1993: 176, among others). Goddard makes the same argument with reference to Neapolitan women outworkers: 'the re-entry of women into the labour market did not displace the ideals of women as mothers and carers' (1996: 13). The author notes that her informants worked at home often with an unfavourable arrangement because they were trying to achieve a 'compromise between economic needs and their primary obligations as housewives' (ibid.). Gender ideals seem to be the result of a continuous dialectic relationship between cultural imagery and subjective experience, between discourse and practice. The identification of women with the household proves to be a rather fragile one in practice, but at the same time is a fairly resistant ideal in Greek cultural consciousness indicating the power of gender ideologies to conceal the effects of their contradiction.

None the less, assessing the theoretical and ethnographic importance of Elena's story I agree with Dubisch's argument that women's roles (and generally gender roles), in the Greek context are much more flexible than was assumed (1986: 28–9). Due to the fact that both at a local and at a wider level there are multiple and competing models of gender, the categories male and female in Greece often become 'epiphenomena of a fundamental concern with display and concealment, extroversion and introspection, pride and self-criticism' (Herzfeld, 1986a: 217). Thus although one cannot but acknowledge the enduring character of gender roles, many of the gender-related beliefs are categories that stand for and symbolise rather than define the nature of their subjects (ibid.: 217). Many qualities like *filotimo* (love of honour) (Dubisch, 1995: 202) or *levendia* (ability to fight) (Seremetakis, 1991: 237) as the ethnographers themselves assert, are not strictly the qualities of men as conventionally portrayed. The symbolic construction and realisation of gender in Greece follows much less rigid processes than is sometimes presumed (Cowan, 1990), and different groups often foster distinct and opposing views with reference to gender realisation (ibid.: 1990, 1991, 1992). It is mainly for this reason that the *parea* can engage in a series of mixed performances that do not appear offensive to its cultural periphery. Undoubtedly, the actor is constrained by certain cultural constructs and expectations 'imposed from without [but also] self-imposed' (McNay, 2000: 80). It is true that often 'individuals act in certain ways because it would violate their sense of being to do otherwise' (ibid.). Nevertheless, one cannot easily talk about irreconcilable contradictions or strictly defined paths in the fashioning of gender subjectivity. Ordinary actors, in conventional contexts, often find themselves in betwixt and between performative circumstances, occupying 'multiple subject positions' (Moore, 1994), while what is at one time defined as female can be itself permeated by male elements and vice versa. The contextuality of the self, which is the main theme of the present chapter, is indeed inseparable from the fluidity and indeterminacy of everyday performance, be it gendered or otherwise.

The case of Carolina

Carolina is one of the earliest and most distinguished members of the *parea*. In her mid-thirties, she is married, she has a teenage son and she runs an *haute coiffure* salon. Her husband is a journalist and they have been together for some 14 years. Carolina's time is divided between her family, the *parea* and her business, although not necessarily in that order. It was never clear to me whether her husband knew about her extra-marital relationships with women, but Carolina always tried to be as discreet as possible. The caution she was exhibiting, however, never stopped her from joining the *parea* more often than any other married woman member of her age, or from following the girls on trips and excursions. The fact that she had a family and a business to run did not seem to considerably constrain her from being actively involved in the group's life. In reality, Carolina was putting in a lot of effort in order to be available both for her family, her business and the *parea* supporting the claim that in relation to women 'living one's life is in conflictual relation with the conventional expectation of being there for others' (McNay, 2000: 41). I happened to stay at her home for several days and follow her truly exhausting daily schedule. Indeed, Carolina was not only investing much in the house and the salon, but she also tried to predict any unexpected changes in her family's routine brought about by her involvement in the activities of the *parea*. For instance, she always had a surplus of cooked food in the fridge, just in case she needed to be away for a couple of days, and she was always careful to arrange the laundry in such a way that there were always plenty of clothes available. Although her husband claimed to be fully capable of running the home, Carolina always made sure that the family's habits would not be disturbed in any way by her absences. As far as her business was concerned, she was 'lucky to have found an extremely efficient manageress', as she put it, 'who is able to deal with any problems when I am absent. Unfortunately, I still have to be there, since most of the customers come because of me rather than the quality of the service provided.'

Carolina's house has three large bedrooms. One of them is the guest room where she often sleeps especially when she returns home late, with company. It was to this perfectly tidy, tastefully decorated, spacious house that we arrived one day, at 6.00 in the morning after another long night at *Harama*. Carolina's first task was to prepare coffee and squeeze some oranges. Soon, Akis, her husband, woke up and appeared in the kitchen door with a bright smile. He saluted us with a 'hello girls! You went wild again didn't you?' (*To kapsate pali apopse*), drank the coffee, kissed Carolina and left. 'I'll call you later today', were his last words as he closed the door. Carolina wrote a maternal message to her son, left it on the top of a glass filled with orange juice and, next to it, ten thousand drachmas (the equivalent of £20). I pointed out that ten thousand drachmas is rather a lot for a teenager's daily needs. 'It is his job to control his spending my dear, not mine', Carolina remarked before we went to sleep.

Later that day, I followed her to the salon, where I realised that she was not exaggerating the necessity of her presence for the well-being of the business. Virtually every woman who walked into the place wanted to talk to *her*, to be given a style by *her*, to consult her on beauty as well as strictly personal matters. Carolina was radiant as if she had not had only a few hours sleep and an exhausting night behind her. She was smiling and charming to everybody, caring for each woman individually while, almost at the same time, she managed to arrange a surprise for her girlfriend and a late lunch with her husband. Around 6.00 in the afternoon, we sat in a quiet corner of the salon over a cup of strong coffee and talked. I began my 'exploration' of her highly demanding life from the spatial arrangement of her home, that is from the 'third bedroom':

'Akis [her husband] *sleeps very lightly. I always go to the guestroom when I come home late at night, that is almost everyday* [she laughs]. *With or without company, I avoid going to the bedroom and waking him up. Of course, since most of the time I come home with Fillipa* [her girlfriend at the time] *I need this extra bedroom anyway. However, I have to admit that many days Akis is starting his day at the time that I am returning home. I also have to admit that I never had problems with Akis. He is an outgoing person too, but his work does not allow him to enjoy himself as much as he wants to. He would be out every night if he could and he understands my need for privacy. I would not have married Akis in the first place if he were a person to restrain me and impose upon me. I love him really. When he has his day off work I always try to spend it with him. He is a lovely person. One of those people you are happy to be with. I am mostly concerned with my son rather than my husband. He is the one who probably does not see much of me. But I think this is not so bad after all. He will hopefully grow to be an independent person. He knows that he can communicate everything to me. He knows that I am there for him, although I do not believe that teenagers really go to their parents for a particular problem. The important thing is not how you present yourself to them. You might be liberal, friendly and so on, but you never stop being a parent, and kids know that too well. They are right not to trust us, not to mix the roles. Friends are friends and parents are parents. Friends are for the problems and parents for the real mess that happens once in a blue moon . . .'*

The discussion turns to her almost obsessive care for the home. Carolina comments:

'I care for the home. I want everything to be in order. I want the house to be warm and welcoming for everybody, not only for my husband or my son. How many times have I invited the girls [the *parea*] *to come over at six o'clock in the morning for a nibble? I want the house to be able to accommodate family and friends at any given time.'*

I remarked that I found her life too busy and too demanding. My impression was that she was literally 'split in three' and quite needlessly so, since the *parea*, being an open and relaxed group does not require each and every member to join the outings in such a dramatic frequency. She immediately responded:

'You describe it very well. I am split between three places, three roles, almost three selves to be precise. But I like this. I like the quick rhythms of life, the change, the shift between one Carolina and the other. I love my three selves which are maybe four because for me being a wife and a mother appeals to different parts of my psyche; I cannot imagine myself as one-dimensional, as only something and nothing else, as stuck and stagnated. Stagnation is rust and death that does not transform into anything. It is the ultimate waste of human energy and potential. I manage to deal with each and every one of my responsibilities as separate from each other and as equally important. Because they **are** *equally important! They all relate to a different part of me.'*

One could safely argue that with the exception of her involvement in the *parea*, Carolina is a typical urban woman of her age (cf. Faubion, 1993: 174–6). She is not confined to the private space of her household, she enjoys a relative independence, and her ethos is rather removed from 'the ontological stereotypes that rural ethnographers continue to report' (Faubion, 1993: 175). In many ways, she approaches Faubion's 'Athenian woman' who is free to 'set foot in traditional male domains' (ibid.: 176), who does 'not believe or portray herself as being inferior to men' (Faubion, 1993: 175), who has an independent career and the luxury of a private life. Nevertheless, as Cowan notes, all these are in 'addition to her domestic duties and responsibilities to care for her children' (1990: 54). Carolina is still a proficient *noikokyra* (housewife, mistress of the house) who tends to her chores and is expected to excel in all her domestic duties (Faubion, 1993: 176).

It could be argued that Carolina maintains a double and conflicting identification with conventional and 'alternative' ideals of femininity. Whether her 'conventional self' is enacted and celebrated because of a 'deep-seated often unconscious investment' in a historically and culturally rich ideal of femininity (McNay, 2000: 41, 18, 97–8) or it is the result of a conscious choice is I believe almost besides the point. What is probably more important is that through a series of conflicting but equally significant identifications 'the dialectics of sameness and difference is resolved into a kind of difference *in* sameness' (Sax, 2002: 190). Through occupying different contexts and persisting in being loyal to multiple relations Carolina abolishes the dichotomies between self/other, homosexual/heterosexual, traditional/alternative (cf. Corber and Valocchi, 2003). In this manner, the discourse of the other does not merely transform into the discourse of the subject (McNay, 2000: 152) but the very quality of otherness – whether this is taken to be the conventional, heterocentric patriarchal norm or the alternative homocentric ideal – is incorporated and creatively reworked to become part of the self and indistinguishable from it.

Significant is perhaps also the observation that Carolina is not unique. Like most Greek women, she is expected to be a 'vassal and an executive, eternal maiden and eternal Circe, child and mother at the same time' (Faubion, 1993: 177). She can be the girl of the *parea* and the housewife and the prominent business woman, not only because she is an exceptionally capable individual, but also because many of the women of her age and circumstances 'exist as a set of multiple and contradictory positionings and subjectivities' (Moore, 1994: 55). Her multiple constitution, like that of most Greek urban women in their thirties, is 'composed of diverse relations' (Strathern, 1988: 324).[17] Carolina's belonging to a certain idiosyncratic group is actually her only peculiarity. Even if she was not part of any alternative group, she would have still been expected to be desirable as well as cultivated, to work in the public arena and shine in the domestic domain (cf. Faubion, 1993), to be the intersecting point of a series of conflicting discourses about femininity in the highly *disemic* context of Greek culture (cf. Herzfeld, 1987). Most Greek women in the subject position of Carolina have to reconcile at least two 'significant alters', the oriental traditional past and the western European future of the modern Hellenes (Harrison, 1999: 12; Herzfeld, 1987).

With reference to their sexuality, as Maro, Faubion's fictional character notes 'Greek women should never be flirtatious . . . should never be the seductresses of men; but should always be flirtatious . . . should always be the seductresses of their husbands' (1993: 176). Or, as a Greek proverb states: 'the perfect woman should be a chef in the kitchen, a lady in public and a slut in bed'. In fact, the ambiguous character of femininity might not even be an urban phenomenon of late modernity. Du Boulay has rightly pointed out that women were traditionally seen in Greece as both 'Eves' and 'mothers of God' (1991). As her informants stated, pointing out the two-fold character of femininity as conceptualised in Ambeli: 'From one woman came sin and from another woman came salvation' (du Boulay, 1991: 76).

Carolina, like many other Greek women, is used to impersonating more than one role and as such she is an 'agent who acts because of relationships' (Strathern, 1988: 273). She can afford to be a 'partible entity' (ibid.) because all her different selves are sustained intersubjectively, in *relation* to her social others. These relations are, in turn, 'immediate' but at the same time 'extensive ones mediated through impersonal, symbolic and material structures' (McNay, 2000: 12). Thus, she can be: the mother of her son and *a* mother, the wife of Akis and *a* wife, the owner of a beauty-parlour and *a* businesswoman, a seductress of men – and since her initiation to the *parea*, also a seductress of women – in a manner similar to any rural woman who is seen as both an Eve and a *Panayia* (mother of God) (du Boulay, 1991). Still, Carolina, not the mother, not the girl of the *parea*, neither the wife, nor the lover, but just Carolina, the combination of all the above, 'the site of differences' (Moore, 1994: 58), has daily to confront her conflicting ideas about what is and what is not a fulfilling life. Towards the end of our discussion, when I asked her how she felt about her life she told me:

'Some days pass with no sleep at all. Sometimes my mother-in-law visits me and makes my life hell. Some times I quarrel with my husband and at other times with my girlfriend. There are moments when I receive criticism from both my friends and my family for not being there. As if I can be everywhere! On the other hand, there is nothing more pleasurable than this constant change. Each day is different and each day is a challenge.'

The case of Aphrodite – the case of Maro[18]

Aphrodite

Aphrodite, in her early thirties, was one of the first people who created the *parea*. She had studied graphic design in Athens where she was involved in various political groups, mostly leftist. A radical feminist during the 1980s, she now criticises the feminist movement as 'leading women down the wrong path'.[19] Politics are not part of her life anymore, although she still remains an idealist (*ideologos*). Aphrodite returned to her home town after finishing her degree in Athens. At first she was living alone, but later she decided to return to the family home.

'My father's health started deteriorating. My mother could not cope alone, neither physically nor financially. My eldest brother had already married, and my younger sister too. So I went back to my parental home because I felt I was needed. I still live with them although I do not like it. The rhythms of the house are totally different. They get up at the time I go to bed, and a couple of hours later my sister brings her son to us. Although I love Stavros [her nephew] *it is unbearable. He comes to my bed and wakes me up at eight o'clock in the morning in order to play with and tell him stories. I can't say no to him. Stavros is more my child than Fotini's* [her sister's]. *Fotini stays with Stavros a couple of hours at night. Not even that sometimes, as the kid often sleeps at our house. I have him day and night. The whole* parea *has him day and night sometimes!* [Indeed, Stavros often escorts us to taverns and coffee shops] *Now we have to get him in to a nursery school. He is turning four and he has to socialise with other kids . . .'*

Stavros's nursery school became the *parea*'s collective business. Aphrodite preferred a private nursery whereas Carolina insisted upon the public option. The girls were discussing the matter for a week, and every 'specialised' person was asked for her opinion. In the end, the boy was sent to a private nursery run by a friend who was not, however, a member of the group.

The times that Stavros was escorted to the nursery by a girl of the *parea* were frequent. The little boy was driven to his school by car and on motorbike depending on who was available on any given day. On Valentine's day he gave us a present. He had drawn all the girls of the *parea* that he knew on a huge piece of paper with his name scribbled at the bottom. We could hardly read his script, as he could not write properly yet, but the piece of paper was stuck on a wall at *Harama* for many many months.

Aphrodite's family knows that the girls are 'friends'. Her two-year relationship with Daphne remained a carefully kept secret.

'I vividly remember the day that my mother returned from the market really upset. "I've heard something terrible today", she said. I asked her what. "Somebody told me something about Daphne, your friend." I remember my blood going cold. My mother went on to explain to me that this "person" told her that Daphne was "one of them". I demanded to know what she really meant. "You know she likes women they say", she said finally. I tried to laugh and reassured her that it was all nonsense. She never told me who this person was.'[20]

I asked Aphrodite why her mother's opinion was so important for her. She was a grown up, economically independent person, and her mother could not interfere with her life anymore. Her perspective was different though:

'When I was a little girl, kyra-Efi [her mother] *used to take me along with her when visiting friends. I had specific instructions to be well behaved. Kyra-Efi was a very strict woman, very disciplined. She was the "captain" of the house. My father's opinion did not count, especially because he was getting the family into troubles with his political ideas* [Aphrodite's father was a communist]. *So, every time we were visiting somebody I was sitting on a chair without moving or talking. I was barely breathing, in order to please her. When the hostess was offering me a sweet, I was looking straight into kyra-Efi's eyes. If she nodded "yes" I would take it. Otherwise, no matter how much I wanted the sweet, I was politely refusing it. If you asked me before, I would tell you that I did not care whether my mother found out about my relationship with Daphne or not. But when the time came, when kyra-Efi* ***actually*** *asked me about it, the only thing I could see were her eyes; black and straight, exactly the same eyes that were telling me not to take the sweet. I never took it back then, and I realise that, metaphorically speaking, I would not take it today. It seems that I never grew out of the power of those eyes. . . . It might seem peculiar to you but in a way I do not want to. Part of me is unable to do it and part of me does not even want to try.'*

After finishing her story, Aphrodite remained silent for 10 minutes, staring at the ceiling. It was the only instance when she talked about the subject, and the longest 10 minutes of my fieldwork. During all the years that I knew her, she kept her private life carefully out of her family's gaze, but she never offered any explanations about her behaviour. She simply chose to 'compartmentalize her life by developing two distinct groups of people: those who know and those who do not' (Savin-Williams, 1998: 141; cf. Davies, 1992). In turn, 'those who do not', are first and foremost her family and more specifically her mother. Aphrodite's case testifies to the relevance of kinship as a source of personhood 'located within the broader contexts of civil society'

(Goddard, 1994: 86). Kinship here, and particularly the mother–daughter relationship, is definitely not a domestic affair (cf. Moore, 1988: 25). The authority of *kyra*-Efi, not over her daughter's choices, but over a part of her persona, proves to be of major importance. Motherhood, in this case, goes beyond the 'natural process' of giving birth to a child (ibid.) and becomes the source of intersubjective identifications that force Aphrodite to adhere to certain 'parental fantasies' (de Lauretis, 1994) that have significant and explicit consequences in the fashioning of her subjectivity. In turn, these parental fantasies are themselves originating in and are shaped by a specific socio-cultural and historical context that defines sexuality 'proscriptively' (Rubin, 1975; Dunne, 1997: 6), presenting heterosexuality as the only 'normal' option (Dunne, 1997) while constructing homosexuality as the 'Other' (Fuss, 1991).[21] However, as Aphrodite's involvement in the *parea* demonstrates, there can be many contexts other than the familial one where a person can form different kinds of relationships as well as enact different identifications. Furthermore, as Maro's story will demonstrate, one can safely argue that family as a context and a source of gender ideas is itself an 'uncertain form' (Donzelot, 1980: xxv, quoted in Goddard, 1994: 74) that frequently becomes 'a point of intersection of a number of often contradictory discourses and practices' (Goddard, 1994: 74–5).

Maro

Maro is 25 years old and works as a physiotherapist. She is my best friend in the *parea*[22] and one of the most active members. She, too, lives in the family home, but her mother is one of the very few in the context of the group who knows almost everything about her daughter's sexual preferences. The reason most of the girls keep this part of their lives secret from their kin is not only their fear of rejection or marginalisation but also, as Maro explains, because many members of the group feel that their families would force upon them an identity they do not wish to have:

'I have never decided to tell her that I have sexual relationships with women, precisely because I felt that she would not understand. My mother could never distinguish the difference between sleeping with women, or having relationships with them and constructing a so-called lesbian identity.[23] *For her, things are "either" – "or". She cannot share my approach to things and she has totally internalised the social stereotypes. Anyway, at some point she found out. She first suspected it when I was with Rania* [one of Maro's first relationships]; *she asked me and I did not deny it. In the beginning she was shouting and threatening she'd die if I don't "change" but as time passed she got used to it. She still shouts at me from time to time: "Those women are going to destroy you"* [*autes oi gynaikes tha se fane*], *but who cares? She never had the guts to tell my father. In fact, lately, she started having opinions about the various girls. Well, she cannot conceptualise the fact that I am in a relationship now, so every woman who calls or passes by the house she thinks I am sleeping with her. It's amazing. Lately she saw*

Marina, a colleague from work who's not very pretty, and she commented: "I see that you have lowered your standards lately." I tried to explain to her that I never lower my standards and that I do not sleep with Marina, but alas, once she has set her mind on something you cannot persuade her otherwise.

Our relationship has improved a lot over the past five years. Once I asked her how she feels about the fact that I am erotically involved with women: "It's not what I dreamed for you but still it does not change the fact that you are my daughter and part of this family. I do not see the point of making an issue out of it anymore. After all, who is to say what is wrong and right, what is acceptable and not when it comes to ***my child****?' she replied* [original emphasis].

The funniest story ever, is when an aunt visited us for my name day. The aunt brought a piece of embroidery with her as a present, She gave it to me and told me not to let my mother use it because it is supposed to be for my dowry. My mother took it and – on the spot – spread it on the coffee table replying to my aunt: "Of course I will use it because if I wait for Maro to marry it will never be used." The poor aunt was watching us without being able to catch the hint. My mother looked at me and laughed. It was one of those moments when I felt that we were actually communicating. Anyway, I still care for my mom. How do they say it? The mother is always the mother and there is only one [mother]*!*[24] [laughter] *No, seriously, this is why I do not leave the house. I like being her child. Even if this takes a lot of effort sometimes. And to tell you the truth, I enjoy very much having coffee with my mother in the mornings. I like family dinners, and I always try to be present at the Sunday table. My relationship with the extended family is a part of my life I do not wish to abolish. We might have different ideas about things, but I want them to be part of my reality . . .'*

The case of Emily

Emily is a lawyer. She does not work regularly but she is never short of money. At present, she lives alone in a rented flat and her relationship with her parents is not always smooth. The only child of a very religious family, she grew up in a rather conservative environment. Some of her relatives are high-ranking priests, one of them is an abbot while a very close kinsman is a bishop. Emily claims that from the very early years of her childhood, her family suppressed her sexuality and attempted to 'deform' her.

'My whole upbringing revolved around what I call deformation, or the abolition of desire. It is not only because of the religiosity of my family. Many families, religious or not, believe that "apatheia" [lack of desire, apathy] *is the normal state of human beings. Individuals with no desires are considered as liberated, while desire itself is regarded as constraining. People like my parents believe that one's "true self" is somewhere there, hidden, a prisoner of desire, passion and pleasure. Once passion and desire are dead the "true self" is supposed to shine like a diamond cleaned from the mud. These people view desire as an impediment of the soul. From as early as I can remember, they were struggling to abolish my desire to desire and I was struggling to keep my desire*

alive. Every time I go to some family reunion in the parental house my kin-group gathers around me. They try to decode me. They do not exactly succeed . . . I still go to these reunions though. I pay visits to my parents and I like going to the church with my mother during holy week [week before Easter] *where I become a participant observer* [*paratiritis kai synama symmetoxos*] *of a world without desire and pleasure, a world which, mind you, is the universe I grew up in. But, I would like to repeat it: this attitude is not directly related to religiosity. The sweeping, overpowering denial of hedonism is about "spirituality", a kind of monastic spirituality. Philosophical, more than religious, are the beliefs I was nurtured with. I say philosophical because these ideas pertain to the "care of the self", which in this case is misapprehended as advancement of the self. The self here is identified with the spirit and radically separated from the body and subsequently from the senses. In turn the superiority and advancement of the spirit is ensured through its conquest over the body. The self is split in two irreconcilable parts that are always fighting each other. This is the "paradigm". As to the use of it, this is another story. People in this corner of the globe struggle continuously for social capital. The mortification of the body, the abolition of desire, the ostracism of pleasure are capitalized. They are means to "difference", means to distinction . . .'*

During the same meeting, Emily was very keen to relate her ideas on gender. According to her, female sexuality is considered by 'spiritual' people (i.e. according to Emily, the people who are involved in religious and philosophical quests) dangerous precisely because it represents the fear of the body:

'Before I begin to explore the issue of female sexuality with reference to "spirituality", I have to tell you that women become women, as men become men through a forced identification with a feminine or a masculine model respectively. In other words, the category woman is a political and not a biological entity. Nevertheless, the sexuality of the people who belong to the political category woman is always feared more because the female body has come to symbolise desire; it is historically related to pleasure and hedonism. The paradigm of spirituality is itself a gendered paradigm. If the spirit is to successfully prevail upon the body, it has to prevail first upon its representation which is female sexuality. But female sexuality is in a way a simulacrum devised to stand for sensuality. Priests should not be female-like [*thyliprepeis*] *because female stands for sensual . . . In the environment I grew up in, one had to first become a woman and then, in order to transform into a truly worthy spiritual being, she had to stop being a sexual entity. What is left? Well, reproductive capacity of course. Thus, to recapitulate, you first become a gendered being, you then abolish your sexuality/sensuality/desire/need for pleasure, to finally develop into a true Panayia* [Holy Mary]. *Who is Panayia? A mother who never had sex, the perfect reproductive vessel of pure spirit. Some call it Panayia, some others might call it something different. The way to distinction for the spiritual people always passes through the same basic process.'*

Emily has the reputation of being a very good lawyer. She usually takes 'big' cases, such as drug trafficking or whatever seems interesting enough to her and although she practises selectively, she adores talking about law. She believes that her studies on the particular subject have shaped her thought.

'Law taught me a lot. Firstly, I came to realise how powerful certain consortiums can be when they wear the cloak of the "de-jure". Law is a powerful institution, but its basic difference from the church or the family or the psychiatrist, is that the people who serve it, lawyers and judges alike are fully aware of the fact that what they are worshipping is man-made, and transitory. Law is a parody of philosophy based on the premise of "let's all assume that this is the truth until a new truth comes and takes its place". Adultery used to be a crime, now it is not. From one moment to another what once constituted grounds for conviction, take abortion for instance, can be perfectly legal. Law is perhaps the only institution where manipulation of symbolism and connotation is so overt. The principles of the legal system have shown me how to avoid seeing things as natural, how not to structure an argument on the basis of "nature".'

As we were talking, my eye caught a photo of Emily in a suit holding a briefcase and wearing smart glasses. I picked up the photo and showed it to her remarking that she looked different in that outfit. She smiled. I could still remember some moments from her recent separation when Emily was dancing with her hair untidy, without the smart glasses, wearing jeans, immersed in the performative of pain. She was really beautiful on the dance floor, really powerful. I took a look at the photo again and asked her whether she uses her charm in the courtroom: *'Of course I do', she replied. 'I always try to charm the judge. Especially so, if she is a woman!'*

Emily is, in many ways, like Faubion's fictional character of '*Maro*'[25] (1993). In fact, *Maro* combines in more than one instance both Emily and her kin group in so far as they are all engaged in the project of self-realisation (Faubion, 1993: 164). Emily, like *Maro*, is the only child of a family who is 'secure in the distinction of her heritage' although she does not belong to any particular socio-cultural élite (cf. Faubion, 1993: 168). Unlike *Maro*, however, she values leisure precisely because she is aware of the ancient Greek association between the élite and leisure (ibid.). Emily can afford to practise law selectively and defies any kind of work ethic whatsoever. Labelling herself as a 'worker', like Faubion's character, would remind her too much of her mother who often includes such 'self-consciously populist remarks' in her rhetoric in order to *sound* like one of the élite (1993: 168).

Both *Maro* and Emily received a good education, work and live independently of their families, but the latter's relationship with her parents is expressly confrontational since her radical separation from her mother has become an indispensable part of her own game of distinction. Emily and *Maro* read a lot. The former enjoys Foucault, Kristeva, Bourdieu and Derrida while the latter prefers Dumont, Nietzsche and Foucault (Faubion, 1993: 178). For Emily, the knowledge she acquires through reading comprises her 'armory' (*oplostasio*), an armory that makes her *unique* and turns her into the 'historically authentic self' she feels she ought to be (Faubion, 1993: 164). In many respects, Emily's attitude towards life is a typical example of what Giddens calls 'institutional reflexivity', that is 'the adoption by people and groups of terms originally used to describe social life' (1992: 29). Emily does not only read/study social analysis, she introduces it into her life and becomes inspired by it (ibid.). Her radical separation from her mother follows an almost therapeutic/psychoanalytic model of personal autonomy based on the achievement of one's emotional independence from her parents (Giddens, 1992: 108). Her continuous inquiry into her present and past renders her self 'a reflexive project' (ibid.: 30), one that cannot be conceptualised separately from a scholastic process of thinking.

On the other hand, Emily is also an attractive and stylish young woman who, nevertheless, would never go to such lengths as wearing flowing skirts and embroidered slippers in order to distinguish herself from her contemporaries who follow the changing fashion (Faubion, 1993: 178). This would have been very much her mother's style. On the contrary, Emily changes her wardrobe according to the latest fashion, she dares to paint her toe-nails, she wears mini-skirts and high heels as well as suits and smart glasses. She treats herself to expensive cosmetics and writes with a *Mont-Blanc*.[26] She is a *bon viveur*, a girl of luxury and frivolous avocations, who leaves everything spiritual to her family and prefers to indulge instead in a life full of hedonism. Even her intellectual quests are expressed in a relaxed albeit self-confident manner. Much like *Maro*, Emily, a true daughter of her mother, is convinced of one thing, namely, that the self can be *made* (cf. Faubion, 1993: 159–83) and she is struggling to make her own self very different from what is expected by her kin-group.

As Faubion (1993) very acutely pointed out, the realisation of the self is a common and popular project in Greece. Be it through spirituality, hedonism or the reinvention of cultural idioms, constructivism, historical or otherwise, always entails an 'elaborate objectification of the self which is subject to historical and culturological analyses' (Faubion, 1993: 163). Emily's 'objectification of her self and her culture' (ibid.) place her with her mother as well as with the girls of the *parea*, who are engaged in the same process of deconstructing and reassembling an authentic self and an idiosyncratic private culture. All of them are characters who engage in a process of synthesising mixed performances by creating new combinations out of already existing, often conflicting, cultural elements. As a result, both the self and the vernacular culture that supports its existence are founded at once on difference and 'self-willed' – as well as unconscious, I would add – 'mannerism' (cf. Faubion, 1993: 164). In this context, the 'stability of personhood' emulates the 'obligation to be unique' (ibid.: 165) and the subject is revealed to be contextual and multiple instead of homogenous and undifferentiated (Moore, 1994). In this sense, Emily, both as an individual and as a girl of the *parea*, is no different from her mother, who is herself in a way, very similar to Herzfeld's Cretan men. All of them know how to cultivate an *agonistic* self who is *made* to perform 'not so much within everyday life as in front of it' (Herzfeld, 1985: 11).

Elena, Maro, Aphrodite, Carolina and Emily, were familiar figures even before this chapter focused on their individual circumstances. They were 'the girls' who initiated other women into the group, who started relationships, separated, danced and drank as members of the *parea*. The present ethnographic material threw some light on their lives as daughters, wives and mothers of people who do not share the group's experiences. Through their narrations, I was able to reaffirm my conviction that 'in a world with too many voices speaking all at once, a world where syncretism and parodic invention are becoming the rule . . . it is increasingly difficult to attach human identity and meaning to a coherent "culture" or "language"' (Clifford, 1988: 95). As a consequence, I would argue that in the midst of this intra-cultural polyglossia it becomes almost impossible to talk about unchanging selves and homogenous subjects. The women present in this chapter are culturally and historically syncretic selves, *persons* (cf. Strathern, 1988) who occupy 'a variety of subject positions within different discourses' (Moore, 1994: 55).

Agreeing with the approach that views culture as an interminable 'dialogue of subcultures' and language as the 'interplay of dialects' (Clifford, 1988: 46), I cannot but approach the subject as an inherently polyphonic entity who oscillates between different discourses, idioms and contexts, embodying constraint but also creativity. The girls of the *parea* live in a state of contextual flux. For most of them the world always consists of dominant and less dominant discourses, of more and less alternative contexts, of various subject positions which ultimately collapse on to each other blurring the boundaries between difference and sameness. In this sense my informants are no different to any other social actor whose self-awareness depends on a series of intersubjective identifications. As Cowan argues with reference to the Sohoian girls, who like the *parea* 'doubt the natural basis of their destiny' (1992: 146): 'we need to examine the interplay of gender ideologies in relation to the choices the girls can imagine as desirable and feasible in the actual conditions of their life' (ibid., my translation). Many of the choices of the women I studied are dictated by a similar logic, of 'what is desirable' *vis-à-vis* what is 'feasible' with reference to their positions in a specific, Greek, provincial socio-cultural milieu.

The initial question posed at the beginning of this chapter pertained to the influence of dominant discourses on individuals and groups. Through a slightly more holistic ethnographic exploration of the lives of the women of my *parea*, I can safely argue that the importance placed on the fashioning of the self is certainly a larger cultural project that the girls adhere to. One of the common denominators of this polysemic culture to which the *parea* belongs is the constant engendering of personhood, but not in the sense that the 'I' 'authors experience', or 'guarantees the authenticity of their knowledge of self and of the world' (Moore, 1994: 30). Quite the opposite, in this specific multi-textual cultural setting, identity is performatively constructed against and in the midst of different models, which enjoy variant degrees of sanctioning and consequently distinct weight and desirability. Precisely this textual and highly intersubjective mode of constructing the self (cf. Moore, 1994: 119) is what promotes the 'elaborate objectification of the self and the culture' (Faubion, 1993). It is a kind of poetics of personhood based on analysis and deconstruction of some of its cultural determinants (ibid.: 183).

In turn, the highly syncretic character of gender identity that the *parea* promotes can be said to be part of the greater cultural project of self-realisation. A project that governs a wide array of cultural enactments: the Herzfeldian 'poetics of manhood' (1985) along with the competitive suffering of Elena's mother, the excellent performance of the proficient housewife and business woman in which Carolina engages, or Emily's counter-spirituality are all expressions of the same collective undertaking. The fact that culture can be objectified along with personhood itself, does provide us with powerful analyses of anthropologically conscious selves (Faubion, 1993: 163). Nevertheless, it does not always guarantee the ability or willingness of the person to threaten the magnitude of certain cultural discourses, or their 'bearing on individual experience' (Moore, 1994: 16). The policing of sexuality and desire is not only externally enforced but also sometimes internally established (McNay, 2000: 80). As Goddard has noted:

> Gender models which derive substantially from parental ones and which involve an ideological elaboration of motherhood, are effective on the one hand as collective discourses and on the other are formative at the level of the intimate and unconscious dynamics involved in the process of creation of the self.
>
> (1996: 203)

Or else, as Aphrodite puts it:

'But when the time came, when kyra-Efi ***actually*** *asked me about it* [her relationships with women], *the only thing I could see were her eyes; black and straight, exactly the same eyes that were telling me not to take the sweet. I never took it back then, and I realize that, metaphorically speaking, I would not have taken it today either. It seems that I never grew out of the power of those eyes. . . . It might seem peculiar to you but in a way I do not want to. Part of me is unable to do it and part of me does not even want to try.'*

On the other hand, precisely because people are not only socially confined subjects, but also actors, and persons 'who act because of relationships' (Strathern, 1988: 273) the possibility that dominant discourses crumble under the weight and culturally defined importance of these relationships is also a very strong one. The self, although very well situated, is never in stasis. What Maro's mother claimed when asked how she feels about the fact that her daughter is erotically involved with women, attests to the ability of the subject to effectively undermine – even briefly – certain dominant stereotypes through the power given to her by these very same idioms. Maro's mother talks with the authority of the Greek mother whose suffering entitles her to the only opinion that actually counts:

'It's not what I dreamed for you but still it does not change the fact that you are my daughter and part of this family. I do not see the point of making an issue out of it anymore. After all, who is to say what is wrong and right, what is acceptable and what is not when it comes to ***my child****?'*

7

DIFFERENT PEOPLE, SAME PLACES – DIFFERENT PLACES, SAME PEOPLE

This chapter focuses on the continuity between the *parea* and the socio-cultural environment that surrounds it, seeking to establish a narrative link between experience, practice and discourse. It has been argued that actors discover and position themselves *vis-à-vis* a narrative repertoire and interpret their experience in relation to the episodic but contextual plot of their individual life histories (Munt, 1998: 4). In turn, the reciting and sharing of narratives facilitate not only the positioning of the actor within a wider web of relationships, but also enable the formation of an ontological definition of the self with reference to relationships and discourses (ibid.). In so far as all identities are provisional (Marshall, 1998: 66) and in a continuous state of 'becoming', the experiential process of narrative informs and is informed by both discourse and practice. In my attempt to acknowledge the socio-cultural circumstances within which the *parea* was/is formed, I had to rely on the narratives of different people who were directly or not related to the group. For their stories seem to constitute a reservoir of knowledge for the *parea* that helps the girls not only define who they are, but also decide what to do, what not to do and how to relate (cf. Munt, 1998: 4).

I treat these narratives as expressions of a shared culture and try to determine how the life and decisions of the women of the *parea* reflect and are reflected in different stories suggestive, albeit not necessarily representative, of distinct spatial and temporal contexts. The central theme of all the stories to be presented is women's homoerotic experiences as these unfold in space and time. The following accounts provide an excellent context for the discussion of a number of issues such as the relationship between financial independence and the ability to sustain an alternative lifestyle, the institutionalised character of heterosexuality (Dunne, 1997) and the aestheticisation of desire. Some of the stories relate to experiences of empowerment gained through questioning normative idioms of desire and relatedness, while some others reveal the feebleness of the actor against powerful, hegemonic discourses that constrain her creativity. In many ways this chapter is a journey through time and space that seeks to approach the relationship between the particular and the general, the circumstantial and the representative, through an examination of the continuity between cultural context and personal narrative. My central argument is that the *parea* belongs to a specific socio-cultural collectivity (cf. Green, 1997), or else to a certain web of socio-cultural narratives with which it maintains a continuous dialectical relationship. In other words, the women of the group are an audience to other people's performances and at once performers for a wider audience. Within this context of exchange and mutual influence, however, some utterances can be heard louder than others.

The journey

One of the best-guarded myths of the group is its actual origin. The women who first started building this all-female network maintain that there was no plan, no intention, no objective behind the creation of the *parea*, which is perceived as 'a bunch of like-minded people who happened to be travelling together in life', as Emily often likes to describe it. All I knew throughout the years I was close to the *parea*, was that it started with four girls developing gradually into a fairly complex and wide web of relationships between women of various socio-economic and educational strata. What I also knew was that all these four pioneers came from Kallipolis and met while at university in Athens during the early 1980s. They were Emily – a lawyer, Aphrodite – a graphic designer, Lina – an architect and Rosita, who studied philosophy and literature. Emily and Rosita used to be friends before entering the university and it made sense to live together as students in a small apartment and later in a house that Emily inherited from her grandmother. This house that nowadays frequently accommodates the women of the *parea* who travel to Athens, 'saw the beginning of one friendship and two loves', as Rosita poetically puts it. When Emily inherited the property, during her second year in law school, she moved in with her friend-cum-flatmate Rosita, and decided to share the old but spacious and centrally located house with two additional girls. Aphrodite and Lina proved to be ideal choices, not only because they too came from Kallipolis, and were thus deemed to be trusted, but also because they were renowned party animals and hence expected to be good company. From this point onwards, however, the story of the four girls, whenever reluctantly told, always became vague. According to one version, Rosita fell in love with Emily and then somehow Aphrodite started flirting with Lina. At other times, I was told that it was Lina who fell in love with Aphrodite, and she decided to tell Rosita who then realised that she felt the same about Emily. On one occasion Maro, Martha and myself were told that Rosita actually fell in love with Aphrodite and this is how they started to explore this aspect of their sexuality. Each time the story was recounted in a different way, while the reason they all returned to Kallipolis was constantly and, as it were, strategically omitted.

I never thought much about the 'Athens years', as they were frequently referred to by the quartet. I always thought, even after I had finished the original fieldwork, that it was another instance of myth-making on the part of the girls who liked to mystify parts of their own lives and of the *parea*'s history in order to credit them legendary status. Reinforcing each other's mythology was the girls' favourite pastime and an indispensable part of the group's culture.[1] Towards the later stages of the research upon which this book is based, it became apparent that I should somehow account for the origins of the *parea*. I was frequently asked, and justly so, to account for the early stages of the group and to contextualise this *parea* in time and space. There was no other way for me to accomplish this other than ask them about the 'Athens years', and so I did. I boldly went to Emily, Aphrodite, Lina and Rosita and explained my social/analytical problem and the need for more information on the origins of the group. 'I sit there reading other people's work and they all know the full story of the communities they study', I told them and I insisted:

> The ethnographers usually know the political background of the communities they write about, the wider debates that influenced them. And I look back to my material and all I have is some vague stories about how you met and things seem to have been 'just happening'. Why is the *parea* the way it is? How did it start? How did it happen that the group came to have today's ideological orientation?

They decided to settle my questions through a long journey into the backstage of their lives and occasionally on the streets of Kallipolis; a journey in time and space that set sail from the very house where everything began.

Greece: from Kallipolis to Athens during the early 1980s

It is no accident, I think, that the *parea* started as a small circle of four women who during their university years began exploring their sexuality. Dunne argues for a positive association between education and the prospect of interpreting one's sexuality outside the confines of a heterocentric model (1997). As it arises from previous chapters of this book,[2] there is a definite relationship between education and financial independence on the one hand and the potential to lead an alternative lifestyle on the other. In the case of the women of the *parea*, education and employment might also come as a consequence of belonging to the group[3] since the community also functions as a support network to its members. There is no doubt that social and economic improvement are important factors in sustaining an alternative lifestyle. Higher education and university life, apart from facilitating social and economic mobility, are also thought to comprise a context for the development of critical thinking which can be applied to the rethinking of sexuality and the positive evaluation of same-sex relationships (Dunne, 1997: 125). With reference to university, however, the opposite argument might also hold true. The institution itself, as well as student life in general, can be excellent fields for the reproduction of class and gender stereotypes instead of their critical evaluation (Holland and Eisenhart, 1990: 6). Holland and Eisenhart (1990) found that there was enormous peer pressure on young women in the US to form romantic relationships during their university years. The urge to conform to gender stereotypes, often at the expense of career prospects, was experienced by most young women who 'faced constant evaluations of their worth on the basis of their sexual appeal to men and they made "life decisions" in the shadow of that reality' (ibid.: 21).

With reference to the Greek context, education at least up until the early 1990s was extremely formalistic and over-inflated (cf. Mouzelis, 1978: 145). The entry examination to university (*Panellinies*) was for years the line that separated the successful from the failed, but not necessarily the knowledgeable from the unlearned. Mouzelis reports how Greek gymnasium students used to study for years the grammar and syntax of ancient Greek texts but not the content of the classical writers (ibid.). Faubion argues that in contemporary Greece, the educational system shapes the actor and is the context for the enactment of collective and recognised rites of passage from childhood to youth and subsequently to young adulthood (1993: 163). Higher education is not only the route to social and symbolic capital, for the acquisition of which Greek parents often go to considerable lengths (ibid.: 59, 190; Stewart, 1991: 126), but also a collective ritual of initiation to independence. The four women who established the *parea*, but also many of those who joined it afterwards, experienced the *mise-en-scène* of Greek university life. As their narratives that follow demonstrate, the reinterpretation of their sexuality was connected to student life in a complex and intricate way. Their university years were for the four women who founded the group the context *par excellence* of being 'educated in heterosexual romance' (cf. Holland and Eisenhart, 1990). On the other hand, the experience of heterosexual romance combined with freedom from the provincial gaze led them to question not only heterosexual relations but also politics, ideological orientations and even education itself. As McNay observes, challenging conventional ideas about gender relations might not come simply as a result of the subject's exposure to alternative notions of femininity but 'from tensions inherent in the concrete negotiation of increasingly conflictual female roles' (2000: 69). The narratives of the women I address here, sketch an era, that of the early 1980s, and shed light on their subsequent choices that developed almost organically within the social and cultural ambience of the time. Emily, Aphrodite, Lina and Rosita were not like the young people described by Faubion, who during their studying outside Greece became familiar with homosexual communities, and brought back to their town the 'strategies and technologies' they had acquired in European cities (Faubion, 1993: 234). What these four women brought back to Kallipolis was the knowledge that political movements can be utopian and sometimes dystopian, that university and student cliques are frequently the very spaces where gender and class hierarchies are reproduced and last, but not least, that women's networks can sometimes be the safest and most creative places to be and to become.

It would be perhaps useful at this stage to address the issue of 'lesbian continuum' with reference to 'woman-identified' experience (Rich, 1993: 238–9). As Alsop *et al.* point out, lesbianism is often taken to be not simply about sexuality *per se* but about a culture of sisterhood, networking, political and practical support and the creation of safe spaces for women (2002: 119). Although I acknowledge the significance of the notion of lesbian continuum and its possible applicability to other ethnographic contexts, due to a number of reasons my analytical position moves away from such a theorisation of homoerotic experience with special reference to the *parea*. It is true that the ethnographic textualisation of the life of the group and especially the narratives and stories presented in this chapter, demonstrate the importance of the *parea* as a homoerotic space, but also as a network of women who are often provided with emotional and practical support in matters of everyday life. The girls, however, avoid any identification with stable and already given categories such as those of lesbian, homosexual or woman because of their naturalistic overtones (cf. Alsop *et al.*, 2002: 120). Furthermore, as Rubin argues conflating lesbianism with supportive relations 'evacuates' the concept 'of any sexual content' (Rubin with Butler, 1994, cited in Alsop *et al.*, 2002: 122).

The purpose of this book has never been to prioritise either a gender-based analysis, or a sexuality-oriented one. I tend to agree with McNay that to an extent the transformatory potential of libidinal practices might have been overstressed (2000: 18, 68) and that 'the processes of gender restructuring are far more complex than the distinction between the normal and the excluded allows' (ibid.: 15). The fact that my informants resist all identity-based classifications, or that I frequently refer to a culturally specific shared experience of womanhood and marginality in my ethnography does not necessarily denote my desire to commit this analysis to any single specific branch of gender or feminist scholarship. My wish has rather been to avoid a theorising of identity that remains trapped to dichotomous politics of oppression/resistance, homosexual/heterosexual, marginal/central and so forth, for I believe that subjectivity, agency and social change are not matters that can be effectively explicated in either/or frameworks, which in their model-like structure only manage to oversimplify otherwise extremely complex matters. What I consider the life of the *parea* and the following narratives to entail mostly is the claim that power can be found within powerlessness, marginality within centrality, oppression within resistance, reification within challenge, otherness within selfhood and so on, and vice versa. It is in this sense that I understand the subject to be the site of contradiction and difference, but also the source of creativity and autonomous action. Viewing identity as relational and contextual implies crediting supremacy neither to the actor nor the social structure – nor any one single field of experience, be it gender, sexuality, or marginality – but rather understanding the formation of subjectivity as result of a lived, embodied, intersubjective, discursive and practical existence, or else, as a complex *biography*. For the contexts of life are not separate, sanitised, quarantine-like compartments but historically and culturally invested, interrelated sites that both shape and are shaped by social actors. More than any other theoretical and analytical concern, it is the journey of a group of women through and across such contexts that I wish to document remaining sensitised to the complexities of their lives and biographies rather than to any specific theoretical manifesto.

The following narratives were given to me within a short period of time, and serve to demonstrate the reasons behind these women's decision to distance themselves from official political discourses and the organisations that represent them.

ROSITA: *The word university was a magic one both for the eighties' youths and their parents; for different reasons of course! All* ***we*** *cared about was to go away and all* ***they*** *cared about was the kudos of higher education. To 'pass in the university'* [i.e. enter the university[4]] *was thus everybody's dream. I remember the afternoon after the results came out, all the 'successful' were allowed to go out for coffee and all those who 'failed' had to stay at home. Not a single person who did not pass dared showing her/himself at the cafes downtown. I remember the mother of a girl friend of mine mourning over the phone: 'Poor kids from villages passed. Kids without any help, without any background . . . and mine, mine stayed out'. You see, she was a philologist, a teacher in high school and she couldn't tolerate the idea that* ***her*** *daughter was unsuccessful. The mother of a male friend almost suffered from a nervous breakdown because her son did not enter the school of architecture. Allegedly, she was banging her head against the wall and addressing herself to her dead father she was screaming: 'not even in the KATEE, not even in the KATEE'* [i.e. he did not even enter a technical school]. *My boyfriend at the time had not passed either. His father was beating him the whole afternoon. Of course, other families took the results a lot more lightly. Some had even already arranged for their kids to go to Italy, or Bulgaria to study, especially those who were aiming at medical school. All in all, I am telling you this in order to understand how important it was that* ***we*** *passed. We felt successful, worthy, and mostly, free. Four and even five years away from the parental home and the small town! Free to explore life away from the despotic gaze of the neighbourhood, the parents and the kin group.*[5] *The next step was to go to Athens to find accommodation. It made sense for me and Emily to live together because we were good friends and from the same town of course. So Emily's father and my mother escorted us to Athens where we found a small apartment. I still remember the moment they left. I was staring at the car as they drove away and then I looked into Emily's eyes. We were alone.*

EMILY: *We decided to start exploring the city. I remember walking for hours and hours, and exploring all those cafes and bars and the clubs at night. Nothing that fanciful mind you for we did not have much money although some other people had even less. You see we were middle-class kids, well-off by the standards of the time. Anyhow, the university was so politicised back then. Endless student gatherings, endless discussions, endless arguing and of course endless flirting! It did not matter to which student party you were affiliated, as far as I am concerned everybody was going there to woo. Yes of course there were some people who joined the parties for more genuine reasons but generally that was the situation. You were approached by people from all sides and talked into joining the 'struggle'. They were always struggling for something. I remember a guy from the Panspudastiki* [the left student party] *telling me about how I should join the party that fought for the emancipation of women. Meanwhile by emancipation he meant going to bed with him, 'liberated from the moral pseudo-dilemmas that the capitalist society imposed on the masses',*[6] *and then march against the Americans and declare my 'absolute disagreement with imperialism'* [*tin pleria antithesi mou ston imperialismo*]. *Well, I did. I was both emancipated by the guy and marched to the American embassy in order to express my disagreement with imperialism. It was there that I met Aphrodite who was also from Kallipolis and an otherwise sober woman, but at the time very much in love with someone from the same student party.*

LINA: *It was not all marching to the American embassy of course! But generally the first year of the university was about sexual relationships. As the saying goes, all the girls were virgins when they left their hometowns but not when they returned. Most of the relationships formed at the time were short-lived. Some though lasted for years, and it was during those university years that many of my girl-friends learned how to put up with cheating, to practise it themselves, to be housewives to boyfriends who often settled in their homes and expected to be fed and taken care of . . . There were of course men and women who were devoted to their studies but romance remained a central aspect. Student life was, for me at least, romance and parties, romance and exam periods, romance and girlfriends, and cliques. The student cliques were the best thing; large and complicated and full of frays and arguing and also love and support. They were the real forums for exchanging ideas, they were communities in a sense with all their faults and problems. Friendship was so important! What marked my university years were the webs of friendships and different companies* [*parees*] *around which one's life was organised. I was very close to Aphrodite who was always an idealist and I remember discussing the most weird things with her and analysing and sharing boyfriend experiences. I met Emily and Rosita through Aphrodite and it was nice because we had our own little clique and it was extremely handy. I failed to mention that when you were involved with a guy, you met 'his company' and he met yours, but as soon as you broke up you were supposed to refrain from hanging around with his close friends and vice versa. So, it was nice to have three girl friends prepared to stand by you through thick and thin. We had moved into Emily's place by then, the one she inherited from her grandmother and the second year of the university was just starting.*

The importance placed on higher education in Greece is undoubtedly great as Rosita's narrative demonstrates. A place at university did not only signify achievement for the family as a whole, but also the adolescent's effective transition to young adulthood (cf. Faubion, 1993: 163). A student who failed to secure a place (*thesi*) in the 'higher educational institutions' (*AEI*), as these are called in Greece, could suddenly become a problematic figure in the eyes of his/her parents. Not only because heavy financial sacrifices made by the parents were often proving fruitless, but also because the young person and subsequently the whole family entered a liminal state and remained temporally excluded from the world of successful young adults and accomplished parents, respectively.

For those who managed to find themselves in the envied world of higher education, university life was, and still is for many, the first real taste of freedom from the family's gaze as well as a unique opportunity for self-realisation and identity shaping. The student political parties of the early 1980s were for Emily and Aphrodite sites *par excellence* for exploring not only their ideological orientation but also their sexuality. In this sense, the individual did 'become the site of political activity' (Echols, 1989: 17, in Green, 1997: 127) only in the literal sense. The self, as depicted by Emily, actually becomes the site where political rhetoric is being enacted. Being a politically conscious female in the early 1980s meant, according to Emily, being a sexually liberated female. In turn, sexual liberation in the women's narratives seems to be taking the form of sexual availability under heterosexual jurisdiction. The encounter with politicisation and emancipation becomes thus a brief but effective introduction to a hegemonic politic of sexuality, thus substantiating the argument that sexual desire is deeply implicated in socio-cultural processes, local and global gender ideologies (Wieringa and Blackwood, 1999: 16). According to Emily and Lina, women's sexual possibilities were being constructed 'away from home' but, none the less, mostly within the same prevalent array of discourses that crystallise and perpetuate well-known gender stereotypes.

APHRODITE: *By my third year I felt I had done pretty well. An active member of student movements and feminist circles, an accomplished and sociable friend, I felt quite sure about where I stood and where my loyalties held. My studies were going well and I was growing very close to the girls* [i.e. Emily, Lina and Rosita]. *Everything was to change though very soon. Sometime in February 1986, Lina discovered she was pregnant. I remember she was going out at the time with a guy from the maths department, so when she told us about the pregnancy we immediately thought of him. But no, she said. 'He has nothing to do with it. I am pregnant by a professor of mine'. I still remember the scene. All four of us were sitting around the kitchen table petrified. A professor? How the hell did she end up sleeping with a professor, and why on earth did we know nothing about it? It was a terrible moment. I felt angry and I couldn't quite decide whether I was more angry at her for not telling us anything, at the professor for sleeping with his student – mind you he was at least fifty years old – or at her for sleeping with a guy who could be her father! I always thought Lina as my best friend and I guess I felt utterly betrayed because she did not tell me about it. I left the room screaming to her 'you are totally crazy'!*

EMILY: *We tried to calm Lina, and asked her why on earth did she actually sleep with the guy. In the end she admitted to us that he left her no choice. She was sitting his course three consecutive times and he was consistently failing her. When she went to his office to enquire about it he admitted that there was nothing wrong with her progress. He just wanted to see more of her and that was the reason he failed her. All this had happened the year before. Lina apparently ignored him and sat the exams again in September when he failed her once more. Around November the professor invited her out to dinner. She thought that it was a good idea to eat out with him and hoped to persuade him to discontinue his blackmailing. Instead, she ended up sleeping with him. The situation was even more complicated because the exam period was starting. She was scared that if she told him about the pregnancy he would fail her again. On the other hand, she felt extremely angry about it. She was scared and angry with herself and with him. I immediately thought of the student union and all those people we were marching to the American embassy with. They ought to be notified I thought and we, as a student political party, should be able to sort this out. Mister Powerful should not be able to get away with it! I reasoned with Aphrodite and we went to one of the leading figures of the party. When we told him the problem and the name of the professor he turned back and told us that after all it was not such a good idea to take action about it. His argument was that it would be difficult to prove anything and that Lina's reputation would be seriously compromised. He believed that Lina should not have slept with her teacher in the first place, and he claimed that had she reported the problem when it started, the party might have been able to help her. In reality they did not want to touch the guy because he was a leftist.*[7]

APHRODITE: *We even turned to some of the so-called feminists for help and encouragement. But we did not see much from that side either. You see the feminist circles at the time were fighting for 'equality with men' and this practically meant equal occupational opportunities. An important goal I have to admit, but far greater than our concern for a harassed student. There was no room in their big plans for our little problems. Political organisations were fighting against imperialism and feminist coalitions against unequal opportunities. Who could possibly have time for silly Lina who slept with her professor? Actually what I was told by a 'feminist' friend was that, had Lina attended some of 'our' meetings, she would know how important contraception was in the project of women's sexual liberation! In the end we raised some money for the abortion between us and decided not to talk about it again. This is what Lina wanted and it was the least we could do for her. The exam period was starting soon, so we indulged in some collective work therapy and turned more to each other. After that we broke away from the student movement and the feminist circles. They were just . . . how shall I put it, not persuasive anymore.*[8]

As it becomes apparent from the narratives of Emily and Aphrodite, the student organisations and feminist circles of early 1980's Athens were spaces for cultivating ideological consciousness and, as such, their efforts were mostly directed towards large national and international projects. The youth parties as experienced by Aphrodite and Emily were aiming at raising their members' awareness of global political discourses, while the feminist coalitions are portrayed in these women's narrations as being chiefly preoccupied with national policy. Indeed the impact of the feminist movement, at least until the late 1980s, was not great in Greece. As Faubion argues, feminism in Greece was rather a reformist than a revolutionary movement that encouraged women's political and occupational claims but did not engage in a radical reappraisal of femininity and masculinity (1993: 176). Furthermore, unlike other feminist and lesbian communities (cf. Green, 1997), the Athenian cliques were not necessarily striving to provide a safe space or a support network for women. Green reports the desire of feminist and lesbian communities in London for physical and conceptual niches of safety based often on the acknowledgement of sameness, and consequently on the exclusion of difference (1997: 42–3). Despite the problems that arose especially from the policing of certain ideas that were considered as hetero-patriarchal and thus potentially threatening (ibid.: 41, 43), these communities seem to be a lot more involved in their members' personal lives than the Athenian feminist circles.

It can be argued that identity shaping is not only enmeshed in specific sociocultural processes but also inextricably related to the shape and form that the actor's personal life-history takes in the course of random encounters with cultural and societal idioms. In this sense, the narratives of the four women adduced here shed light on the historically and, to an extent, culturally specific bases of their subsequent denial to embrace any specific political and gender ascription. Their personal encounters with greater ideological contours, be it the student movement or the feminist clique of 1980s Athens, proved to be less an act of radical criticism of existing stereotypes and more a hegemonic substantiation of them. Additionally, the aims and objectives of these formal configurations were a lot less about one's personal circumstances and life choices than my informants hoped. What probably turned these women away from political associations was the latter's reported stifling engagement with power that resulted in conformism. The disappointing confrontation of the actor with the formalistic and depersonalised character of political action at the time, grew in the case of the girls into a complete loss of faith in the attainability, as well as the honesty, of collective and extended sites of struggle.

Albeit suggestive of an era, the narratives of the four founders of the *parea* cannot form the basis for generalised claims about the nature of student movements, universities or feminist cliques in Athens during the 1980s. It might very well be the case that all such institutions and communities followed similar practices to those described, while it might also be true that the experiences recounted here are rare and even unique. The typicality of those narratives is an altogether different subject that does not directly concern the present study. What is central to the understanding of the *parea* as a community with specific historical and cultural foundations is that these events, representative or not, comprised specific conceptual sites for the negotiation of one's identity *vis-à-vis* local and global discourses as these came to be experienced circumstantially by the actor. The manner in which the plot of these four women's lives developed demonstrates how their later choices were directly related to specific socio-cultural circumstances.

ROSITA: *Almost a year later, that is around October 1987, we had to deal with yet another problem, this time a lot more serious and somewhat even more frightening than Lina's pregnancy. I remember it was one of those last sunny days of October and we were sitting outside, at a central Athenian café called the Magnum, discussing (ironically!) how much weight Emily had lost over the past year. At some point Emily left, allegedly to see some friends of hers, and the rest of us started commenting on how distanced she had become lately. She always had 'something to take care of' and 'a party she wished to go to alone', and she didn't seem to look very well either. Physically I mean. She was getting thinner and thinner and had what seemed to be a semi-permanent flu. We decided it was all due to that lousy, unsociable boyfriend she was with for the past eight months. We didn't like the guy, mostly because we felt he was taking her away from us. As we were chatting about this we noticed a really beautiful woman sitting almost next to us, alone. She was in her early thirties, slim, tall and 'imposing' [typissa]. She leaned slowly towards us and said: 'Why don't you come inside? I'll buy you some more coffee'. It was Marika, the owner of the place and as far as I am concerned she had the most beautiful green eyes I've ever seen. We sat at a table towards the back. Marika lit a cigarillo, and looked searchingly at each and every one of us. Finally, she asked: 'That girl who was sitting with you, she is your friend right?' We nodded 'yes'. 'And how long do you know her'? We replied that we knew her for four years, that we studied together and lived in the same house. 'Well', she said, 'it's probably none of my business, but your friend might be in trouble.' I remember jumping off my chair and asking her loudly 'What kind of trouble?' 'Don't scream', she replied, 'I normally wouldn't even involve myself. You see I am thirty-two years old and I've learned not to stick my nose in other people's business, but your friend is rather different.* ***She*** *is different. She is on drugs and I think you ought to do something about it.'*

LINA: *Heroin [preza] was spreading so quickly during the eighties. But what was worse than heroin itself, was the image of heroin and the image of the junkie that was constructed by the media and those who wished to inform the public.*[9] *The junkie was synonymous with the delinquent, the person that would do anything to secure his/her 'fix', the dangerous. Preza was portrayed as something that inhabits the soul, not just the body of the user. It was seen as a substance that once taken inside the body was able to transform the mind and constitution of the addict. As Marika explained to us, however, it was not the substance* per se *that we should be scared*

> *of, but rather the police, the arrests that might come with it, the marginalisation of our friend. I admit not knowing that much about drugs. I mean we all knew what we were told about the subject. But we learned. Marika helped us a lot to put this thing into perspective before we approached Emily.*
>
> *What is interesting though is that Marika was actively involved in one of what you can call 'lesbian' networks of the time. She got interested in Emily because she liked her and she fancied her, something we found out a lot later. We were soon introduced to this network that embraced us. It might sound really naive the way I put it but we felt like we were coming home. It's true. These women were not pretentious, they did not sell ideologies at a price, they were really supportive and caring and mind you very 'connected'. They wanted and they were in a position to help. We were suddenly introduced into a different world of relating . . .*

The four women finally returned to Kallipolis after they had established friendships and erotic relationships with Marika's *parea*, as they referred to it. Emily came off heroin and the four of them thought that Kallipolis might be the best place to make a fresh start. Slowly but steadily they formed their own clique that began growing into the *parea* that I met in the early 1990s. The group formed in Kallipolis bore many similarities to Marika's *parea*, at least as this was perceived by Emily, Rosita, Lina and Aphrodite. It was operating not only as a space for the exploration of an alternative sexuality but also as a support network for its members who were often provided with the very means necessary to live differently. Thus, in many ways the *parea* as a concept was the outcome of the 'Athens years' of the four girls who felt betrayed by student movements and feminist parties, but rescued by a lesbian community concerned to establish a safe homoemotional space for women.

As I have noted above, the life-histories of these four women might or might not be representative of the time and place in which they were composed. Typical or circumstantial, their narratives amply demonstrate that 'individuals negotiate their identities in [a] dense maze of imbricating sociohistorical, political, cultural relations and embodied motivations' (Wieringa and Blackwood, 1999: 16). They also demonstrate that sexual identity is frequently a personal/political standpoint that can be translated into an equally personal/political statement, even outside the confines of an official categorical classification. The girls refuse to legitimise their sexuality by linking it to a politicised struggle against the heterosexual regime (cf. Grosz, 1994b: 153) – thus privileging one definition of oppression against others (cf. McNay, 2000: 61) – while at the same time are not unaware of the personal/political implications of questioning the conventionality of a culturally specific sexual economy. In other words, the fact that the women of the *parea* question the term lesbian as a suitable self-ascription, and do not wish to be open about their sexual preferences, does not necessarily imply that their choices and lifestyles are any less politically charged. The *parea*, as do probably other communities that look towards the issue of gender (and also possibly class, race or ethnicity), constantly strive to establish an identity of difference *vis-à-vis* those societal and cultural idioms that are restraining the self. In this sense, it is true that the sexual desires and experiences of the women of the *parea* should not be treated as 'other', or simply as differences within the female Kallipoliot/Greek[10] population for these are not strictly private matters (cf. Dunne, 1997: 226–7). In the case of the group I present here, the choice to live in the company of women and love women closely relates to their experience as women (ibid.). Thus, it can be argued that the *parea* maintains a dialectic and mutually constructive relationship with the greater community of the Kallipoliots/Greeks. As Braidotti argues: '[s]elf reflexivity is not an individual activity but an interactive process which relies upon a network of exchanges' and triggers the production of new 'figurations' that 'materially embody stages of metamorphosis of a subject position' (2002: 13). The group consists of women whose decision to join it and to stay in it cannot be decontextualised from their socio-culturally informed life-histories, circumstances and narratives. As such, the *parea* is an inseparable part of the Kallipoliot/Greek female experience and grows, changes and moves in directions common with the rest of the people, subject to the same socio-cultural actuality (cf. Green, 1997: 23).

Greece: Thessaloniki and Kallipolis in the 1960s, 1970s and 1980s through the stories of Julia, Nena and Soula

A lot has been written about women's same-sex friendships and homoemotional worlds before the twentieth century, especially in relation to whether these passionate friendships could be actually termed lesbian or not (cf. Faderman, 1985, 1993; Smith-Rosenberg, 1975; Jeffreys, 1985; Brehony, 1993; Raymer, 1993, among others). Even synchronically, the applicability of the term lesbian to any relationship between women who do not share the western or Euro-American notions of gender is also questioned by anthropologists such as Wieringa and Blackwood (1999). The latter argue that the ascription lesbian when used to describe women's relationships universally might possibly undermine and even disguise the variability and cultural contextuality of sexual and emotional expression (1999: 20). Despite these debates it is true that the diachronic study of western culture, as well as contemporary studies of other cultures, reveal that women form close relationships with each other, frequently of a sexual and/or deep emotional character (cf. Dunne, 1997: 3; Kendal, 1999; Elliston, 1999). It can also be argued that in the twentieth century western cultural context, secrecy in relation to gay life has been as common a phenomenon as gay life itself (Worton, 1998: 41). In my attempt to account theoretically and ethnographically for the invention and the subsequent mistreatment of the term lesbian and its bearers as well as the social silencing of homosexual practices, I found myself travelling in space and time with the guidance of the women of the *parea*. Due to their patience and willingness to escort me along narrow paths, I traced three valuable stories which I adduce as a starting point for a theoretical review and discussion of women's homoemotional worlds as well as of the central issue of 'compulsory heterosexuality'.

An early afternoon in Julia's house

Julia was a member of the *parea* that I had not personally met although I had seen her partner Artemis a few times at *Harama* before. Only very close friends of Julia were invited to her house, that is Shanell, Rita, Emily and Sia who visited her quite often. When Emily suggested to me that 'I should meet Julia and listen to her story', I happily accepted especially since I suspected that she must have tried hard in order to persuade Julia to invite me. On the day of the visit, Shanell, Rita, Emily and myself decided to walk to her house. I was warned that I should not take notes until after we have left the place and told that Artemis, originally from Kallipolis, had met Julia during her university studies in Thessaloniki. Artemis was a member of the *parea* before she entered the university and had a formal relationship with Shanell with whom she separated as soon as she met Julia. Julia is extremely beautiful, I was told. 'She was studying modern dance and she was such a performer!', Emily informed me and continued: 'She was often coming to Kallipolis to visit, and when she was walking towards the dance floor and started dancing everyone was stepping down. People wanted to just sit and look at her.'

When we arrived at the house we were received by Artemis, who showed us into a spacious living-room with large windows, and disappeared into the kitchen, escorted by Rita, to prepare some coffee. The place was immaculately clean and furnished in a minimalist fashion with a few but imposing pieces; an old table and a credenza, two tall cocktail tables with marble tops and a sofa that matched the orange organza curtains. Rita came back with the coffee and told us that Julia would be coming soon. A few minutes later a stunningly beautiful, naturally blonde young woman with blue eyes entered the room in a wheelchair. She was discreetly made up and smelled of Chanel No. 5. She greeted the girls with a smile and a wink and me with an inspecting glance. Artemis brought her coffee and cigarettes and placed them next to her on one of the cocktail tables along with a silver ashtray. She lit a cigarette, sipped some coffee and began her story:[11]

'The part of the story that probably interests you starts on a Saturday night in Thessaloniki just before Christmas. Artemis was in Kallipolis for the Christmas break [Artemis was studying in Thessaloniki] *and I was out with friends. On the way back the driver lost control of the car and we crashed. The next thing I remember is being in the intensive care room. I was asking for Artemis and the nurse thought that I was referring to one of the people who were in the car with me, so she kept replying that Artemis was fine and I shouldn't worry. When I managed to communicate sensibly with*

my mum I told her to notify Artemis. My mother did not know at the time that we were a couple, and as soon as Artemis came it was extremely difficult for me to explain to the medical staff why she had to be allowed into the intensive care since she was not immediate family. As soon as I went to a normal room, things got better. Artemis and my mum were taking turns keeping me company, trying to cheer me up and make me forget my predicament. At nights I could often sense one of them leaving the room for a cigarette and returning back to check on me. One morning I was woken up by Artemis who had just arrived so that my mum could go and rest. Realising that I was holding a packet full of old letters and a pendant, I began to look at them. From the dates and the names I understood that these letters were sent to my mother during the sixties by somebody named Stella. I started reading them to find out that Stella and my mother had an affair. In the beginning they were mostly passionate letters but somewhere in the middle Stella started expressing her anxiety for my mother's forthcoming wedding. My mother was being match-made[12] *by her older brother to a supposedly wealthy guy, my father, who had migrated to Germany and owned a restaurant. She was supposed to marry him and follow him to Germany, which she eventually did. The content of the letters was becoming more and more desperate to the point that they were even considering to run away together. But where could they go? Without a job, without support and how could they justify their relationship? The last letter was rather short and it ended like this: "How will I learn to live without you? How will I ever get used to the idea that someone else will be caressing your soul and body? It is a question that will always remain; suspended like a hanged person, a tragic suicide."*[13] *It came together with the pendant, a small golden heart, and a photo of Stella with a dedication: "To the one I loved; never forget." These letters were my mother's way of expressing her understanding of my relationship with Artemis. She has supported us right through, financially and emotionally, but always silently. She is still unable to discuss Stella and their relationship. She did not even have the courage to give me the letters herself. That's why she left them in my hands that morning. They were tokens of love and affection, but also of pain and frustration [mataiosi]. Write about this story. I guess it should be recorded somewhere.'*

For the rest of the visit Julia talked little. Artemis and the rest of the girls talked about music and the latest news of the *parea* for a while until it was time for us to leave. Still dazzled by her aura, I thanked her for sharing this story with me. She looked straight in my eyes and granted me a smile for the first time that afternoon.

The story of Julia: a comment

What I find as the most interesting aspect of Julia's story – or rather Antigone's story since this is the name of Julia's mother – is that it came to be known by pure coincidence. Julia herself only found out about it because of the tragic turn her life took during a night out. If Julia had not been a victim of an unfortunate car accident, and if she had not been in a relationship with

Artemis, her mother may have continued to keep her old affair with Stella carefully locked in her memory and her private drawer. The highly conditional character of the disclosure can thus be seen as intriguing in itself, so long as it is suggestive of the silence around women's homoerotic relationships. This silence seems to be deeply implicated in the perpetuation of the myth that heterosexuality is the prevalent form of sexual expression. The concealment of homosexual relationships helps position them in the realm of the unconventional, the rare, and finally the socially marginal and the excluded (Fuss, 1991: 3). In turn, the portrayal of certain forms of sexual expression as unorthodox and infrequent renders them partially unattainable. The social impossibility of Antigone's and Stella's relationship is hence two-fold. On the one hand, due to specific historical social and economic reasons it was seen by its protagonists as non-viable (cf. Dunne, 1997: 3, 230), while on the other, precisely because such a relationship was deemed impossible it was kept secret. The silence around similar relationships helps perpetuate the myth of their rarity, which in its turn contributes to their perception as socially unthinkable.

By means of selective presentation, 'definition' and 'regulation' (cf. Foucault, 1976; Dunne, 1997: 7), the wide spectrum of sexual expression has been, at least in the Greek context, energetically reduced to the one socially rewarded possibility of heterosexuality, preferably practised in a monogamous and conjugal(like) model. Nevertheless, as feminist historians attest, women not only formed romantic relationships in the past, but these relationships were socially condoned and even encouraged[14] (Faderman, 1981; Wolfe and Penelope, 1993). With the emergence of the feminist movement, the status of these romantic friendships between women was to be re-evaluated in the light of sexologists' theories that deemed love for the same sex as abnormal[15] (cf. Faderman, 1981). There is no doubt that the medicalisation of sexual life, as well as the promotion of the idea that sexual practices were constitutive of one's identity, led to the construction of the category homosexual and the pathologisation of the people thought to belong to it (cf. Faderman, 1981: 240; Dunne, 1997: 10; Green, 1997: 124; Gunter, 1998: 86; Weeks, 1987: 32). Homosexuality was not only manufactured as a distinct identity category but it was also placed outside the norms of the sexual economy 'as an indispensable interior exclusion' (Fuss, 1991: 3). The alleged abnormality of homosexual relationships served thus as a proscriptive (cf. Rubin, 1975) definitional mark of what was deemed to be socially acceptable and normal sexual expression (cf. Corber and Valocchi, 2003: 3). Heterosexuality is thus best understood as the outcome of specific societal idioms that render it a socio-economic institution, and not simply a sexual practice (Dunne, 1997: 12). The view that heterosexuality is a socially produced political institution was especially supported by Rich (1980) who also claimed that lesbianism constituted a resistance to the compulsory character of heterosexual relationships.[16] Sexuality, far from a 'natural given . . . is the name that can be given to a historical construct'

(Foucault, 1976: 105), and as such it must be understood within its socio-historical context (Wieringa and Blackwood, 1999: 11). Blackwood and Wieringa shift the emphasis from the institutionalised character of sexuality towards the importance of context and argue against the universal applicability of the theory of compulsory heterosexuality, maintaining that non-heterosexual practices can often be legitimate expressions of sexual desire (1999: 55).[17]

Nevertheless, although cross-cultural studies demonstrate that homosexuality is not always a marginal form of sexual expression, it is also true that hegemonic ideologies serve to privilege certain idioms of desire over others (Blackwood and Wieringa, 1999: 183; Dunne, 1997: 58). Individual creativity is capable of producing a range of masculinities and femininities but sexual and emotional outcomes enjoy societal and cultural sanction to different degrees (Dunne, 1997: 58). With reference to Julia's story, heterosexuality and conjugality were the only available options for Antigone. First, because anything other would be characterised as immoral, or abnormal and, second, because of the economic constraints placed on her, which dictated – to paraphrase Levi-Strauss (1969) – that she should marry out or die out. Thus, it is easy to agree with Dunne who argues that 'the movement beyond heterosexuality . . . necessitates financial self reliance' (1997: 227).

Concealment and display: Nena, Stasa and Soula

Nena and Stasa

Nena and Stasa are two women in their fifties who have been in a long-term relationship for the past 25 years. They are friends with some of the older women of the *parea*, but strictly speaking, they do not belong to the group. I was introduced to them by Eleana, one of the oldest members, who thought that the story of their relationship might help me illuminate the status of women's relationships outside the confines of the *parea*. Both Nena and Stasa held clerical posts in the public sector, something that allowed them to be financially independent. They lived with their parents, until the latters' deaths[18] and alone thereafter. Since the two women never made their relationship known, in the consciousness of the Kallipoliot milieu, they are designated as spinsters (*megalokopeles*, or *gerontokores*) and friends. Nena and Stasa spend a lot of time together, go on holidays and trips abroad and generally enjoy each other's company for prolonged periods of time as they always did.

Nevertheless, they continue to hold separate houses and still wish that their relationship remains secret, under the rubric friendship, while they do not particularly like to be thought of as lesbians. The narratives that follow were given to me in Eleana's house and contain some interesting views of marriage and conjugal life, as well as Nena's and Stasa's feelings for each other and their relationship.

STASA: *Nena is family for me. She has always been my company* [*i parea mou*]. *At all times . . . When my mother was sick and I had to look after her . . . hospitals, problems, financial difficulties. We went through everything together but we had good times too: trips, holidays, we've been all over Greece. We shared a good life. You should have seen us younger, when we were going to the balls and parties . . . We were always energetic and happy, free from responsibilities. I am glad I didn't marry. Do you think those who actually married are happier? They were loaded with a husband to carry on their backs, to wash, to feed and listen to his nagging.*[19] *And some are lucky but some others . . . A friend from work is married to a guy who cheats on her, beats her and she is still staying with him. Whereas me, I was always free to go wherever I cared to, do as I pleased. I had nobody there to check upon me. I was saying to Nena: shall we go to the movies tonight? and off we went. We didn't have to account for our actions. Listen, I had my salary and now my pension and I don't need anybody.*[20] *I remember the people from work were continuously trying to set me up with various men.*[21] *I was agreeing to see them and go out with them, partly in order not to insult the 'matchmakers' and also because I was curious. I mean, you never know, somebody might actually prove to be worthy. But they were all so bad! I remember one asking me whether I would inherit my mother's house or not, and I said to him: 'is it me you want, or the house? If it is the house you want, go and work and buy one'. Do you get it? This is what they want, a house ready made and the maid inside, the whole package.*[22] *My Nena and I never had these problems. We had love, genuine love and understanding. We were meant for each other. If one day I said I liked to go to the gym, the next day Nena would go and buy a membership to the best gym in the town. If she said she'd like to read some poetry I would go to the bookshop and buy her four books of Seferis who is her favourite poet. This is because we cared for each other.*

NENA: *That's true. I had proposals to marry too, but as soon as I met the guys I would ask myself: will they love me as much as Stasa does? I don't know whether Stasa was the reason I didn't marry, but I don't think so. I am being honest, I did not find anyone that I could imagine spending my life with. I am happy I stayed with Stasa, I am content. I got everything I wanted out of this relationship: affection, love, understanding, erotic fulfilment, company, stimulation, joy, name it. I know people call us 'spinsters'* [*gerontokores*], *but I'd rather be a happy spinster than a miserable wife. I don't want people to know that we are sleeping together, although I guess some might have figured it out. But you see, if they knew for certain they would point at us and say 'the lesbians', and I don't think I am a lesbian to tell you the truth. I mean, I am not attracted to women, I am attracted to Stasa, but Stasa is different.*[23] *I would do anything with her. It's also the gossip I want to avoid. It's better this way. At least we have our peace and privacy. When we have a fight sometimes and I don't want to make the first move, I stay home alone and I feel so bad! And when I hear the phone ringing and it's her I forget everything. There is nothing I wouldn't do for my Stasoula* [tender nickname for Stasa].

Nena and Stasa: a comment

Both the narratives of Nena and Stasa revolve around the theme of marriage. It has been noted that within the context of institutionalised heterosexuality, matrimony is presented as the 'normal adult goal' (Dunne, 1997: 16, 20). Especially in Greece marriage is seen as 'a matter of destiny' (cf. Hirschon, 1989: 107) although many women recently and especially in urban settings express their lack of motivation to fulfil the expectations of a long-term heterosexual commitment (cf. Faubion, 1993: 177). Faubion's fictional character of Maro puts forward her own reservations about men, which although different in many respects from those of Stasa and Nena are indicative of the ambiguous position of women in the Greek cultural context (cf. Cowan, 1991). Women, according to Maro, a bourgeois Athenian of about the same age as Stasa and Nena, are expected to be mothers and children simultaneously, carers and nurturers of men but not their equals (Faubion, 1993; 177). In this sense, Stasa's narrative can be seen as the refusal to play the double persona of the wife whose rewards are furthermore regarded as highly questionable: *'Do you think those who actually married are happier? They were loaded with a husband to carry on their backs, to wash, to feed and listen to his whining.'* Stasa's relationship with Nena, unlike marriage, is thus being portrayed as positive and rewarding, a continuous 'source of practical and emotional support throughout life' (Dunne, 1997: 5).

Nena focuses more on the quality of love inherent in her relationship with Stasa. When presented to potential husbands, she doubts whether these men will ever love her like Stasa does and decides, instead, to cherish a relationship that has over the years kept her consistently content. Although Stasa seems to be the most important person in Nena's life, and vice versa, they are both unwilling to be open about the sexual dimension of their relationship. Wieringa and Blackwood argue that social acceptance of close relationships between women might at times depend on 'their not being associated with the word lesbian' (1999: 28). As Jivani maintains, what is more threatening to the social establishment than lesbianism itself is the visibility of lesbian sexuality, and he goes on to state that '[t]he best way to deal with lesbianism was not to talk about it' (1997: 34). It can be observed in this case that the presence or absence of sexual activity and not simply lifestyle *per se* marks out whether a relationship is deemed as socially acceptable or not. On the other hand, it is also true – as I have pointed out with reference to other cases – that 'societal repression relates mostly to social rebellion rather than sexual preference' (McNay, 2000: 157). Nena and Stasa, by exploiting the social space of spinsterhood – an 'undesirable' but nevertheless not provocative state of being – avoid being associated with both marginal expressions of sexuality and a rebellious (anti)-social existence.

From Nena's narrative, it also becomes obvious that her conceptualisation of the term lesbian is distinct. Placing sexual attraction for women instead of/as opposed to men at the core of her definition of lesbianism, she claims that a lesbian is a woman who is attracted not to another woman, but to women in general. According to Dunne, in the western cultural context 'adult primary relationships . . . must be heterosexual and the base should be *sexual*' (1997: 13–14, original emphasis). In so far as this is true, lesbianism appears to be understood by Nena not as a possibly different way of relating altogether, but as the mirror image of heterosexuality. In turn, if the absence of sexual activity is a criterion for the social acceptability of women's relationships, it seems that Nena's definition is not strictly personal but collectively shared by a number of actors in the Greek cultural context. Faubion argues that women's sexual relationships are seen as less threatening than men's because women are regarded as 'phallically inactive' (1993: 221). His pointed observation further substantiates my claim that lesbian is often defined in opposition to heterosexual, and in direct relation to sexual activity rather than as an alternative idiom of relatedness. The image of the homosexual woman as someone who likes women – and is thus unable to sustain a 'normal' marriage – constructs the term lesbian as an unattainable category of self-ascription, for it not only relates a person directly to an 'abnormal' sexual desire. It also describes a woman who *has* sexual desires and is actively pursuing them constituting thus a threat to the existing sexual economy (cf. Cowan, 1991).

Nena and Stasa experience a relationship founded on deep emotional commitment, characterised by support and equality as well as freedom to exist as women independently of men. The sustainability of such a relationship is directly related to their financial self-sufficiency that allowed them to question the idea and practice of marriage as destiny, and to distinguish love and sexuality from conjugality. By exploiting the socially condoned institution of friendship, they were able to stay together since the 1970s thus accomplishing what seemed, in the context of Julia's story, an impossibility. In this case McNay is probably rightly implying that social change is not a matter of even and synchronous phenomena (2000: 27) but the result of 'the negotiation of complex relations of power by individuals in their movement within and across fields of social action' (ibid.: 69). The narratives of Nena and Stasa demonstrate the fragility of the boundaries between affection, sex, friendship, emotional and physical consummation (Kendall, 1999: 161), as well as the contextual meaning of formal classificatory terms. Loving a woman in this case, might not be a straightforward matter of being committed to a lesbian identity. It remains however a defiant statement about the self who chooses a personally rewarding existence over a socially awarded life managing to 'act autonomously despite constricting social sanctions' (McNay, 2000: 5).

Soula

Soula is the first woman presented here without a pseudonym. Born in the 1950s, she is a lesbian, one of the few in Kallipolis who are open about their sexuality. She does not belong to the *parea*, but is befriended and respected by the girls for her style and character. Soula makes a good living by being a psychic although she privately admits that she does not believe anybody can predict the future. I think that her narrative is a valuable addition to this chapter for it illuminates the politics of a 'heroic' (cf. Munt, 1998) quest for visibility and difference in the context of a changing culture which nevertheless still remains largely heterosexual.

I visited Soula in her consulting rooms, a top floor apartment located in the centre of the town, on a late afternoon. The sign on her door read: 'Soula: tarot and palm reading, numerology, recovery of lost people and items, restoration of faith in your internal powers'. Soula opened the door, dressed in a dark blue suit and a tie. She was tall slim, muscular, with short hair pulled back with plenty of gel and a tan in the middle of winter apparently acquired during her recent skiing trip. She gave me a strong handshake and a wide smile and ushered me in. We sat in the lobby, a spacious room, furnished with two brown leather sofas and a mini-bar. She served herself a straight whisky after offering me one, sat opposite me cross-legged and lit a cigar with an authentic Dupont[24] lighter. This was not the first time that I had seen Soula, nevertheless her style never ceased to impress me. She always managed to be particularly attractive cultivating an exhibitionist butch style that was at the same time subtle and dainty. Everything on her, from her clothes to her Gucci accessories, was exaggerated, but the aesthetic outcome was always chic and original. Born in the 1950s, Soula must have been at least 45 but she looked a lot younger. I could not but observe her beautifully cared for hands and the tiny ring on her little finger. She must have read my thoughts because she looked at her hands and said to me:

SOULA: *Hands are everything!*[25] *In my job at least. The client looks at your hands all the time, when you shuffle the tarot cards, when you uncover them, when you hold their palms . . . Future reading is about hands, voice and the ability to persuade. Most of the people who come to me, and especially women who are the majority, do not need to know their future. They need reassurance and indirect advice. This is what I provide them with. I listen to their problems patiently and then highlight some options they haven't thought about or encourage them to take calculated risks. I have been doing this job since 1979 and I've seen so many people, so many cases . . . but I guess work is not quite the reason you came here today. Contrary to what you might believe though, my job* **is** *one of the main reasons you came to see me. For it is precisely what I do that allows me to be who I am or rather to be how I please. As you know I was not born in Kallipolis. I came here in 1978 because of a woman who I guess you can call 'my first love'. I was trying to pursue a career as an athlete, a swimmer actually, but I fell in love with Nana. Nana was the daughter of a wealthy bourgeois family who decided to marry the equally wealthy offspring of her father's close friend, almost as soon as we came to this town. Despite this, she continued to want me in her life and all I wanted was to be near* *her. This is how I started the psychic business. It was easy, did not require any special knowledge, and Nana connected me with all the wealthy ladies who had plenty of time, energy and money available to spend. Soon I realised that as a 'psychic' I was free to do as I pleased. I was per definition something exotic*[26] *and, no matter how idiosyncratic a style I adopted, I was accepted and even feted by the Kallipoliot circles. Professional success, personal style, and social acceptability fed one another in a systematic manner. I discovered how much it pleased me to flirt with women and more importantly how much it pleased* **them** *to flirt with me. As soon as I got over Nana, I realised that I could sleep with nearly any woman, if I wanted to. Don't misread me though, it was not because I was pretty, or essentially irresistible, but rather a peculiar mixture of what I did and how I looked that promised women a different experience. 'Butch'*[27] *was challenging and I liked being butch. I was a 'dyke' and I wanted people to know it. Style was something I slowly but steadily internalised and made it part of who I am instead of just employing it in order to succeed. Style became the story of my life and the means of my expression not only of sexual desire but also of my whole self. My social life was always very busy and I still get a kick out of entering a place – be it a private party, a club or a café – and feeling that my presence alters the space. My sexual desire for women – generally thought to be a private thing – becomes a public matter and influences people around me. Sometimes I actually wonder whether I am an exhibitionist who seeks attention, but I think I am not because all I do is actually embody desire [somatopoio tin epithimia]. It's not only about the surface. The surface is a way of expressing the interior. It is a means of externalising a lesbian energy . . . No I take that back. It's not one-dimensional. The relationship between my 'dyke' style and my 'dyke' feelings is one of mutual reinforcement [amoivaia enisxytiki].*

Kallipolis accepts me as a lesbian. I am a persona grata because I constructed a different self, an exotic self, but what was exotic ten years ago it's today just another identity. As a result I have to constantly reinvent my self [na efeurisko ton eauto mou] in order to remain unique, for it is precisely this originality that grants me social acceptability. I am celebrating life, exploiting people's need for challenge and making visibility [to na fainesai] work for me instead of against me. In Greece you are what you announce. I'm a lesbian and thank god I found a way to declare it!

Soula: a comment

Soula's story is a testimony of how much and, at the same time, how little the cultural response to homosexual practices has changed in Greece over the past four decades. While during the 1960s, according to Julia's account, a woman's relationship lacked the financial and social basis necessary in order to be viable, in the 1980s a provincial town accepted and even embraced a lesbian who was open about her sexuality. On the other hand, one can argue that as recently as about a decade ago a homosexual woman had to engage in a systematic process of self-exoticisation in order to be accepted by a Greek urban milieu. Indeed, one may claim that all three stories presented so far are in fact circumstantial since two women like Stasa and Nena could have stayed together even in the 1960s, while such a highly entrepreneurial woman as Soula would have lived through almost any decade. Still, I argue that although attitudes towards homosexuality might not have changed drastically over the last four decades in Greece, what has changed is the availability of financial and social opportunities open to women. The steady expansion of women's socio-economic prospects had undoubtedly created new spaces and allowed novel identities to form creating – at the same time – new kinds of uncertainties for women.

What is interestingly common between Soula's narrative and those of Stasa and Nena is that all three women related non-heterosexuality with individual 'experiences of empowerment' (Dunne, 1997: 21). With special reference to Soula's case, the quest for visibility seems to be interwoven with a sense of empowerment. Munt describes a very similar feeling to that reported by Soula: 'My butchness makes me indiscreet; its visibility alerts those around me to my lesbianizing of space' (1998: 173). Similarly, Soula is aware that she transmits a 'lesbian energy' to people and spaces and it is precisely the stylistic 'imposing' of this energy that makes her feel powerful. She is engaged in a constant politic of display within the context of which her self-definition becomes 'the narrative product of a heroic quest of identity' (Munt, 1998: 5). In so far as her 'feelings of dykeness mutually reinforce her dyke style', she constitutes her identity in practice and through practice.

The originality of Soula is epitomised in her ability to create a socially legitimate space within which she asserted and even celebrated her sexuality. By constructing her professional self as 'other', she obtained initially poetic licence to manifest a different erotic self as well. What began, however, as a 'privileged margin' (Faubion, 1993: 191) soon became an instance of venerated difference and subsequently an accepted identity. The narrative of Soula is one of self-poesis and aesthetic distinction and in so far as it constitutes a claim to authenticity it is deeply rooted in modern Greek culture (cf. Faubion, 1993). By linking lesbianism to a stylistic pursuit of originality, the protagonist of this story accomplished her personal goal but, nevertheless, at the same time she managed to shift the focus from politics to aesthetics. Her 'butchness' was transformed from a sexual/political statement into an artistic one and was thus socially neutralised. This might actually be the very reason why Soula was so easily incorporated into the Kallipoliot society, in the same manner that a nude fresco can adorn the wall of a church. From the moment she became a lesbian persona instead of a lesbian person, her actions belonged not to the realm of ethics but to that of aesthetics and their content was thereby semantically altered. As Emily put it: 'Soula's uniqueness makes her untouchable. Especially because she cannot be imitated, the Kallipoliots enjoy her refreshing and challenging presence being confident that she will not be a model for anyone else, for there can be only one Soula.'

The *parea* – a last note

The narratives presented in this chapter relate either directly or indirectly to the women of the *parea* and the manner in which they decide to negotiate their daily lives and identities. Unlike other groups of women, the community I studied does not claim to be lesbian/feminists (cf. Green, 1997). Nevertheless, they share many similarities with communities who accept a lesbian/feminist self-ascription. Not unlike other lesbian collectivities, the *parea* place great emphasis on friendship-relationships, which often play the role of 'fictive' kinship (cf. Weston, 1991/1997), they establish short-lived instead of long-term erotic relations, they are concerned with identity politics and difference and they opt to threaten the content of conventional idioms through mixed (cf. Butler, 1990) performances (Green, 1997: 9–10, 115–20). Paradoxically, the same communities that share so many similarities with the *parea* seem, from another angle, fundamentally different. In direct opposition to other lesbian groups, the *parea* has never believed in the authenticity of lesbianism or any other identity category (cf. Green, 1997: 10, 130). The women I studied refuse to be 'open' about their sexuality or to accept the title lesbian and for them gender and sexuality, more than cultural categories, are matters of subjective experience (Blackwood and Wieringa, 1999: 182). According to the *parea*, identity and desire are not necessarily linked (Marshall, 1998: 55; Vance, 1989: 11, quoted in Wekker, 1999: 119). Their attitude can be recognised in Wieringa and Blackwood's argument:

> The adoption of an identity, a process that might involve enormous suffering and defiance, always implies the closing off of other options . . . Further, adopting a 'lesbian' identity, and the naturalising discourse associated with it by many gay and lesbian activists in Europe and America at this time, carries with it the risk of essentializing, an essentializing that is also employed by the heterosexual culture one wants to challenge.
>
> (1999: 15)

The lack of the *parea*'s motivation to commit themselves to a lesbian identity cannot be attributed solely to their concern with viability. They definitely respect the slower pace of change that characterises Greek culture, and they fear the potentially dramatic effects of publicity on their community. Still both individually and collectively they are not in a particularly weak subjective position. As individuals, most of them are socially and financially able to live as 'lesbians'. As a group, especially due to their large number and various affiliations, they could possibly resist ostracism and marginalisation quite effectively. The defying of the term 'lesbian' by the *parea* relates to their questioning of identity as a fixed constellation. It is important to clarify that resisting various identifications in this case does not relate to a wholesale rejection of identity as a quality of the self, but it is rather an attempt to highlight the 'non-synchronous', non-fixed and externally defined attribute of 'life and experience' (McNay, 2000: 113). The collective political objective of the *parea* is epitomised in the questioning of heterosexuality and homosexuality alike, in favour of a more flexible and polymorphous kind of desire that sets erotic energy free from taxonomic classifications and specifically politicised idioms. In this sense, the women of the group compose their 'biographies in transition' (ibid.). They are 'flâneurs' who appreciate that change comes as a result of movement in time and across social contexts and who constantly seek to blur discursively and performatively the boundaries between masculinity, femininity, self, other, homosexuality and heterosexuality (Munt, 1998: 43–4).

The ideological project of the *parea*, which I should note is not expressed in the rigid form of a manifesto, definitely relates to the women's cultural experiences and life histories. The origins of the group are to be found in four women who, frustrated by student movements and feminist cliques, found support and novel ways to express erotic desire by joining a women's network. Most of the girls know the moral of Julia's story, even if they never heard the actual narration, namely that women's options were traditionally restrained by financial, social and ethical boundaries constructed to limit their life-choices. The narratives of Stasa and Nena are also pertinent to many members of the group who effectively question the 'joys' of marriage and conjugality. Finally, Soula's example reminds the community how effortless it is for a largely heterosexual culture to process, digest and transform an actor's quest for visibility and difference. All these stories, and many more that cannot possibly fit in a chapter, are instances of culture the contextual meaning of which is continuously negotiated by the *parea* in their constant endeavour to remain a meaningful collectivity, an enterprise that is by no means simple or unconstrained by cultural and personal limitations.

This chapter sought to illuminate the conceptual links between the *parea* and the wider culture that surrounds it. The women of the group move into a dense maze of culturally specific discourses and practices, which inform their ideological and performative occupations. Similar to the community of lesbian/feminists studied by Sarah Green, the *parea* is constantly regenerated 'out of historically specific conditions' (1997: 130) that can only be partially captured by the ethnographer. The group is formed within and out of a provincial Greek culture that negotiates wider influences in its own particular way. In this context, being a 'lesbian' does not always have a fixed or clear meaning or one that corresponds to the actual practices of women who find themselves in homosexual relationships. Hence, the women of the *parea* prefer to remain unclassifiable, not because they treat lesbian as 'other' (cf. Dunne, 1997: 226) but due to the conceptualisation that their definition of women's relationships will not be able to undermine the hegemonic discourse about homoeroticism. The feeling of non-feasance is characteristic of the narratives of the Greek periphery (cf. Herzfeld, 1992; Loizos, 1975; Theodossopoulos, 2000), as well as suggestive of the deeply hierarchical nature of available discourses. To be able to construct alternative social arrangements does not always imply the power to negotiate and alter the meaning of existing stereotypes. The manner in which the *parea* voices its sexual and erotic feelings is thus proved to be powerfully shaped by the cultural environment (Dunne, 1997: 3) to which the group ultimately belongs.

8

THE LONG *ZEIMBEKIKO*

This book has been concerned with the lives, the ideas and practices of a community of women who refer to themselves as the *parea*. The term *parea* is used in the cultural context of Greece to describe 'emotional alliances' between people governed by the politics of 'fellow feeling' (*sympatheia*) (Papataxiarchis, 1991: 156; Loizos and Papataxiarchis, 1991: 18). Making *parea* (to keep company) and the making *of* a *parea* (to *create* and maintain a company) is a 'laborious' and in many ways a 'utopian project' (Cowan, 1990: 226). For the sustaining of a *parea* presupposes a commitment and a continuous effort on behalf of its members towards the creation of an atmosphere of trust that allows the different actors to release themselves emotionally and to co-exist harmoniously in an egalitarian ethos. Most of the adult *parees* in Greece exist in the spatio-temporal bounds of eating and drinking commensality, and although 'making *parea*' is a treasured experience it usually belongs to the marginal leisure time (cf. Papataxiarchis, 1991; Cowan, 1990; Madianou-Gefou, 1992). The *parea* I studied is an 'affective community' of people who come together not simply in order to eat, drink and have a good time, but mainly in order to be and to become gendered subjects in ways different to those prescribed by the local culture.

The community upon which this study has focused consists of female persons who prefer to think of themselves as 'girls', although some of them enjoy officially the adult status of 'woman' that comes in Greece with marriage, rather than age (Cowan, 1991: 180). Their wish to conceptually remain girls is closely related to another utopian project, that of sustaining an adolescent spirit which allows them to keep their distance from authority. As Cowan argues, women in Greece 'act as agents of control of females on behalf of men' (1990: 199).

> The married woman's voice coming from women as well as attributed to them, upholds the dominant gender ideology because, ironically, it is against her interests (as a wife, mother and a lady of the community, a *kyria*) to assert her interests (as a woman, an autonomous person).
> (ibid.: 82)

My informants do not aspire to be 'ladies of the community' (*kyries*). They prefer to assert themselves and have freedom over what they see as being their interests to the prestige attached to the status of being a woman and a lady. The position of the socially unimportant girl (cf. Cowan, 1992: 147), 'the nothingness to which [unmarried] women in patriarchy have been assigned' (Marshall, 1998: 59), is paradoxically invested with possibilities denied to 'ladies'. Because 'nothing is all. By a kind of heretical-mystical and then baroque conversion, this "nothing of being" changes into an infinity of ecstatic delight, a plethora of forms' (Benjamin, 1984: 109).[1] The 'girls' – through being girls – are after this 'infinity of ecstatic delight', the feeling of being able to assume more than one role, to occupy more than one position, to be members of more than one conceptual world.

The girls of the *parea* are modern 'dandies', Baudelairian 'flâneurs',[2] educated women who exploit their intellectual sophistication – and share it between them – while, at the same time, they repudiate the vested interests of both the middle class and the élite. The reading of Foucault, Lacan and French poetry, the possession of a Harley Davidson-type motorbike, the articulation of aesthetic claims, together with an emphasis on beauty and the enactment of a 'working-class' *mangia*[3] comprise the syncretic personae of the members of this community. Social and aesthetic capital, the quest for authenticity and originality (cf. Faubion, 1993) are for the *parea* not only the means to distinction, but also, and perhaps more importantly a way of legitimising their lifestyles, of establishing their art of living as a rightful one in the context of provincial Kallipolis (cf. Bourdieu, 1979: 57).

This syncretic idiom of personhood, one that is particular to the *parea*, constitutes the common 'social sense' of a community of women who are bound, as they claim, 'by sentiments of elective affinity' (cf. Bourdieu, 1979: 241–3).[4] What brings together these women of various ages, vocations, socio-economic and educational strata, and what keeps them together as a group, is desire for other women. This desire is nevertheless articulated by the girls, not in the form of a clear lesbian identity based on object choice, but in terms of a 'multiple', 'nomadic' subjectivity. As Braidotti claims explicating Deleuze:

> the affirmation of difference as pure positivity inevitably entails the abolition of the dialectic of negation, in favour of a multiple nomadic thought. 'Multiple' does not mean the dispersal of forces in a given field, but rather the redefinition of the embodied subject in terms of desire and affectivity . . . The multiple is whatever is not attached to any principle of identity and unity, anything that knows how to put into play the differences that constitute the affirmative powers of the bodily subject, and through a game of differences produces meaning. (1991: 111)

Or as one of the girls put it:

> Difference is a blessing, not a curse. But in order for difference to work for you instead of against you, you have to treat it as temporary. There is no meaning in substituting one identity for the other. Play with difference in all the fields of your life. Constitute your self as the incarnation of difference and ambiguity. This is the only way to defy the system, by not letting it categorise you. Desire and *pathos* [passion] is the only authentic rule by which you can measure things. Desire women but don't let your object of desire define you. Be here, be there, be everywhere.[5]
>
> (Clio)

Through the promotion of a multiple and nomadic type of subjectivity, the women of the *parea* attempt to articulate homoeroticism as a discursive practice which, although specific to the group, can best be understood in terms of larger narratives of resistance to both institutionalised heterosexuality and homosexuality as an authentic identity. The policing of sex, the medicalisation of sexuality and its naturalisation as a universal human drive (cf. Foucault, 1976; Abramson, 1987: 195, 197; Caplan, 1987) established the exclusivity of heterosexuality as the only 'normal' sexual outcome (Dunne, 1997) and homosexuality as its 'interior exclusion' (Fuss, 1991: 3). In the western hierarchical model of a sexually divided society (Jackson, 1987: 52), homosexuality has been constructed as the abnormal, the deviant, the rare predicament of a few, the 'contaminated other' (Fuss, 1991: 3). As Foucault argued, however, 'sexuality is not a drive but a specifically dense transfer point for relations of power' (1976: 103). The institutionalised character of heterosexuality founded on the establishment of a causal relation between sex, gender, identity and desire is then interwoven with idioms of power that relate to all aspects of self-realisation. The *parea* resists any identification with essentialist stereotypes of the 'other' through renouncing the terms lesbian, homosexual or bisexual as categories suitable for self-ascription, and by attempting to break the link between sex, gender, identity and desire (cf. Corber and Valocchi, 2003).

The decision of the community to remain outside the 'realm of the visible, the speakable and the culturally intelligible' (Fuss, 1991: 4) relates, however, not only to their anti-essentialist ideological beliefs but also to issues of viability and survival. The *parea* is located in a Greek provincial town where publicly to admit to a lesbian identity is equivalent to signing one's social death warrant. The women of the group are thus forced to engage in a constant game of concealment and display employing ambiguity, not only as a conscious gender performative (cf. Butler, 1990), but also and most importantly as a strategy for surviving (cf. Battaglia, 1999). The *parea* lives literally in the fissures of the sexual economy exploiting the socially condoned idiom of friendship in order to exist as a collectivity.

Same-sex desire and homoerotic life in the community are realised away from the ethos of stability that permeates heterosexual conjugality and procreation, in terms of a kind of 'pure relationship' (Giddens, 1992) that stresses passion, desire and the celebration of the ephemeral. Seen in this light, homosexuality in the context of the *parea* is not simply understood as a set of sexual practices but as a site for self-realisation. To be with women pertains to one's experience as a woman and takes for the group the form of an alternative idiom of personhood that, although different from the one prescribed by hegemonic discourses of gender, is nevertheless directly related to the cultural context within which it is articulated. The *parea* belongs to a certain web of socio-cultural narratives with which it maintains a continuous dialectic relationship (cf. Green, 1997) by engaging in a constant and consistent process of self-poesis based on the elaboration and creative redefinition of familiar cultural material.

In the repertoire of the *parea*'s idiosyncratic poetics of selfhood there is first the 'masculine' competitive self, who is realised on behalf of the collectivity (i.e. the community as a whole) according to the ethos of *eghoismos*.[6] It appears when one of the girls flirts with a woman with the view of initiating her into the community, when she engages in conspicuous consumption of alcohol while remaining (or acting) sober, when she dances a *zeimbekiko* in order to express her infatuation for a member of the same sex, or even, when she rides her motorbike in the cold air dressed in a white open shirt, jeans and boots. A girl's *eghoismos* is primarily the display of toughness and indifference towards a lover who left her, to the society, even to the elements of nature, to all the things she is tortured by: love, marginalisation, physical suffering or exhaustion. In the display of *eghoismos* the self is made to be larger than emotional or physical obstacles, larger than life itself, liberated, legendary and defiant on behalf of a community that struggles with the contradictions of provincial reality. Through this agonistic (Herzfeld, 1985) idiom of genderhood a new kind of introspective femininity arises, namely the female *mangia*, fashioned according to what is conventionally perceived to be a masculine performance. The female *mangia* relates to sentiments, articulated in the form of statements, symbolic of specific values and particular representations of the self (Abu Lughod, 1986: 34). As a woman of the *parea* explained to me:

> *Mangia* means to be in touch with your sentiments but not let them drag you in places you don't want to go. *Mangia* is to be fully aware of what is torturing you and yet be fully capable of controlling it. It means to have *filotimo* [love of honour], to be able at any given time to feel as you feel and to act as you should, or as you want. To suffer and smile. This is *mangia*.[7]

The woman/*mangas* acts according to certain values, either personal or shared and is inspired with honour, instead of being controlled through shame, defying the stereotypical image attributed to young females as being weak, or even naïve and in need of protection (cf. Cowan, 1990; du Boulay, 1974; Hirschon, 1989; Collier, 1997). At the same time, *mangia* as enacted by the girls is a specifically female performative that employs suffering as a 'language of the self' (Lutz and White, 1986: 417).

The archetype of the suffering woman (cf. Dubisch, 1995; Goddard, 1996) is a dimension of the 'feminine' competitive self as enacted in the *parea*. The idiom of suffering provides Greek women with a shared language, and ties them to a collective narrative of pain that aims to articulate the experience of being a woman and a mother (Dubisch, 1995: 217–23).[8] Similar to the male *eghoismos*, female suffering is about self-assertion on behalf of a collectivity and presents the self as being unique in her endurance of pain. Dubisch pointedly notes that:

> Suffering may also serve as a basis for a woman's identification with other women. This can be seen in the concept of *ponos* (pain), especially as it is applied in the experience of death and mourning . . . [W]omen's performances of mourning laments speak of a 'community of pain' that unites women . . . The laments themselves are a major form of female performance, created by women from traditional forms and the painful materials of their own lived experience, and they serve as vehicles to express their sufferings and those of others and to protest against injustice on behalf of the weak and the downtrodden of the world . . . Thus being a woman in this case means not only identifying with other women but also with others who share women's experiences of marginality.
>
> (1995: 214)

Suffering in the *parea* as it is performed mainly in the context of separation, is then not only about employing a shared female expressive idiom. It is also the source of a poetics of the self that is both about being a woman and being a (gay) woman/girl on the margins of culture. Marginality, suffering, 'staying outside the system', being tortured by love and anxiety as well as by societal constraints, are the main themes of the girls' narratives that combine 'female' suffering and 'male' *mangia* in a mixed performative that strives to animate the lived contradictions of the *parea*'s existence. I prefer to call these 'surreptitious narratives of the periphery', for the common thread between them – besides their gendered character – is that they explicate a paradoxical feeling and state of empowerment and powerlessness.

The experience of homosexuality in the *parea* is tied to a sense of empowerment (cf. Dunne, 1997), mainly because the community I studied is also a women's network that aims at providing its members with emotional and practical support, and often with the very means to live differently. As was demonstrated in Chapter Four, the girls have formed an alternative model of relatedness that is nevertheless based on a culturally specific understanding of close relationships. Through the idiom of the 'best friend' who is expected to perform the role of kin, the women of the *parea* form kin-like bonds based on emotional affinity. These 'families by choice' (Weston, 1991/1997), otherwise found in many lesbian and gay communities (cf. Green, 1997; Nardi, 1992), are enacted in the *parea* according to the specific cultural pattern of self-sacrifice and unconditional support found in biological Greek families.[9] The best friends – like kinsmen – 'must be loyal' to each other (du Boulay, 1974: 156) and will often go to considerable lengths to ensure not only their friends' emotional well-being, but also their access to 'social and symbolic power' (Faubion, 1993: 59). Indeed, the whole *parea* as an alternative family operates according to the logic of *symferon* (self-interest), 'in a cultural context where self-interest and well-being are understood in terms of household-oriented priorities' (Theodossopoulos, 2000: 74; Hirschon, 1989: 174; Loizos, 1975: 66, 291), 'since individuals do not act outside the family context' (Hirschon, 1989: 260). The model of relatedness that the *parea* promotes is certainly different from conventional Greek kinship, in so far as it concentrates on emotional instead of blood-based affinity and so long as it supports the girls' sexual choices. Nevertheless, the group as a network of women is established by and promotes the establishment of relationships that animate the culturally specific familial ideals of mutual trust, support and collective self-realisation, which invoke in its members a sense of empowerment and belonging.

Empowerment in the *parea* does not only come from the security of relationships, however, it is also embedded in defiant performances of *mangia* and suffering. The girls, like other male and female actors in Greece, draw considerable power from the politics of self-assertion, either through the display of an audacious masculinity (cf. Herzfeld, 1985) or through compelling performances of pain (cf. Seremetakis, 1991; Dubisch, 1995). None the less, all these actors, the girls of the *parea*, the Maniat mourners (Seremetakis, 1991), the female pilgrims who crawl on their knees in public (Dubisch, 1995), the rebellious Cretan men (Herzfeld, 1985), seen from another angle occupy similar positions of marginality.

The suffering mother, as much as she might be empowered by her pain, remains the representative voice of the 'weak and the downtrodden of the world' (Dubisch, 1995: 214). The original *mangas* is a mere petty thief 'impoverished and disenfranchised' (Cowan, 1990: 174), while the prototype of the Herzfeldian man is permeated by feelings of insecurity and inadequacy when confronted with the agents of the state. The feebleness of these rebellious men, 'outside the immediate locality of their communities' (Theodossopoulos, 2000: 68) is effectively demonstrated in the following ethnographic example given by Theodossopoulos. Theodossopoulos eloquently describes the 'performative excellence' (cf. Herzfeld, 1985: 16) of certain Zakynthian men, who tried to stop the officials from pulling down some buildings constructed by the villagers illegally on land they owned, but which was deemed to be part of a marine conservation area. One of his informants narrates:

> they tried to pull down the new illegal constructions today. But one of the owners . . . was waiting for them. He went down the road with a gun and he stood in front of the bulldozer and the Public Prosecutor. He said: 'Get down, if anyone dares [*opoios einai antras as katevei kato*]'.[10]
>
> (Theodossopoulos, 2000: 67)

A couple of pages later, the same informants reflect on their feelings once they have left the protected enclave of the village and tried to confront the bureaucrats and the state officials in the latter's offices and courts of law: 'What could the unpolished and illiterate villager (*o aksestos ki agrammatos xoriatis*) do in front of the people of the law?' (*brosta stous anthropous tou nomou?*) (ibid.: 68).

Similarly, the girls of the *parea* whose daily life is devoted to powerful assertions of a competitive and rebellious self, feel their weakness and inability to confront dominant discourses, or to impose their definition of homoeroticism over hegemonic stereotypes of lesbianism. For this reason, the women of the community decide not to stand in opposition to hegemonically instituted heterosexuality. They live as cultural symbiots, side by side with the rest of the Kallipoliots without openly provoking the heterosexual establishment. Like the Zakynthian men, however, there are times when the *parea* from the secured position of performative ambiguity display themselves not just in front of the Kallipoliots, but also 'against them' (Cowan, 1990: 177) thus articulating surreptitious narratives of resistance.

The experience of being a woman and loving women becomes in the *parea* a site for the realisation of the self in a gender-syncretic manner. The combination of masculine and feminine performative idioms (cf. Butler, 1990) is, nevertheless, perhaps the only innovative aspect of the *parea*'s project. The competitive self, the one that is realised at the same time s/he is asserted, is a familiar Greek performative theme. The presentation of the self coincides in Greece with the fashioning of personhood and it is more often than not a variation upon the same theme, namely the discursive and embodied display of power frequently enacted from the margins of power. Although one cannot be blind to the fact that different subject positions enjoy in Greece different degrees of empowerment and prestige, the model of the 'defiant' self is always constituted competitively *vis-à-vis* some hegemonic discourse, proving that power is not 'a general system of domination exerted by one group over another' but a 'multiplicity of force relations' (Foucault 1976: 92). Power is constituted and established in practice and it is the ability to *act* in certain contexts and not others that renders the self the paradoxical interface of empowerment and powerlessness in the *parea*, and also in Greek culture as a whole.

The women of the community enact a gender-syncretic self through culturally specific poetics of personhood. The co-existence of intellectual sophistication, *eghoismos*, *mangia* and suffering in the image of the 'girl', which is nevertheless permeated by a tough swaggering sense of masculinity, effects a mixed performance that attempts to undermine conventional dichotomies of gender, class, location and status in favour of a polysemic subjectivity that appropriates more than one expressive idiom. In turn the subjectivities of these women are informed by certain cultural conditions that 'shape their aspirations, their choices, their capacities to deal with the challenges of everyday life' (Goddard, 1996: 239). As Goddard puts it: 'These [conditions] are important because they help explain how and why men and women accept, reject or modify the ideals and expectations defined for them, and how they *act upon them and reproduce them*' (ibid., my emphasis). Butler has argued that gender identity is not only socially constructed, but also performatively realised, produced in the rehearsal of a 'set of norms' that acquires an 'act-like status' (1990: 147, 1997a: 538). These gender performances, however, are not enacted by some 'volitional subject . . . who decides which gender it will be today' (Butler, 1991: 24), but by culturally constituted actors who stand in a dialectic relationship with the 'cultural conditions' of their gendering. Thus, through repetition the girls' syncretic performances at once challenge and reify traditional conceptualisations of gender. As Battaglia has argued, 'the porous boundaries of performative texts problematise as certainly as they reiterate social identities and relationships' (1999: 128). With reference to the girls, even their desperate attempt to escape essentialist discourses of lesbianism helps – through their consistent refusal to identify with the term lesbian – perpetuate local myths of anomalous man-like women, almost exotic and rare deviants. One can argue then, that in many ways resistance and reproduction are frequently enmeshed in the same intersubjective play of identity-making. The realisation of the gendered self is characterised by an episodic quality where the conscious and unconscious, the self-willed and the cultural enactment, the forced, the random and the premeditated are interwoven instances of the same complex process of gendering.

The acquisition of a homoerotic subjectivity in the *parea* is accomplished by the conscious questioning and the not so conscious reproduction of gender stereotypes, and is certainly established both practically and discursively. The appropriation of culturally specific femininities and masculinities presupposes an involvement of the body that 'incorporates social meaning through day to day practices' (Cowan, 1990: 23). The corporeality of gender meanings invested in bodily postures demonstrates in the context of the group how the body can become the threshold of subjectivity, the site where the material and the symbolic overlap (Braidotti, 1991, 2002; Moore, 1999), the meeting point of conventional and alternative praxis. Sex, gender and sexuality are not located in the body, but rather established through the body constituting it as the material post of subjectivity. The flirtatious, defiant, suffering, desiring bodies of the girls are culturally informed tangible evidences of a gender-syncretic politic of identity, the loci of actors who are conscious of their homoerotic desire, but nevertheless, not necessarily strategic in relation to the embodied and discursive production of their gendered selves. One cannot but identify instances when the person is totally aware or completely oblivious of her embodied subjectivity. Most of the time 'she is a body' and 'she has a body', and therefore her performance is not simply a text to be read – or misread – by a given audience but a site where the embodied self is intersubjectively realised (Cowan, 1990: 24).

The ethnography presented in the previous chapters has documented the movement of bodies through *space* and *time*. The girls have been dancing, consuming, flirting, being thrilled by their love and also suffering because of it, working, travelling, making sense of the world and attempting to act upon it by means of their bodies. The women of the *parea* were also depicted as they were articulating sophisticated verbal narratives. Indeed, in many ways this book has been an ongoing storytelling about persons and their life-circumstances, about selves as the 'heroes' of stories and the products of narrative (Alasuutari, 1995: 77), about 'biographies in transition' (McNay, 2000: 113). I have claimed that the group engages in a consistent rewriting of its collective history through the individual stories of its members. Through heroic tales of achievement, beautified accounts of prominent relationships, and continued references to a legendary past, the girls create a ravishing image of homoerotic life that aims to deconstruct and destabilise the negative connotations that homosexuality bears in provincial Kallipolis. These narratives are instances of collective identity-making and also sites for the dissemination of alternative ideals of same-sex desire. The girls belong to the *parea* partly through sharing the same chivalrous past, one that consists of noble moments of passion, an almost baroque portrayal of an otherwise difficult daily life. I have employed many of these narratives in my ethnography, but not because I wish to partake in my informants' mythicisation. Instead, by documenting their heroic rhetoric, I aspired to convey, more than data, the *parea*'s ambience, the lived experience of belonging to a group of intrepid women who, through dramatisation, attempt to encompass the difficulties and conflicts of their conditional existence.

The *parea* has been founded by four women who grew up during a highly politicised time, but whose encounters with agents of politicisation (student parties and feminist coalitions) left them feeling misled. At a critical point in their lives, they were introduced to an Athenian lesbian community the atmosphere of which made them feel, as they say, 'like they were coming home'. Lina, one of these girls, pointedly described to me this company of lesbian women in the following way:

> These women were not pretentious, they did not sell ideologies at a price, they were really supportive and caring and mind you very 'connected'. They wanted and they were in a position to help. We were suddenly introduced into a different world of relating.

From that point onwards, the four Kallipoliot women and many more afterwards, tried consistently to reproduce and even amplify the original experience of safety and belonging they enjoyed in this Athenian company. For the love of women they established a *parea* that is 'both part and a reflection of the culture and city in which they exist' (Green, 1997: 2). Through the *parea*, the girls promote an alternative gender idiom. Their 'version' of gay existence, as it is ethnographically captured in this book, serves to highlight that different groups of people hold distinct and even antithetical views with reference to gender realisation (Cowan, 1990, 1991, 1992), while at the same time it demonstrates how their experiences resonate with culturally specific categories of identity. As is true for other European lesbian communities (cf. Green, 1997), homosexuality in the *parea* is not just about sexual practices but rather about the politics of desire and resistance. The model of lesbianism as a political stance of resistance to heteropatriarchy in Euro-American societies has been articulated by a number of gender theorists (cf. Rich, 1980) and thoroughly criticised for its inability to explain homosexuality cross-culturally (cf. Wieringa and Blackwood, 1999). I certainly do not wish to articulate any grand narrative about homosexuality that would potentially aim to encompass the meaning of same-sex desire in other field-sites. Furthermore, I cannot claim that homoerotic desire in the *parea* is about resistance to heteropatriarchy. This is a specific project undertaken by other lesbian communities, inspired by feminist ideas that 'reflected the circumstances of their cultures, and their cities' (cf. Green, 1997). Feminism in Greece has largely remained 'less a revolutionary than a reformist movement' (Faubion, 1993: 176). As Cowan argues, although feminist ideas are being increasingly incorporated into the local discourses, 'one needs to examine how the ideas of equality and feminism are employed in specific arguments pertaining to men and women, by whom and against whom they are used' (1992: 146, my translation). In other words, it is not always self-evident how feminist discourses that originate in specific contexts and at specific times will be incorporated into various local narratives.

Homosexuality in the *parea* is, nevertheless, about resistance albeit not to heteropatriarchy. The community I studied aims to negotiate another theme that pertains to power, namely, the culturally specific understanding of the defiant self as always being positioned *vis-à-vis* some hegemonic discourse. At one level, this confrontation might take the form of the gallant Greek heir of a glorious ancient past who, nevertheless, 'seriously and frequently asks [him/her self] if perhaps [s/he] now belongs politically, economically and culturally to the Third World' (Herzfeld, 1987: 3). In this case, the self is seen as being at once the intellectual centre and the pariah of Europe who is proud of his/her celebrated past but feels unable to overcome the peripheral character of his/her present. At some other instance, the paradoxical play of empowerment and powerlessness might be exemplified in a conspicuous local display of *eghoismos*, which nevertheless seems ineffective when it comes to the dealings of the actor with 'powerful' idioms of the state and the law (cf. Theodossopoulos, 2000).

The *parea* negotiates its existence and articulates its resistance in relation to another hegemonic discourse, that of gender. But in the case of the girls the self does not need to go as far as Europe, or even outside the village, in order to feel its weakness. The Kallipoliot representatives of this hegemonic discourse are right there, on the edge of the dance floor sitting side by side with the girls. Normative ideas of gender, ones 'that are known and felt but not articulated' (Cowan, 1990: 14) saturate every movement of those otherwise rebellious women. But because as Cowan notes, hegemony is 'a process that always entails the possibility of resistance as well as of accommodation' (ibid.), the girls spend their lives *resisting and accommodating* discourses that are more powerful than those they themselves wish to articulate. In many ways, my informants are like archetypal *zeimbekiko* dancers. In the same manner that the *mangas* in a *zeimbekiko* performance resists what is torturing him, the women of the community through acrobatic embellishments of balancing a life in and out of the group, and defiant postures enacted both in discourse and practice, try to conjure that which haunts them. In this sense, the fashioning of a homoerotic subjectivity takes in the *parea* the form of a long, long *zeimbekiko* that has lasted for the past 15 years.

NOTES

1 FOR THE LOVE OF WOMEN

1 Although my informants consistently refuse to identify themselves as lesbians or homosexuals, they occasionally employ the term 'gay' (in English) more as a political marker than as an identity category. Likewise, I use the term 'gay' to refer to a particular standpoint rather than to a fixed sexual identity.

2 *Parea* (company) is a term documented by many ethnographers who specialise in the area of Greece (Loizos and Papataxiarchis, 1991a; Papataxiarchis, 1992; Cowan, 1990; Madianou-Gefou, 1992). I will discuss the connotations and use of this word in the beginning of the following section.

3 I employ the term 'context' here in the sense that Loizos and Papataxiarchis use it: 'to suggest spheres of activity in which ideas of gender can be identified' (1991a: 4).

4 As Marcus has argued, ethnographers 'work intensively and locally with particular subjects . . . but they no longer do so with the sense that the cultural object of their study is fully accessible within a particular site, or without the sense that a site of fieldwork anywhere is integrally and intimately related to sites of possible fieldwork elsewhere' (1998: 117).

5 With special reference to male drinking parties, egalitarianism is probably one of the most basic prerequisites for a company (*parea*) (cf. Papataxiarchis, 1991, 1992).

6 My informants employ the term 'girl(s)' to refer to each other and the group. The word girl is used in Greece to describe 'all unmarried females regardless of age' (Cowan, 1991: 180). As Cowan observes, in Greece 'gender categories for females (and *not* males) reflect how it is marriage rather than age that precipitates the status change from girl (*kopella* or *koritsi*) to "woman" (*yineka*)' (1991: 196). The same author pointedly notes the overtones of 'immaturity', 'naivety' and even social unimportance that the term girl bears (1992: 147). The word girl also has affective connotations and it can be used to describe even married women in informal settings. I believe that the women of the *parea* use the term girl(s) with all of the above connotations, and because the term woman, or women, would sound somewhat formal. Throughout the book I use the expression 'girls' or 'girls of the *parea*' to refer to the women of the community I studied in the same manner that they themselves use it.

7 The youngest girl was, at the time of the fieldwork, seventeen while the oldest member was approximately thirty-eight. Today, more than ten members of the

group are well into their thirties, while the majority of the women are in their twenties.

8 The married members of the *parea*, and especially those who have children, often rely on the help and support of their mothers, sisters, or other female members of their family in order to be able to participate in the group's night-adventures. It may be probably worth noting that not all women manage to be in *Harama* every night. Nevertheless, due to the fact that the *parea* consists of more than seventy members, at least twenty to twenty-five of them are gathered in the bar each night.

9 The fact that the women of the *parea* do not reveal their sexual preferences greatly contributes to this. This issue is discussed later in this chapter.

10 Discussing Felski (1995) Adkins points out that 'during the late nineteenth century the literary avant-garde pursued a self-conscious textualism as a strategy of subverting sexual and textual norms' (Adkins, 2002: 95).

11 For a detailed and ethnographically substantiated account of male homosexuality in Athens see Faubion (1993: 213–41).

12 Please note that this particular woman is not a member of the *parea*.

13 Compare with Faubion's account of why sexual relations between women remain 'licit' quoted by a juridical source: 'because of the difficulty of proving and the difficulty of defining the terms of criminal practice' (Pandelidhis, 1982: 87, quoted in Faubion 1993: 221).

14 In fact my discussion with these men closely resembles Cowan's encounter with Sohoian men who argued against the practice or wish of women to go to the local cafeteria (1991, 1992). Although paradoxical it is probably not surprising that both in her case and mine a woman who goes to the cafeteria and a woman who establishes sexual relationships with other women are both metaphors for the 'female person actively taking her pleasure' (Cowan, 1991: 197). Although going to the cafeteria is a much less serious slippage than being a lesbian they both pertain in some ways to female pleasure away from the jurisdiction of men. What is probably worse in the case of lesbians is that whereas a woman who goes to the cafeteria runs the risk of being led to a sexual encounter by a man other than her husband, a woman who sleeps with other women irreversibly defies the male order itself.

15 Please note that all the women I refer to in this paragraph, with whom I discussed about same-sex female sexuality were not members of the *parea*.

16 Watching porn with one's girlfriend or wife, although not unprecedented, is by no means a standard practice, since most women in Greece tend to regard porn as 'filthy' and 'revolting'. Porn has nowadays become even more widely available in Greece since it is included in the broadcasting of a local cable/satellite movie channel, the equivalent of Sky Premiere in Britain, usually between 12.30 and 1.30 in the morning.

17 The women of the community regard most Euro-American discourses put forward by activist groups as essentialist (cf. Corber and Valocchi, 2003: 2–3).

18 In fact, they borrow this term directly from Bourdieu (1979). Bourdieu defines elective affinity as: 'taste that brings together people who go together' (ibid.: 241).

19 In such an image of the past homosexuality does not have a place, and it is thus systematically de-emphasised.

20 For a more inclusive discussion of nationalism in terms of Greece's classical past, see Herzfeld (1986b, 1991b). For a discussion of national identity especially in

Aegean Macedonia, see Karakasidou (1997), Danforth (1995), Mackridge and Yanakakis (1997).

21 The *parea*'s contribution to the bar's atmosphere is actually manifold. First, it ensures that the women customers are more than the men which gives *Harama* the reputation of being a women- and family-friendly establishment. Second, the girls, mainly through dancing, create a positive ambience and last but not least the *parea* brings to *Harama* more customers through introducing it to friends and acquaintances.

22 The girls call *Harama* their *steki* (haunt).

23 Generous spending is practised in Greece, in places called 'skylladika' (literally dog places). 'Skylladika', as opposed to *Harama*, are frequented mostly by men, play heavy popular Greek music and sometimes provide paid female companionship at the customers' tables. The most characteristic attribute of a 'skylladiko', apart from the poor-quality singing, is competitive spending. The typical customers of such bars are 'working-class men who seem to be particularly conscious of their masculinity' (Argyrou, 1996: 19), and who often dispense large sums of money in flowers and champagne. A good 'skylladiko' client is one who does a lot of 'damage' (*zimia*), that is one who pays a large bill by the end of the night. For an account of a typical Cypriot 'skylladiko', see Argyrou (1996: 20–1). For a detailed account of different music trends in Greece, see Cowan (1990: 175–6).

24 Treating someone to a drink should not be confused with the traditional *kerasma*, the offering of hospitality performed by women. The traditional *kerasma* takes place in the home and consists of coffee, preserved fruit or other sweets, water and sometimes sweet liqueurs like cherry. For a description of a traditional *kerasma*, see Cowan (1990: 65–6).

25 Note that some musicians from Smyrna arrived in Greece even before 1922.

26 For a contemporary description of *paraggelia* as well as its gendered connotations, see Cowan (1990: 115).

27 Note that Petrides (in Butterworth and Schneider, 1975: 28–9, quoted in Cowan, 1990: 175) gives a slightly different – older – account where not even the man's *parea* follows him to the dance floor. What I am describing is the form that the practice took from the 1960s onwards.

28 The practice and importance of initiation are explicated in the third chapter of this book.

29 *Grapse gia tin parea, na mathei o kosmos oti kapou iparxoun kapoies gynaikes pou tolmoun na fantazontai mia diaforetiki zoi. Grapse gia tis zoes mas, kai gia tis idees mas, grapse tis istories, alla mi mas doseis apokalyptontas tin pramatiki mas tautotita.*

30 Thus a woman who is a psychologist might be referred to as a sociologist, but not as a teacher or a beautician.

31 Most ethnographers, however, admit that keeping fieldnotes is not a straightforward task (Dubisch, 1995; Hammersley and Atkinson, 1995; Kemp and Ellen, 1984).

32 I use the terms representation, validity and verisimilitude in Denzin's (1997) sense where representation refers to 'how well a text can capture reality' (418). Validity relates to legitimacy whereas verisimilitude, as the most important criterion of validity concerns: 'a text's relationship to reality, whether a text is accepted by the relevant scientific community and whether a text is able or not to permit generalisation' (see Denzin, 1997: 4–18).

2 THEORETICAL REFLECTIONS

1 See, for example, the volume edited by Peristiany (1965), and John Campbell's monograph 'Honour Family and Patronage' published in 1964.

2 For a thorough critical evaluation of the honour and shame literature, see Goddard (1994) and Goddard *et al.* (1994). For a critical review of the approaches that influenced the theorisation of gender in the context of Greece, see Cowan (1990) and Dubisch (1995).

3 Goddard observed a very similar attitude in Naples where women's work was valued but did not threaten local conceptualisations of women as mothers and carers (1996: 13).

4 It is worth noting here that the opposition between mind and body is present in the writings of ancient Greek philosophers such as Plato and in Christian tradition (Grosz, 1994: 5). As Grosz maintains, 'what Descartes accomplished was not really the separation of mind and body (a separation which has long been anticipated in Greek philosophy since the time of Plato) but the separation of soul from nature' (ibid.: 6).

5 I refer here to Mauss's article '*Les techniques du corps: Sociologie et anthropologie*' (1934). Csordas (1999: 175) notes that the term had been also used by Max Weber (1934/1963: 158) in *The Sociology of Religion*.

6 The 'field' is understood as being a context of certain objective limits – presumably of historical and cultural character – within which habitus can be understood as an open system of dispositions (cf. Bourdieu, 1992: 133; McNay, 2000: 38–44).

3 FLIRTING WITH THE 'OTHER': RITUALISTIC INCORPORATION IN THE REALM OF THE *PAREA*

1 With reference to 'spiritual' kinship, see Chapter Four.

2 I have borrowed this extremely eloquent term from Cowan (1990: 173).

3 Those events take place quite often and bear similarities with Cowan's *Horoesperides* (1990). They are less formal than the *horoesperides* and their main goal is the socialisation of the students. At least four times a year different departments organise parties, usually in a place with live music. As a result there is a large party every month or so and of course more than that before Christmas, at the end of each term and during the Greek Halloween. The profit, if any, is usually kept for the organisation of the next party.

4 Shots served 'on the house' should not be confused with the traditional *kerasma* in Papataxiarchis' sense (1992). It is a standardised practice nowadays in Greek night-spots that some shots be served on the house to customers who have already consumed more than two or three drinks, to big companies and so forth as a means of tempting them to build *kefi* (high spirits) and dance. The latent meaning of the gesture is the recognition on the part of the barman that the celebrant is actually a loyal customer, *pelatis*, a person who frequents the place and can be trusted to consume generous amounts of alcohol. Since many girls and, less so, boys introduced the practice of dancing *on* the bar, usually a shot is offered to the daring dancer after her performance, this time as a means of recognition of her contribution to the building of the high spirits of the customers in general. In this case, the barman has his own reasons for offering free shots.

5 *Zeimbekiko* is a solo dance, one of the two favourites of the *parea* with the other being *tsifte-teli*. For a detailed description of both these dances, see Cowan (1990) and the relevant section of my ethnographic introduction.

6 Such a glass is often put in front of the person who dances a *zeimbekiko*. By performing difficult embellishments without knocking the glass over, the dancer proves her skill as well as her state of sobriety. Sometimes, depending on the manner in which a person puts the glass in front of the dancer, this can take the form of a challenge.

7 *Rembetiko*: a musical tradition associated with refugees from Asia Minor and a certain subculture that thrived between the mid-1920s and the mid-1950s. *Laiko*: popular music especially favoured among the working class that varies from *gnisio laiko* (authentic popular) represented by singers such as Kazantzidis to *skylladiko* (literally dog song). The latter is regarded as the poorest expression of *laiko* culture and it is banned from places like *Harama*, which is considered a cultured night-spot. In turn, political songs assume traditional rhythms such as the *zeimbekiko* but the lyrics, often based on poetry, refer to the ordeals of the communists during the time that the party was illegal, poverty and social issues. For a detailed account of the different musical trends, see Cowan (1990: 176).

8 *Levendia* can be translated either as upstandingness, dash, ability to fight, or manfulness. The latter term is probably the one closest to the original meaning, but – like *filotimo* (love of honour, see Dubisch, 1995: 202) – *levendia* is not solely associated with men. Thus a man can be *levendis* and a woman *levendissa* (cf. Seremetakis, 1991: 237). As Herzfeld has argued, the categories male and female in Greece often become 'epiphenomena of a fundamental concern with display, concealment, extroversion and introspection, pride and self-criticism' (1986a: 217). For a similar discussion, see Chapter Six.

9 It is important to note that not every woman stays at the bar for a whole night, every night. Depending on individual responsibilities and circumstances the visit to the bar might be short or long and the consumption of alcohol heavier or lighter. As different women hold different kinds of jobs, some go to *Harama* earlier or later during a specific night. The *parea* is thus more complete on Fridays and Saturdays.

10 It is important to stress at this point that, according to Papataxiarchis, drinking commensality is precisely the field where men can co-exist as equals in the ethos of *kefi* (high spirits). However, he refers to instances where the socio-political reality penetrates the world of the coffee-shop in the form of what he calls 'dependent' commensality (1992: 226–7).

11 The connotations of the term misunderstood (*pareksigoumai*) are explicated later on in this chapter.

12 In addition to *Harama* which is the night haunt of the *parea*, there are other places like small taverns and coffee-shops that can be considered as the *parea*'s haunts.

13 'Our' (*mas*) is used here to indicate proximity. The girls 'are of this place', that is they belong to it, they are not *kseni* (outsiders) but precious and favourite customers.

14 Coffee-drinking (that takes place in the house as opposed to the coffee-shop) is a traditional form of female commensality observed throughout Greece. Cowan (1990: 68) describes coffee drinking among women in Sohos who – similarly to my *parea* – exchange during these sessions news and information about the social life of their town.

15 As Cowan notes, while men 'are misunderstood to each other' women always become the object of misunderstanding, and while misunderstanding among men has a personal or a political tone 'misunderstandings over a girl or a woman are assumed to have a sexual tenor' (1991: 203). Generally, a certain behaviour or act is 'misunderstood' when it is considered to be outside the cultural bounds of propriety.

16 Compare with Herzfeld's expression 'stealing to be friends', describing how Cretan men employ sheep-stealing as a context for the establishment of social relations (1985).

17 The two identical rings Maria and Chrisa wore are the symbol of the relationship. They are called the 'bonds' and they stand for the confirmation of an erotic relation. The 'bonds' substantiate a couple's commitment in the eyes of their friends and in the minds of the partners. There have been cases where relationships had practically ended but the respective partners still kept wearing their 'bonds', and the latter was a sufficient reason for the relationship to be considered still valid by the *parea* and by the partners themselves. For more information, see also Chapter Four on 'erotic relationships'.

18 The Greek equivalent is given by the personification of the word 'kamaki'. As such, the person who does 'kamaki' is a 'kamaki'. See also Zinovieff (1991, 1992).

19 Zinovieff's informant said literally: 'How can I have respect for a woman if I screw her?' (1991: 210).

20 As Herzfeld has noted, the term *eghoismos* can only be conceptualised as a 'social category. The fierce mustache and insouciant cigarette of the truly successful *eghoistis* are recognisable precisely because they fit a pattern. One has *eghoismos* on behalf of a collectivity, be it kin group, patriline, village, region, island or country' (1985: 11). Similarly, the girls' *eghoismos* is enacted in familiar and culturally recognisable ways and it is a sentiment performed on behalf of the *parea* as a whole.

4 RELATIONSHIPS

1 The importance of relationships for the construction of personhood and the conceptualisation of agency has been particularly noted in Melanesia (Strathern, 1988; Carrier, 1999). Although a cross-cultural comparison between Greece and Melanesia would be daring in addition to being outside the scope of the present study, it can be safely argued that relationships are pivotal for the fashioning of subjectivity and the understanding of agency in the Greek cultural sphere as well. The same argument has been made in relation to work invested in family-oriented collective enterprises by Theodossopoulos (1999).

2 Contrary to other cases, the community I studied does not treat same-sex relations as a form of open rebellion to heteropatriarchy (cf. Green, 1997: 104). The political agenda of the *parea* is realised in a symbiotic manner.

3 Cohen has observed a similar attitude in New Guinea, where incest taboos exist with reference to a friend's close female kin (1961: 356, noted in Bell and Coleman, 1999: 3).

4 A practice that resembles this has been registered by Johnson (1997) who studied gay men often employed in, or owning beauty parlours in Jolo, Southern Philippines. His informants often use kinship terms to refer to each other, especially if they are in a working relationship in the same parlour. Johnson states

that: 'knowledge and the act of "coming out" to one's parents and other family members not only replaces "blood" as the key symbol and narrative marker of belonging but also opens up new possibilities for rethinking what family and kinship are' (ibid.: 175).

5 Athena's refusal to reveal her friend's secret relates to the deeply rooted cultural ideal of loyalty. Suggestively, I quote du Boulay: 'The way in which kinsmen must be loyal to each other in the matter of gossip is threefold – they must not reveal their secrets, they must back them up in any deceit or evasion they think fit to practice, and, particularly, they must not speak evil, true or false, about them' (1974: 156). The fact that Athena was not related to the rest of the girls through kinship ties demonstrates how friendships are expected in the *parea* to be as important as kin relations.

6 For the importance of higher education in Greece, see Faubion (1993: 59) and Stewart (1991: 126) as well as the relevant ethnographic analysis of Chapter Seven. Goddard also documents that Neapolitan working-class families value education, and parents or older siblings often have to make sacrifices so that the children continue their schooling (1996: 172–3).

7 I will again cite Johnson and his work on Filipino gay men: 'it is not only that "coming out" establishes a shared identity as an excluded "other" but also that it exposes the social fictions of affection and solidarity based on, or rooted in consanguinity' (1997: 175). 'If families can abandon and reject their gay or lesbian children . . . if family love is conditional, then the lesbian or gay man may choose to form a family on another basis' (Lewin, 1993, quoted in Johnson, ibid.).

8 For a more substantiated discussion of this, see Chapter Seven.

9 I do not wish to imply here that Loizos and Papataxiarchis suggest something different. I am rather reflecting further on the claim that friendship as developed in the western world is often empty of structure and function (Papataxiarchis, 1991: 160; Rezende, 1999).

10 Back in the 1970s, Hirschon's informants disapproved of romantic love as a basis for marriage (1989: 114). Collier found a similar attitude prevailing among the inhabitants of Los Olivos during the 1960s (1997: 68), which the author explains in terms of the socio-economic idiom of inherited property that made a family's income and occupation much more important than romantic attraction (ibid.). The superiority of logic over emotion is also noted by Abu Lughod in the context of Bedouin society (1986: 210).

11 Even in Faubion's account of homosexuality in Athens, the local interlocutors present us with a naturalised exegesis of alternative sexuality. As the author pointedly observed: 'A great majority of my "homosexual" acquaintances in Athens insisted that their "homosexuality" was the result of an "inborn predisposition"' (1993: 228).

12 I have to stress here that age and occupational standards are nowadays major considerations. At least in urban contexts a woman is not supposed to marry very young, or before she finishes her studies, and a man's marriageability is seriously compromised if he is not financially/occupationally 'settled'.

13 McNay's observations that Giddens tends to disregard the embodied and pre-reflexive features of subjectivity, offering a largely abstract account of sexuality in the *Transformation of Intimacy* are certainly pointed (2000: 42).

14 The attitude of women towards self-presentation has changed dramatically in

Greece over the past 20 to 30 years. The black shapeless clothes that aimed to disguise one's physical attributes gave way to a fashion-conscious style of dressing, while women are becoming experts in the art of make-up and personal beautification (Dubisch, 1995: 209, 281).

15 All three expressions: 'cure', 'illness' and 'adventure' were used by Zina herself to describe her state at the time. Especially the terms cure (*na gino kala*) and illness (*arrostia*) are frequently employed by people who use drugs in Greece to refer to their predicament.

16 The expression 'somebody's table' refers to the person who made the reservation who is a kind of symbolic representative of the company that occupies the space. So, Kosta's table means Kosta's company and implies that he took the initiative to reserve the table and organise the night out. Sometimes, it can also mean that he is responsible for the expenses.

17 I am referring here to the stereotypes of masculinity, femininity and sexuality enacted in dance events.

18 *Kefi* as the emotional state of happiness and festivity is intrinsically related (though not exclusively as Cowan, 1990, noted) to alcohol and/or food consumption in a celebratory context where music and dance are frequently indispensable elements. For detailed accounts of *kefi*, see Cowan (1990: 107), Loizos and Papataxiarchis (1991a: 17), Caraveli (1982, 1985), Papataxiarchis (1992).

19 In the sense that since they do not get drunk they remain within the bounds of feminine propriety.

20 Note how the *parea*'s ideology with reference to the politics of erotic seduction is one that discourages internal conflict.

21 This is actually a proverb frequently used in the Greek army and translates as: '*O neos einai oraios alla o palios einai allios*'.

22 Pure alcohol, or surgical spirit as it called in Britain, is widely available in Greece and sometimes used in bars for disinfecting purposes. It is not scented as it frequently is in the UK and thus we were unable to notice the difference before actually drinking it.

23 These verses are part of a wedding song once performed at Misti in Cappadocia, Turkey, by the local Orthodox population. The bride here laments her separation from her mother as she is about to leave her family of birth to reside in her husband's natal home; she will soon be considered part of a new household.

24 To borrow an expression from David Sutton's *Memories Cast in Stone* (1998).

25 I only present these verses of the song here that make sense when directly translated. The lyrics of the song are written by Lina Nikolakopoulou and the music composed by Stamatis Kraounakis.

26 For the importance of food in the construction of identity and the enactment of social memory in the Mediterranean region, see Sutton (1998) and Goddard (1996, Chapter Ten). As Goddard argues, in Naples: 'food provides a most important medium for the exchanges that take place within the family and for the construction and expression of family relations and sentiments' (ibid.: 227). Food commensality also relates to the fashioning of a local Neapolitan identity since the consumption of certain foods 'contribute in important ways to creating a sense of belonging' (ibid.). Likewise, the *parea* through eating commensality create and strengthen their emotional and familial ties, and enact group solidarity. Food, like alcohol, is linked to the construction of one's identity as a member of the group.

5 SEPARATION

1 Thekla and Lillian, both members of the *parea*, work as professional singers at *Harama*.

2 *Xenitia*, a person's departure, usually to a foreign country, directly relates in the Greek context to the phenomenon of emigration.

3 For a detailed account of the 'bonds', see Chapter Four.

4 I have chosen to begin the chapter with this particular scene as it was the first ritualistic separation that I participated in, not as an audience, but as the best friend of one of the partners. For the role of the best friend, see Chapter Four.

5 Please note that the 'subgroups' as I call then do not consist necessarily of the same people throughout the course of the invented ritual. The women enter and leave the scene and, depending on other engagements they have, they might offer their support for a few hours or a whole day.

6 The Athenian custom, as Panourgia notes, does not involve overnight mourning since apparently the deceased is buried earlier in the afternoon. However, relatives and friends do come to the house to offer their condolences during the day, and stay for quite some time discussing the details of the death (1995: 111–16).

7 When a person is dancing *zeimbekiko* (solo performance) his/her friends form a circle or semi-circle around him and crouching on one knee they clap according to the rhythm of the song (cf. Cowan, 1990).

8 For an ethnographically substantiated example of suffering as a female performative idiom in Greece, see Chapter Six.

9 Exhumation is a customary practice in Greece, and is usually performed when three years have passed from the date of the burial.

6 CONTEXTUAL IDENTITIES

1 The translation of the girls' narratives has been done by me. All the narratives were documented in the form of notes.

2 In Greece university studies are free. However, since people rarely study in their home town, the family is usually paying for the rent and subsistence of the student. Students supporting themselves are rare, while grants are very difficult to obtain. Thus, the majority of families supports university students for four or more years until they graduate.

3 For the traditional *kerasma*, the 'customary offering of hospitality', see Cowan (1990: 65–7).

4 Note that the last few statements took in Greek the form of consecutive rhetorical questions: Where to start from? And who could help me? Debts? People coming asking me for money?

5 This is how Mrs Evangelia said this in Greek: *'Den fantazesai ti vassana perasame meta to thanato tou paidaki mou. Moni mou, me dyo mikra kai tin kaimeni tin Elena na trexei gia ola. Apo pou n' arxiseis, kai poios na se voithisei? Xrei? Kosmos na 'rxetai na zitaei lefta? To mono pou m' enoiaze itan ta paidia mou. Epefta to vrady ki elega sto Theo: Ton pono tis manas koita Thee mou. Ego vasanistika na t' anastiso auta ta paidia, na ta do na proodeuoun, na ginoun kalytera apo ti mana tous. Ax, i Elena mou, to aksio mou to paidi. Irthe mia mera pou les kai mou lei: "Mana mi fobasai tipota. Ego eimai edo. Tha ta kataferoume".'*

6 For the meaning and importance of struggle as a culturally specific stance towards life, see du Boulay (1974: 56), Kenna (1990: 149–50), Hart (1992: 65–6), Dubisch (1995: 215), Theodossopoulos (1999: 620).

7 The term performance here does not suggest that Mrs Evangelia's emotions are not sincere (cf. Dubisch, 1995: 218). As Dubisch argues '[t]o perform, then, is to present the socially constructed self before others, to in a sense "argue" for that self . . . and thus to convince and draw recognition from others of one's place and one's satisfactory performance of that role' (1995: 204).

8 See Herzfeld (1985: 10–18).

9 As Herzfeld argues: 'it is clear that the successful performance of selfhood depends upon an ability to identify the self with larger categories of identity' (1985: 10).

10 Compare with Herzfeldian *eghoismos*, the 'being good at being a man' (1985: 16).

11 In the same manner that Herzfeldian men claim that: 'I am [the one who matters] and no one else [*egho ime, ce kaneis alos*]' (1985: 11), any mother can claim that her suffering cannot compare to anyone else's.

12 The relationship between suffering and motherhood has also been addressed by Goddard in her study of Neapolitan identity. Goddard argues that motherhood is seen in Naples as the ultimate destiny of women and at once as the rite of passage to womanhood (1996: 188): 'childbirth was the event, which signified entry into full womanhood. And this entry was marked by pain' (ibid.). Goddard observed that the link between pain, sacrifice and women, established through the bearing of and giving birth to children, provides women with a 'shared language' that connects them with the supernatural and specifically the Mother of God (1996: 201). The Madonna's role as a suffering mother 'is directly applicable to other mothers' lives' (Dubisch, 1995: 215) and establishes the religious theme of pain as a 'gender-bound and gender-specific' experience (Goddard, 1996: 192). The identification of women/mothers with the Mother Mary (*Panayia*) is explicated in the Greek context by du Boulay (1986: 141, 1991: 74, 75); Hirschon (1989: 140, 148, 152); Dubisch (1995: 214–16). The belief that marriage and procreation is the ultimate destiny for women is noted in the Greek context by Hirschon (1989: 148), du Boulay (1974: 107) and Loizos and Papataxiarchis (1991a: 6). It is also worth noting – as Loizos and Papataxiarchis argue – that for men, too, marriage is a social necessity although their attachment to the household is 'more flexible and indirect' (1991a: 6).

13 For the importance of education in Greece, see Stewart (1991: 126) and Faubion (1993: 59), while for Cyprus, see Argyrou (1996: 35). With reference to Neapolitan families, Goddard has observed a similar attitude (1996: 172–3). In fact, the author also notes that sometimes (like in the case of Elena here) 'the division of labour between children results in one child's subsidizing the education of another' (Goddard, 1996: 174). Chapter Seven also attests to the importance of education for most Greek families through specific narratives provided by the girls of the *parea*.

14 Although Cowan does not make this explicit, I see the dancing of the male *zeimbekiko* by Sofia, as a corroboration of her success in performing both the role of the mother and the father. It might be true that this particular woman felt that she deserved to dance to this male rhythm since for so many years she was successful in performing a masculine as well as a feminine role in her family life. In turn, for the importance and meaning of *zeimbekiko*, see Chapter One.

15 For the meaning of the term 'misunderstood', see Chapter Four.
16 One of Hirschon's informants in *Yerania* told the ethnographer: 'money earned by women brings no success' (*ta lefta tis gynaikas den ehoun prokopi*) (1989: 100).
17 Throughout the book I have repeatedly used Strathern's notion of the Melanesian person as being composed of relationships (1988). As I have noted elsewhere, this is by no means an attempt at cross-cultural comparison. Self-realisation in Greece passes through relationships as well as being an individual quest. It is mostly Strathern's notion of agency that I find useful in explaining many actions of the women I studied, whose decisions – with the first being that of remaining a kind of secret society – are taken 'with others in mind' (cf. Strathern, 1988: 272, 273).
18 I have grouped these two cases together for they both deal with one important issue, the relationship between these two girls and their mothers. Aphrodite's mother ignores her daughter's involvement with women, while Maro's has full knowledge of it.
19 For more information on Aphrodite and a contextualisation of her ideas in terms of her personal biography, see Chapter Seven.
20 Actually, as we found out a lot later, that person was Daphne's own mother who knew about her daughter's sexual preferences, and seeing Aphrodite befriending her tried to warn her mother. Daphne's and Maro's mothers are of the very few, if not the only ones in the context of the *parea*, who know about their daughters' involvement with women.
21 For a more detailed account of the history of the term and notion 'homosexual', as well as the institutionalised character of heterosexuality, see Chapter Two.
22 For more information on the role of the 'best friend' in the group, see Chapter Four.
23 For a detailed account of the girls' rejection of socially defined categories such as those of 'lesbian' or 'bisexual', see my ethnographic introduction to the group in Chapter One.
24 In Greek: 'i mana einai mana kai mana einai mono mia'. Compare with the Neapolitan saying: 'mother is always mother' (*la mamma e sempre la mamma*) (Goddard, 1996: 202).
25 Please note that I have italicised the name of Faubion's character, *Maro*, to distinguish her from Maro, the girl of the *parea* whose case I presented earlier.
26 Trademark for expensive and rather extravagant fountain pens.

7 DIFFERENT PEOPLE, SAME PLACES – DIFFERENT PLACES, SAME PEOPLE

1 See also Busiou (1998).
2 See suggestively Chapter Six.
3 I will remind the reader of the case of Athena, who entered the university and studied with the support of her partner Zoi and their best friends (Chapter Four), and the case of Elena (Chapter Six) who was supported by the *parea* in establishing herself as an interior decorator of bars and recreational spaces. These are just two of the many instances that the *parea* has functioned as a support network to its members.
4 To pass in the university, or to succeed in the university (*na peraseis sto Panepistimio, na petyxeis sto Panepistimio*) are indeed two intriguing Greek expressions for entering

the university. To pass and to succeed signify success in the Panhellenic entry exams thought to be the turning point in a young person's life. The two verbs can be seen as suggestive of a *rite de passage*, as they encapsulate both success and transition. Note also that the importance is being placed on the 'entrance' to higher education and not necessarily on the degree. This is because of the nature of the university system that allows virtually everyone to complete their studies.

5 As Cowan argues, 'surveillance as a form of controlling female sexuality arises from and is rationalised in terms of the patriarchal system' (1990: 1999). Women in Greece, particularly young girls, are watched by the parents, the kin group and the neighbourhood, whereas 'boys can do what they like and are independent' (du Boulay, 1974: 124). Hirschon reports on the same subject that 'the vigilant eyes and ears of neighbours were felt as a constant presence' (1989: 171), while Argyrou notes that discos in 1990s Cyprus were places where young people escaped the community's gaze (1996: 19). The reasons put forward by mainly older women – who 'act as agents of control of females on behalf of men' (Cowan, 1990: 199) – for watching girls constantly revolve around the perceived 'nature' of girls as Eves and paradoxically at once as naïve virgins (Cowan, 1991: 134–5). Goddard observed a similar attitude in Naples where working-class girls, although they enjoyed freedom of movement, were controlled by the neighbourhood, kin and friends (1996: 145, 149–50). Collier has also noted that in the village of Los Olivos in Spain (during the 1960s) the community exercised considerable control over young women who were describing themselves as 'tied down' in relation to men who were 'free', or as a female informant put it: 'men are not the same as women; men are free . . . women are the ones who have something to lose' (implying their reputation for being chaste) (1997: 91).

6 *Apeleutheromeni apo ta ithika pseutodilimmata pou to kapitalistiko systima epivallei stis mazes.*

7 Lambiri-Dimaki also argues that in the same period the student movement had developed strong ties with party politics (1983).

8 It worth noting what Mouzelis claims with reference to student movements that were very strong after the fall of the junta in 1974 partly due to the fact that they played a catalytic role in the demise of the regime: 'However, all this enormous potential [of the student movements] was literally squandered in either struggling for the "dejuntaisation" of the universities (i.e. removing from teaching posts all the personnel who had collaborated with the junta) or in ultra-revolutionary rhetoric very much removed from the immediate and pressing educational problems' (1978: 136).

9 About the spreading of heroin, as well as the image of the addict as constructed by the media, see also Busiou (1998: 163).

10 The term Greek is used here under a poetic/anthropological licence in strictly cultural terms.

11 Julia's story is in italics although I was advised not to take notes on the spot. In effect what she told me that afternoon is narrated by me, but I tried to keep as many of the original expressions she used as possible.

12 For the custom of arranged marriage in Greece as well as the pragmatic basis of matrimony, see Hirschon, 1989: 109–18. Hirschon reports that matchmaking was preferred during the 1970s among the Yerania people in Athens who disapproved of romantic love as a basis for marriage (1989: 114). Love was seen by Hirschon's

informants as obscuring the issues of health, economic viability and suitable background of the partner, and it was thus regarded as dangerous (ibid.). Collier also observed a similar attitude in the village of Los Olivos in Spain (1997). It is nevertheless important to note that love had a different meaning in different socio-economic contexts.

13 *Pos tha matho na zo xoris esena? Pos tha synithiso pote stin idea oti kapoios allos tha xaideuei tin psyche kai to soma sou? Mia erotisi pou tha paramenei gia panta. Aioroumeni san kremasmenos, tragikos autoxeiras.*

14 The controversy over whether these romantic friendships can be termed lesbian or not and over whether they were actually sexual is important (cf. Dunne, 1997: 7), but not directly relevant to the argument I am putting forward here. Indeed, since the term lesbian with its current meaning was coined a lot later, Faderman's argument that had these women lived today they would probably identify themselves as lesbians (1981: 20), seems rather speculative.

15 Faderman implies that the invention of the term 'invert' by sexologists was meant to scare women away from feminist ideas and to prevent them from loving each other (1981: 238–40). However, Green carefully points out that romantic friendships were not seen as sexual (1997: 126). According to the same author, it was failure to marry rather than perceptions of lesbianism that caused feminists to be thought of as unnatural (ibid.: 126). In fact lesbians, or rather 'inverts', were seen as belonging to the separate category of 'third sex' (Wolfe and Penelope, 1993: 3; Green, 1997: 126). Green also notes that the womanhood, so to speak, of lesbians was recovered by second-wave feminists who saw homosexuality as a form of resistance to heteropatriarchy (1997: 127).

16 Lesbianism is seen as an alternative to patriarchal domination by other theorists too. Irigary for instance, argues that women's relationships effectively challenge the patriarchal economy (1974) while Wittig also makes the connection between heterosexuality and the domination of women (1992). Female homosexuality as resistance is also a way to view lesbianism as a political stance, and not as a problem that pertains to individual psychopathology (cf. Rubin, 1975: 202). For an extensive critique of Wittig's and Irigary's theses, see Gunter, 1998. For a critical review of Rich's argument, see Blackwood and Wieringa (1999). Although the authors agree that compulsory heterosexuality is the case in many societies, they note that Rich was not informed of the multitude of women's sexual expressions 'and so was unable to imagine women's same sex erotic practices except as resistance to compulsory heterosexuality' (1999: 55). Although I totally agree with such an observation, it could be also argued that Rich never claimed her analysis to be universally applicable. See also note 17.

17 Although Blackwood and Wieringa's argument is extremely important with reference to anthropological analysis, it should also be noted that although not universally relevant, the notion of compulsory heterosexuality is pertinent to the socio-historical understanding of how sexuality has developed in the west. Homosexuality as resistance in Euro-American societies refers not to the sexual practices *per se*, but to the promotion of a different model of femininity, relatedness and self-realisation (cf. Dunne, 1997). It is ethnographically substantiated that for many women in Europe, identification with a lesbian identity is part of a complex process of belonging and dealing with female oppression (cf. Green, 1997: 17). Having said that, it would be – as I have pointed out earlier – theoretically

and analytically problematic to conflate lesbianism with either a politic of resistance or an ethos of supportive relations between women (cf. Alsop *et al.* 2002: 119–23).

18 Nena and Stasa follow the cultural rule, which dictates that women (and men) live at the parental house until they marry. Although this is subject to change nowadays and especially in urban centres, it is still somewhat rare for people to set up their own homes before marriage especially if they continue living in the same town as their family of origin.

19 What she actually said in Greek was: *'ki autes pou pantreutikan ti katalavan nomizeis? Fortothikan enan, na ton plenoun, na ton taizoun, na akoun kai ti grinia'.*

20 *'kai den exo anagki kanenan kerata'.*

21 Women in Greece, especially in smaller communities, bear continuous pressure to marry from both kin and the neighbourhood that takes either the form of remarks like 'Here is to a bridegroom', 'Married next year', or 'Get married and open your house!' (Hirschon, 1989: 108). Cowan reports the anxiety of a 31-year-old woman in Sohos for not having married yet (1992: 141). A great part of her uneasiness was apparently cause by the 'inexorable reprehensions of the community' (ibid., my translation). This woman reported to Cowan: 'I am getting out in the street and people, instead of greeting me they ask: Are you still unmarried?' and shares with the ethnographer the example of a friend of hers who was 'slapped into marrying someone she did not want' (1992: 142, my translation).

22 *Katalaves filenada? Theloun kai to spiti etoimo kai ti doula mesa, olo to paketo.*

23 Nena's statement reminds one strongly of Vance's argument that 'a sexual act does not necessarily carry universal meaning' (1989: 18, quoted in Wekker, 1999: 119).

24 Dupont is the trademark of a specific kind of luxury lighter, usually made out of gold or silver.

25 *Ta xeria einai to pan.*

26 *Imoun per definionem kati to exotiko.*

27 Soula used this word in English as well as the term 'dyke' she employs later.

8 THE LONG *ZEIMBEKIKO*

1 Cited in Buci-Glucksman (1994: 130), quoted in Marshall (1998: 59).

2 The image of the 'flâneur' is explicated in the writings of the poet Charles Baudelaire. The flâneur is a city type, always on the move, masculine and feminine – although most of the time a man. The dandy (the prototype of the flâneur) is found at the beginning of the ninteenth century. He is a well-dressed man, with an 'aesthetic ridicule of aristocratic pretensions' who 'claimed the status of a gentleman through arrogant superiority, whilst simultaneously managing an independent, isolated and subversive disregard of social protocol' (Munt, 1998: 32, 33).

3 The *mangas* (the tough) is a representative of the post-1922 urban subculture of the *rebetes*. A hashish smoker or a petty thief , the *mangas* 'was a person who lived outside the accepted standards of the traditional Greek society' (Butterworth and Schneider, 1975: 11, quoted in Cowan, 1990: 174).

4 Note, however, that this 'taste that brings together things and people that go together' attributed by Bourdieu to a common pre-existing habitus is one cultivated and developed mostly within the *parea*.

5 *I diafora einai eulogia, oxi katara alla gia na einai me to meros sou prepei na tin antimetopizeis perastika. Den exei noima na antikathistas mia tautotita me mia alli. Paikse me ti diafora se olous tous tomeis tis zois. Kane ton eauto sou ensarkosi tis diaforas kai tou amfilegomenou. Mono etsi nikas to systima, ama den to afineis na se katigoriopoiei; i epithymia kai to pathos einai to mono authentiko metro ton pragmaton. Na epithymeis gynaikes alla min afineis to antikeimeno tis epithymias sou na se orisei. Na 'sai ki edo, ki ekei kai pantou.*

6 The Herzfeldian masculine idiom of self-assertion (1985).

7 *Mangia simainei na eisai se epafi me ta aisthimata sou, alla na min ta afineis na se syroun se katastaseis pou den goustareis. Mangia einai na exeis pliri aisthisi autou pou se vassanizei kai synhronos na boreis na to controllareis. Na exeis filotimo kai na eisai se thesi na noiotheis opos noiotheis men, alla na dras opos prepei, i telos panton opos goustareis. Na ponas kai na xamogelas. Auti einai mangia.*

8 The relation between suffering and womanhood/motherhood is also explicated by Goddard (1996: 188–92).

9 The theme of self-sacrifice, as an indispensable part of the role of a mother, is also found in Neapolitan narratives (Goddard, 1996). As Goddard notes, in Naples: 'the theme of sacrifice runs through the experience of being a mother. Typically mothers were totally giving, putting their children before themselves, indeed neglecting their own well-being in order to ensure that their children were as well off as could be expected' (ibid.: 201).

10 Literally: 'if anyone is man enough let him get down' (i.e. and confront me).

BIBLIOGRAPHY

Abrahams, R. (1999) 'Friends and networks as survival strategies in north-east europe', in S. Bell and S. Coleman (eds) *The Anthropology of Friendship*, Oxford: Berg.

Abramson, A. (1987) 'Beyond the Samoan controversy in anthropology: A history of sexuality in the eastern interior of Fiji', in P. Caplan (ed.) *The Cultural Construction of Sexuality*, London: Routledge.

Abu Lughod, L. (1986) *Veiled Sentiments: Honour and Poetry in a Bedouin Society*, Berkeley: University of California Press.

—— (1990) 'Can there be a feminist ethnography?' *Women and Performances* 5(1): 7–27.

—— (1993) *Writing Women's Worlds: Bedouin Stories*, Berkeley: University of California Press.

Adkins, L. (2002) *Revisions: Gender and Sexuality in Late Modernity*, Buckingham and Philadelphia: Open University Press.

Alasuutari, P. (1995) *Researching Culture: Qualitative Method and Cultural Studies*, London: Sage.

Alsop, R., Fitzsimons, A. and Lennon, K. (2002) *Theorizing Gender*, Cambridge: Polity Press.

Argyrou, V. (1996) *Tradition and Modernity in the Mediterranean: The Wedding as Symbolic Struggle*, Cambridge: Cambridge University Press.

Barthes, R. (1985) *The Grain of the Voice; Interviews*, New York: Hill and Wang.

Battaglia, D. (1999) 'Toward an ethics of the open subject: Writing culture in good conscience', in H. L. Moore (ed.) *Anthropological Theory Today*, Cambridge: Polity Press.

Bell, C. (1992) *Ritual Theory, Ritual Practice*, Oxford: Oxford University Press.

Bell, S. and Coleman, S. (1999) 'The anthropology of friendship: Enduring themes and future possibilities', in S. Bell and S. Coleman (eds) *The Anthropology of Friendship*, Oxford: Berg.

Blackwood, E. and Wieringa, S. (1999) 'Sapphic shadows: Challenging the silence in the study of sexuality', in E. Blackwood and S. Wieringa (eds) *Same Sex Relations and Female Desires: Transgender Practices Across Cultures*, New York: Columbia University Press.

Bloch, M. and Guggenheim, S. (1981) 'Compadrazgo, baptism and the symbolism of second birth', *Man: The Journal of Royal Anthropological Institute* 16(3): 376–6.

Boissevain, J. (ed.) (1996) 'Introduction', in *Coping with Tourists*, Oxford: Berghahn.

Bourdieu, P. (1977) *Outline of a Theory of Practice*, Cambridge: Cambridge University Press.

—— (1979) *Distinction: A Social Critique of the Judgement of Taste*, London: Routledge.

—— (1990) *The Logic of Practice*, Cambridge: Polity Press.

—— (1992) *An Invitation to Reflexive Sociology*, Cambridge: Polity Press.

Braidotti, R. (1991) *Patterns of Dissonance*, Cambridge: Polity Press.

—— (2002) *Metamorphoses: Towards a Materialist Theory of Becoming*, Cambridge: Polity Press.

Brehony, K. A. (1993) 'Coming to consciousness: Some reflections on the Boston marriage', in E. D. Rothblum and K. Brehony (eds) *Boston Marriages: Romantic but Asexual Relationships among Contemporary Lesbians*, Amherst: University of Massachusetts Press.

Butler, J. (1990) *Gender Trouble: Feminism and the Subversion of Identity*, New York: Routledge.

—— (1991) 'Imitation and gender insubordination', in D. Fuss (ed.) *Inside/Out*, London: Routledge.

—— (1993) *Bodies that Matter: On the Discursive Limits of 'Sex'*, New York: Routledge.

—— (1997a) 'Excerpt from "Introduction" to Bodies that Matter', in R. Lancaster and M. di Leonardo (eds) *The Gender Sexuality Reader*, London: Routledge.

—— (1997b) *Excitable Speech: A Politics of the Performative*, London: Routledge.

Busiou, P. (1998) 'The Nomads of Mykonos: Consuming discourses of otherness in a polysemic tourist space', unpublished Ph.D. thesis, University of London.

Campbell, J.K. (1964) *Honour Family and Patronage: A Study of Institutions and Moral Values in a Greek Mountain Community*, Oxford: Clarendon Press.

Caplan, P. (ed.) (1987) 'Introduction', in *The Cultural Construction of Sexuality*, London: Routledge.

Caraveli, A. (1980) 'Bridge between worlds: The women's ritual lament as communicative event', *Journal of American Folklore* 93: 129–57.

—— (1982) 'The song beyond the song: Aesthetics and social interaction in Greek folksong', *Journal of American Folklore* 95: 129–58.

—— (1985) 'The symbolic village: Community born in performance', *Journal of American Folklore* 98: 259–86.

—— (1986) 'The bitter wounding: The lament as social protest in rural Greece', in J. Dubisch (ed.) *Gender and Power in Rural Greece*, Princeton: Princeton University Press.

Carrier, J. G. (1999) 'People who can be friends: Selves and social relationships', in S. Bell and S. Coleman (eds) *The Anthropology of Friendship*, Oxford: Berg.

Chafetz, J. Saltzman (1990) *Gender Equity: An Integrated Theory of Stability and Change*, Newbury Park: Sage.

Clark, K. and Holquist, M. (1984) *Mikhail Bakhtin*, Cambridge: Belknap.

Clifford, J. (1986) 'On ethnographic allegory', in J. Clifford and G. Marcus (eds) *Writing Culture: The Poetics and Politics of Ethnography*, California: University of California Press.

—— (1988) *The Predicament of Culture: Twentieth Century Ethnography, Literature and Art*, Harvard: Harvard University Press.

Collier, J. F. (1997) *From Duty to Desire: Remaking Families in a Spanish Village*, Princeton: Princeton University Press.

Collier, J. F. and Yanagisako, S. J. (eds) (1987) 'Introduction', in *Gender and Kinship: Essays Toward a Unified Analysis*, Stranford: Stranford University Press.

Collier, J. F., Rosaldo, M. and Yanagisako, S. (1997. 'Is There a Family?', in R. Lancaster and M. di Leonardo (eds) *The Gender Sexuality Reader*, London: Routledge.

Corber, R. J. and Valocchi, S. (eds) (2003) 'Introduction', in *Queer Studies: An Interdisciplinary Reader*, Oxford: Blackwell.

Cowan, J. (1990) *Dance and the Body Politic in Northern Greece*, Princeton: Princeton University Press.

—— (1991) 'Going out for coffee? Contesting the grounds of gendered pleasures in everyday sociability', in P. Loizos and E. Papataxiarchis (eds) *Contested Identities: Gender and Kinship in Modern Greece*, Princeton: Princeton University Press.

—— (1992) 'I kataskeui tis gynaikeias empeirias se mia makedoniki komopoli', in E. Papataxiarchis and T. Paradellis (eds) *Tautotites kai Fyllo sti Sygxroni Ellada: Anthropologikes Proseggiseis*, Athens: Ekdoseis Kastanioti.

Crapanzano, V. (1977) 'The writing of ethnography', *Dialectical Anthropology* 2: 69–73.

Csordas, T. J. (1999) 'The body's career in anthropology', in L. H. Moore (ed.) *Anthropological Theory Today*, Cambridge: Polity Press.

Cucchiari, S. (1981) 'The gender revolution and the transition from bisexual horde to patrilocal band: The origins of gender hierarchy', in S. Ortner and H. Whitehead (eds) *Sexual Meanings: The Cultural Construction of Gender and Sexuality*, Cambridge: Cambridge University Press.

Dahles, H. (1996) 'The social construction of Mokum: Tourism and the quest for local identity in Amsterdam', in J. Boissevain (ed.) *Coping with Tourists: European Reactions to Mass Tourism*, Oxford: Berghahn.

Danforth, L. (1982) *The Death Rituals of Rural Greece*, Princeton: Princeton University Press.

—— (1989) *Firewalking and Religious Healing: The Anastenaria of Greece and the American Firewalking Movement*, Princeton: Princeton University Press.

—— (1991) 'The resolution of conflict through song in Greek ritual therapy', in P. Loizos and E. Papataxiarchis (eds) *Contested Identities: Gender and Kinship in Modern Greece*, Princeton: Princeton University Press.

—— (1995) *The Macedonian Conflict: Ethnic Nationalism in a Transnational World*, Princeton: Princeton University Press.

Davies, P. (1992) 'The role of disclosure in coming out among gay men', in K. Plummer (ed.) *Modern Homosexualities: Fragments of Lesbian and Gay Experience*, London: Routledge.

de Certeau, M. (1983) 'History: Ethics, science and fiction', in N. Hahn, R. Bellah, P. Rabinow and W. Sullivan (eds) *Social Science as Moral Enquiry*, New York: Columbia University Press.

de Lauretis, T. (1994) *The Practice of Love: Lesbian Sexuality and Perverse Desire*, Bloomington and Indianapolis: Indiana University Press.

—— (1997) 'The violence of rhetoric: On representation and gender', in R. Lancaster and M. di Leonardo (eds) *The Gender Sexuality Reader*, London: Routledge.

Denzin, N. K. (1997) *Interpretive Ethnography: Ethnographic Practices for the 21st Century*, London: Sage.

Derrida, J. (1976) *Of Grammatology*, Baltimore: Johns Hopkins University Press.

di Leonardo, M. (ed.) (1991) 'Introduction: gender, culture and political economy: Feminist anthropology in historical perspective', in *Gender and the Crossroads of*

Knowledge: Feminist Anthropology in the Postmodern Era, Berkeley: University of California Press.

di Leonardo, M. and Lancaster, R.N. (eds) (1997) 'Introduction: embodied meanings, carnal practices', in *The Gender Sexuality Reader*, London: Routledge.

Driessen, H. (1992) 'Drinking on masculinity: Alcohol and gender in Andalousia', in D. Gefou-Madianou (ed.) *Alcohol, Gender and Culture*, London: Routledge.

du Boulay, J. (1974) *Portrait of a Greek Mountain Village*, Oxford: Clarendon Press.

—— (1983) 'The meaning of dowry: Changing values in rural Greece', *Journal of Modern Greek Studies* 1: 243–70.

—— (1986) 'Women – images of their nature and destiny in rural Greece', in J. Dubisch (ed.) *Gender and Power in Rural Greece*, Princeton: Princeton University Press.

—— (1991) 'Cosmos and gender in village Greece', in P. Loizos and E. Papataxiarchis (eds) *Contested Identities: Gender and Kinship in Modern Greece*, Princeton: Princeton University Press.

Dubisch, J. (ed.) (1986) 'Introduction', in *Gender and Power in Rural Greece*, Princeton: Princeton University Press.

—— (1991) 'Gender, kinship, and religion: "Reconstructing" the anthropology of Greece', in P. Loizos and E. Papataxiarchis (eds) *Contested Identities: Gender and Kinship in Modern Greece*, Princeton: Princeton University Press.

—— (1992) 'Koinoniko fylo, syggeneia kai thriskeia: Anaplathontas tin antropologia tis Elladas', in E. Papataxiarchis and T. Paradellis (eds) *Tautotites kai Fyllo sti Sygxroni Ellada: Anthropologikes Proseggiseis*, Athens: Ekdoseis Kastanioti.

—— (1995) *In a Different Place: Pilgrimage, Gender, and Politics at a Greek Island*, Princeton: Princeton University Press.

Dunne, G. A. (1997) *Lesbian Lifestyles: Women's Work and the Politics of Sexuality*, London: Macmillan.

Ellen, R. F. (ed.) (1984) *Ethnographic Research: A Guide to General Conduct*, London: Academic Press.

Elliston, D. (1999) 'Erotic anthropology: "ritualised homosexuality" in Melanesia and beyond', *American Ethnologist* 22(4): 848–67.

Fabian, J. (1985) 'Culture, time and the object of anthropology', *Berkshire Review* 20.

Faderman, L. (1981) *Surpassing the Love of Men: Romantic Friendship and Love between Women from the Renaissance to the Present*, New York: William Morrow and Co.

—— (1993) 'Nineteenth-century Boston marriage as a possible lesson for today', in E. D. Rothblum and K. Brehony (eds) *Boston Marriages: Romantic but Asexual Relationships among Contemporary Lesbians*, Amherst: University of Massachusetts Press.

Faubion, J. D. (1993) *Modern Greek Lessons: A Primer in Historical Constructivism*, Princeton: Princeton University Press.

Felski, R. (1995) *The Gender of Modernity*, Cambridge, MA: Harvard University Press.

Finch, J. (1984) '"Its great to have someone to talk to": The ethics and politics of interviewing women', in C. Bell and H. Roberts (eds) *Social Researching: Politics, Problems, Practice*, London: Routledge and Kegan Paul.

Fisher, M. J. (1986) 'Ethnicity and the post-modern arts of memory', in J. Clifford and G. Marcus (eds) *Writing Culture: The Poetics and Politics of Ethnography*, Berkeley: University of California Press.

Fiske, J. (1994) 'Audiencing: Cultural practice and cultural studies', in N. K. Denzin and Y. S. Lincoln (eds) *The Handbook of Qualitative Research*, Thousand Oaks, CA: Sage.

Foucault, M. (1976) *The History of Sexuality: Volume I: An Introduction*, London: Penguin Books.

—— (1977) *Discipline and Punish: The Birth of the Prison*, London: Penguin Books.

Fuss, D. (ed.) (1991) 'Introduction' in *Inside/Out: Lesbian Theories/Gay Theories*, London: Routledge.

Gatens, M. (1990) 'A critique of the sex/gender distinction', in S. Gunew (ed.) *A Reader in Feminist Knowledge*, London: Routledge.

Geertz, C. (1973) *The Interpretation of Cultures*, New York: Basic Books.

Giddens, A. (1992) *The Transformation of Intimacy: Sexuality, Love and Eroticism in Modern Societies*, Cambridge: Polity Press.

Goddard, V. A. (1994) 'From the Mediterranean to Europe: Honour, kinship and gender', in V. A. Goddard, J. R. Llobera and C. Shore (eds) *The Anthropology of Europe: Identities and Boundaries in Conflict*, Oxford: Berg.

—— (1996) *Gender, Family and Work in Naples*, Oxford: Berg.

Goddard, V. A., Llobera, J. R. and Shore, C. (eds) (1994) 'Introduction: The anthropology of Europe', in *The Anthropology of Europe: Identities and Boundaries in Conflict*, Oxford: Berg.

Green, S. (1997) *Urban Amazons*, London: Macmillan

Greenberg, D. F. (1988) *The Construction of Homosexuality*, Chicago: University of Chicago Press.

—— (1997) 'Transformations of homosexuality-based classifications', in R. Lancaster and M. di Leonardo (eds) *The Gender Sexuality Reader*, London: Routledge.

Grosz, E. (1994a) *Volatile Bodies: Toward a Corporeal Feminism*, Bloomington and Indianapolis: Indiana University Press.

—— (1994b) 'Experimental desire: Rethinking queer subjectivity', in J. Copej (ed.) *Supposing the Subject*, London: Verso.

Gunter, R. (1998) 'Are lesbians women? The relationship between lesbianism and feminism in the work of Luce Irigary and Monique Wittig', in O. Heathcote, A. Hughes and J. S. Williams (eds) *Gay Signatures: Gay and Lesbian Theory, Fiction and Film in France, 1945–1995*, Oxford: Berg.

Hamilakis, Y. (2003) '"Learn history!" Antiquity, national narrative, and history in Greek educational textbooks', in K. S. Brown and Y. Hamilakis (eds) *The Usable Past: Greek Metahistories*, Lanham, MD: Lexington Books.

Hamilakis, Y. and Yalouri, E. (1996) 'Antiquities as symbolic capital in modern Greek society', *Antiquity* 70: 117–29.

—— (1999) 'Sacralising the past', *Archaeological Dialogues* 6(2): 15–35.

Hammersley, M. and Atkinson, P. (1995) *Ethnography: Principles in Practice*, 2nd edn, London: Routledge.

Handman. M. E. (1983) *La Violence et la Ruse: Hommes and Femmes dans un Village Grec*, La Calade, Aix-en-Provence: Edisud (Mondes méditerranéens).

Harding, S. (1991) *Whose Science? Whose Knowledge: Thinking from Women's Lives*, Ithaca, NY: Cornell University Press.

Harris, O. (1980) 'The power of signs: gender, culture and the wild in the Bolivian Andes', in C. P. MacCormack and M. Strathern (eds) *Nature, Culture and Gender*, Cambridge: Cambridge University Press.

Harrison, S. (1999) 'Cultural boundaries', *Anthropology Today* 15(5): 10–14.

Hart, L. K. (1992) *Time, Religion and Social Experience in Rural Greece*, Lanham, MD: Rowman & Littlefield.

Hastrup, K. (1987) 'Fieldwork among friends: ethnographic exchange within the Northern civilisation', in A. Jackson (ed.) *Anthropology at Home*, London: Tavistock.

—— (1992) 'Writing ethnography: State of the art', in J. Okely and H. Callaway (eds) *Anthropology and Autobiography*, ASA Monograph no. 29, New York: Routledge.

Herdt, G. (1981) *Guardians of the Flutes: Idioms of Masculinity*, New York: McGraw Hill.

—— (1994) 'Mistaken sex: Culture, biology and the third sex in New Guinea', in *Third Sex, Third Gender: Beyond Sexual Dimorphism in Culture and History*, New York: Zone Books.

Herzfeld, M. (1985) *The Poetics of Manhood: Contest and Identity in a Cretan Mountain Village*, Princeton: Princeton University Press.

—— (1986a) 'Within and without: The category of "female" in the ethnography of modern Greece', in J. Dubisch (eds) *Gender and Power in Rural Greece*, Princeton: Princeton University Press.

—— (1986b) *Ours Once More: Folklore, Ideology and the Making of Modern Greece*, New York: Pella.

—— (1987) *Anthropology Through the Looking Glass: Critical Ethnography in the Margins of Europe*, Cambridge: Cambridge University Press.

—— (1991a) 'Silence, submission and subversion: Toward a poetics of womanhood', in P. Loizos and E. Papataxiarchis (eds) *Contested Identities: Gender and Kinship in Modern Greece*, Princeton: Princeton University Press.

—— (1991b) *A Place in History: Social and Monumental Time in a Cretan Town*, Princeton: Princeton University Press.

—— (1992) 'I ritoriki ton arithmon: Synteknia kai koinoniki ypostasi stin Kriti', in E. Papataxiarchis and T. Paradellis (eds) *Tautotites kai Fyllo sti Sygxroni Ellada: Anthropologikes Proseggiseis*, Athens: Ekdoseis Kastanioti.

Hirschon, R. (1978) 'Open body, closed space: The transformation of female sexuality', in S. Ardner (ed.) *Defining Females: The Nature of Women in Society*, London: Croom Helm.

—— (1984) *Women and Property – Women as Property*, New York: St Martin's Press.

—— (1989) *Heirs of the Greek Catastrophe: The Social Life of Asia Minor Refugees in Piraeus*, New York: Oxford University Press.

Holland, D. C. and Eisenhart, M. A. (1990) *Educated in Romance: Women, Achievement and College Culture*, Chicago: University of Chicago Press.

Iossifides, M. (1991) 'Sisters in Christ: Metaphors of kinship among Greek nuns', in P. Loizos and E. Papataxiarchis (eds) *Contested Identities: Gender and Kinship in Modern Greece*, Princeton: Princeton University Press.

—— (1992) 'Adelfes ston Christo: I syggeneia se dyo ellinika orthodoksa monastiria', in E. Papataxiarchis and T. Paradellis (eds) *Tautotites kai Fyllo sti Sygxroni Ellada: Anthropologikes Proseggiseis*, Athens: Ekdoseis Kastanioti.

Irigary, L. (1974) *Speculum de l'autre Femme*, Paris: Minuit.

Jackson, M. (1987) 'Facts of life or the eroticization of women's oppresion? Sexology and the social construction of heterosexuality', in P. Caplan (ed.) *The Cultural Construction of Sexuality*, London: Routledge.

—— (1998) *Minima Ethnographica: Intersubjectivity and the Anthropological Project*, Chicago: University of Chicago Press.

Jeffreys, S. (1985) *The Spinster and Her Enemies: Feminism and Sexuality 1880–1930*, London: Pandora.

Jivani, A. (1997) *It's Not Unusual: A History of Lesbian and Gay Britain in the Twentieth Century*, London: Michael O'Mara.

Johnson, M. (1997) *Beauty and Power: Transgendering and Cultural Transformation in the Southern Philippines*, Oxford: Berg.

Just, R. (1991) 'The limits of kinship', in P. Loizos and E. Papataxiarchis (eds) *Contested Identities: Gender and Kinship in Modern Greece*, Princeton: Princeton University Press.

Karakasidou, A. (1997) *Fields of Wheat, Hills of Blood: Passages to Nationhood in Greek Macedonia*, Chicago: University of Chicago Press.

Kemp, J. H. and Ellen, R. F. (1984) 'Informal interviewing', in R.F. Ellen (ed.) *Ethnographic Research: A Guide to General Conduct*, London: Academic Press.

Kendall (1999) 'Women in Lesotho and the (western) construction of homophobia', in E. Blackwood and S. E. Wieringa (eds) *Same Sex Relations and Female Desires: Transgender Practices Across Cultures*, New York: Columbia University Press.

Kenna, M. (1990) 'Family, economy and community on a Greek island', in C. Harris (ed.) *Family, Economy and Community*, Cardiff: University of Wales Press.

Kennedy, R. (1986) 'Women's friendship on Crete: A psychological perspective', in J. Dubisch (ed.) *Gender and Power in Rural Greece*, Princeton: Princeton University Press.

Kirkham, P. and Attfield, J. (eds) (1996) 'Introduction', in *The Gendered Object*, Manchester: Manchester University Press.

Kulick, D. (1998) *Travesti: Sex, Gender and Culture among Brazilian Transgendered Prostitutes*, London: University of Chicago Press.

Lakoff, G. and Johnson, M. (1980) *Metaphors We Live By*, Chicago: University of Chicago Press.

Lambiri-Dimaki, I. (1983) *Greek Society in the Student Consciousness*, Athens: Odysseas.

Leach, E. (1976) *Culture and Communication*, Cambridge: Cambridge University Press.

Levi-Strauss, C. (1969) *The Elementary Structures of Kinship*, Boston: Beacon Press.

Loizos, P. (1975) *The Greek Gift: Politics in a Greek Cypriot Village*, Oxford: Basil Blackwell.

—— (1981) *The Heart Grown Bitter: A Chronicle of Cypriot War Refugees*, Cambridge: Cambridge University Press.

—— (1994) 'A broken mirror: masculine sexuality in Greek ethnography', in A. Cornwall and N. Lindisfarne (eds) *Dislocating Masculinity*, London: Routledge.

Loizos, P. and Papataxiarchis, E. (eds) (1991a) 'Gender, sexuality and the person in Greek culture', in *Contested Identities: Gender and Kinship in Modern Greece*, Princeton: Princeton University Press.

—— (eds) (1991b) 'Introduction, Gender and kinship in marriage and alterantive contexts', in *Contested Identities: Gender and Kinship in Modern Greece*, Princeton: Princeton University Press.

Lutz, C. and White, G. (1986) 'The anthropology of emotions', *Annual Review of Anthropology* 15: 405–36.

MacCannell, D. (1976) *The Tourist: A New Theory of the Leisure Class*, London: Macmillan.

MacCormack, C. P. (1980) 'Proto-social to adult: A Sherbro transformation', in C. P. MacCormack and M. Strathern (eds) *Nature, Culture and Gender*, Cambridge: Cambridge University Press.

MacIntosh, M. (1968) 'The homosexual role', *Social Problems* 16.

Mackridge, P. and Yanakakis, E. (eds) (1997) *Ourselves and Others: The Development of a Greek Macedonian Cultural Identity Since 1912*, Oxford: Berg.

McNay, L. (1992) *Foucault and Feminism*, Cambridge: Polity Press.

—— (2000) *Gender and Agency: Reconfiguring the Subject in Feminist Social Theory*, Cambridge: Polity Press.

Madianou-Gefou, D. (ed.) (1992) 'Exclusion and unity, retsina and sweet wine: Commensality and gender in a Greek agrotown', in *Alcohol, Gender and Culture*, London: Routledge.

Marcus, G. E. (1998) *Ethnography Through Thick and Thin*, Princeton: Princeton University Press.

Marcus, G. and Fisher, M. J. (1986) *Anthropology as Cultural Critique: An Experimental Moment in the Human Sciences*, Chicago: University of Chicago Press.

Marshall, B. (1998) 'Reconsidering gay: Hocquenghem, identity politics and the baroque', in O. Heathcote, A. Hughes and J. S. Williams (eds) *Gay Signatures: Gay and Lesbian Theory, Fiction and Film in France, 1945–1995*, Oxford: Berg.

Mauss, M. (1934) *Les Techniques du Corps: Sociologie et Anthropologie*, Paris: Presses Universitares de France.

Moore, H. L. (1986) *Space, Text, and Gender: An Anthropological Study of the Marakwet of Kenya*, reprinted 1996, London: The Guilford Press.

—— (1993) 'The differences within and the difference between', in T. del Valle (ed.) *Gendered Anthropology*, London: Routledge.

—— (1994) *A Passion for Difference*, Cambridge: Polity Press.

—— (ed.) (1999) 'Whatever happened to women and men? Gender and other crises in anthropology', in *Anthropological Theory Today*, Cambridge: Polity.

Mouzelis, N. P. (1978) *Modern Greece: Facets of Underdevelopment*, London: Macmillan.

Munt, S. R. (1998) *Heroic Desire: Lesbian Identity and Cultural Space*, London: Cassell.

Nanda, S. J. (1990) *Neither Man nor Woman: The Hijras of India*, Belmont: Wadsworth Publishing.

—— (1994) 'Hijras: An alternative sex and gender role in India', in *Third Sex, Third Gender: Beyond Sexual Dimorphism in Culture and History*, New York: Zone Books.

Nardi, P. M. (1992) 'That's what friends are for: Friends as family in the gay and lesbian community', in K. Plummer (ed.) *Modern Homosexualities: Fragments of Lesbian and Gay Experience*, London: Routledge.

Okely, J. (1983) *The Traveller-Gypsies*, Cambridge: Cambridge University Press.

Ortner, S. B. and Whitehead, H. (eds) (1981) 'Introduction accounting for sexual meanings', in *Sexual Meanings: The Cultural Construction of Gender and Sexuality*, Cambridge: Cambridge University Press.

Panourgia, N. (1995) *Fragments of Death Fables of Identity: An Athenian Anthropography*, Madison: University of Wisconsin Press.

Papagaroufali, E. (1992) 'Uses of alcohol among women: Games of resistance, power and pleasure', in D. Gefou-Madianou (ed.) *Alcohol, Gender and Culture*, London: Routledge.

Papataxiarchis, E. (1991) 'Friends of the heart: Male commensal solidarity, gender and kinship in Aegean Greece', in P. Loizos and E. Papataxiarchis (eds) *Contested Identities: Gender and Kinship in Modern Greece*, Princeton: Princeton University Press.

—— (1992) 'O kosmos tou kafeneiou', in E. Papataxiarchis and T. Paradellis (eds) *Tautotites kai Fyllo sti Sygxroni Ellada: Anthropologikes Proseggiseis*, Athens: Ekdoseis Kastanioti.

Peristiany, J. G. (ed.) (1965) *Honour and Shame: The Values of Mediterranean Society*, London: Weidenfeld and Nicolson.

Plummer, K. (ed.) (1992) 'Speaking its name: Inventing a lesbian and gay studies', in *Modern Homosexualities*, London: Routledge.

Pool, R. (1994) *Dialogue and the Interpretation of Illness: Conversations in a Cameroon Village*, Oxford: Berg.

Rabinow, P. (1996) *Essays on the Anthropology of Reason*, Princeton: Princeton University Press.

Radway, J. (1988) 'Reception study: Ethnography and the problems of dispersed audiences and nomadic subjects', *Cultural Studies* 3: 359–76.

Ramazanoglou, C. and Holland, J. (2002) *Feminist Methodology: Challenges and Choices*, London: Sage.

Rapport, N. (1999) 'The "bones" of friendship: Playing dominoes with Arthur of an evening in the Eagle pub', in S. Bell and S. Coleman (eds) *The Anthropology of Friendship*, Oxford: Berg.

Raymer, L. (1993) 'What's sex got to do with it?', in E. D. Rothblum and K. Brehony (eds) *Boston Marriages: Romantic but Asexual Relationships Among Contemporary Lesbians*, Amherst: University of Massachusetts Press.

Reed-Danahay, D. (1999) 'Friendship, kinship and the life course in rural Auvergne', in S. Bell and S. Coleman (eds) *The Anthropology of Friendship*, Oxford: Berg.

Rezende, C. B. (1999) 'Building Affinity through Friendship', in S. Bell and S. Coleman (eds) *The Anthropology of Friendship*, Oxford: Berg.

Rich, A. (1980) 'Compulsory heterosexuality and lesbian existence', *Signs* 5(4).

—— (1993) 'Compulsory heterosexuality and lesbian existence', in H. Abelone, M. Barale and D. Halperine (eds) *The Lesbian and Gay Studies Reader*, London: Routledge.

Ricoeur, P. (1991) *From Text to Action: Essays in Hermeneutics II*, London: Athlone.

Rosaldo, R. (1993) *Culture and Truth: The Remaking of Social Analysis*, London: Routledge.

Roscoe, W. (1994) 'How to become a Berdache: Toward a unified analysis of gender diversity', in *Third Sex, Third Gender: Beyond Sexual Dimorphism in Culture and History*, New York: Zone Books.

Ross, E. and Rapp, R. (1997) 'Sex and society: A research note from social history and anthropology', in R. Lancaster and M. di Leonardo (eds) *The Gender Sexuality Reader*, London: Routledge.

Rubin, G. (1975) 'The wraffic in women: Notes on the "political economy" of sex', in R. R. Reiter (ed.) *Toward an Anthropology of Women*, New York: Monthly Review Press.

Rushton, L. (1992) 'I mitrotita kai o symvolismos tou somatos', in E. Papataxiarchis and T. Paradellis, (eds) *Tautotites kai Fyllo sti Sygxroni Ellada: Anthropologikes Proseggiseis*, Athens: Ekdoseis Kastanioti.

Salamone, S. D. and Stanton, J. B. (1986) 'Introducing the Noikokyra: Ideality and reality in social process', in J. Dubisch (eds) *Gender and Power in Rural Greece*, Princeton; Princeton University Press.

Savin-Williams, R. C. (1998) '*. . . And then I became Gay*'*: Young Men's Stories*, London: Routledge.

Sax, W. (2002) *Dancing the Self: Personhood and Performance in the Pandav Lila of Garhwal*, Oxford: Oxford University Press.

Schneider, D. M. and Smith, R. T. (1978) *Class Differences in American Kinship*, Ann Arbor: University of Michigan Press.

Scott, J. W. (1998) *Gender and the Politics of History*, New York: Columbia University Press.

Seidler, V. J. (1987) 'Reason, desire and male sexuality', in P. Caplan (ed.) *The Cultural Construction of Sexuality*, London: Routledge.

Seremetakis, N. (1991) *The Last Word: Women, Death and Divination in Inner Mani*, Chicago: University of Chicago Press.

Shepherd, G. (1987) 'Rank gender and homosexuality: Mombassa as a key to understanding sexual options', in P. Caplan (ed.) *The Cultural Construction of Sexuality*, London: Routledge.

Skouteri-Didaskalou, N. (1991) *Anthropologika gia to Gynaikeio Zitima*, Athens: Politis.

Smith, D. E. (1989) 'Sociological theory: Methods of writing patriarchy', in R. A. Wallace (ed.) *Feminism and Sociological Theory*, Newbury Park, CA: Sage.

Smith-Rosenberg, C. (1975) 'The female world of love and ritual: Relations between women in 19th century America, *Signs* 1(1): 1–30.

Somerville, S. (1997) 'Scientific racism and the invention of the homosexual body', in R. Lancaster and M. di Leonardo (eds) *The Gender Sexuality Reader*, London: Routledge.

Stake, R. (1994. 'Case Studies', in N.K. Denzin and Y.S. Lincoln (eds) *The Handbook of Qualitative Research*, Thousand Oaks, CA: Sage.

Stein, A. (1997) 'Sisters and queers: The decentering of lesbian feminism', in R. Lancaster and M. di Leonardo (eds) *The Gender Sexuality Reader*, London: Routledge.

Stewart, C. (1991) *Demons and the Devil: Moral Imagination in Modern Greek Culture*, Princeton: Princeton Univesity Press.

Strathern, M. (1980) 'No nature, no culture: the Hagen case', in C. P. MacCormack and M. Strathern (eds) *Nature, Culture and Gender*, Cambridge: Cambridge University Press.

—— (1988) *The Gender of the Gift*, Berkely: University of California Press.

Sutton, D. (1998) *Memories Cast in Stone: The Relevance of the Past in Everyday Life*, Oxford: Berg.

Synnott, A. (1993) *The Body Social: Symbolism, Self and Society*, London: Routledge.

Tapinc, H. (1992) 'Masculinity, femininity, and Turkish male homosexuality', in K. Plummer (ed.) *Modern Homosexualities*, London: Routledge.

Theodossopoulos, D. (1997) Turtles, farmers and "ecologists": the cultural reason behind a community's resistance to environmental conservation', *Journal of Mediterranean Studies* 7(2): 250–67.

—— (1999) 'The pace of work and the logic of harvest: women, labour and the olive harvest in a Greek island community', *The Journal of the Royal Anthropological Institute, incorporating Man* 5(4): 611–26.

—— (2000) 'The land people work and the land the ecologists want: Indigenous land valorisation in a Greek island community threatened by conservation law', in A. Abramson and D. Theodossopoulos (eds) *Land, Law and Environment: Mythical Land, Legal Boundaries*, London: Pluto Press.

—— (ed.) (submitted) 'Introduction: The "Turks" and the Greek imagination' in *Friends and Foe: Greek Views of Turkey in Everyday Life, Memory and Imagination.*

Todorov, T. (1977) *The Poetics of Prose*, Ithaca, NY: Cornell University Press.

Turner, V. (1974) *Dramas, Fields and Metaphors*, Ithaca, NY: Cornell University Press.

Van Gennep, A. (1960) *The Rites of Passage*, Chicago: University of Chicago Press.

Weber, M. (1963) *The Sociology of Religion*, Boston: Beacon Press.

Weeks, J. (1979) 'Movements of affirmation: Sexual meanings and homosexual identities', *Radical History Review* 20.

—— (1987) 'Questions of identity', in P. Caplan (ed.) *The Cultural Construction of Sexuality*, London: Routledge.

Wekker, G. (1999) 'What's identity got to do with it? Rethinking identity in light of the Mati work in Suriname', in E. Blackwood and S. Wieringa (eds) *Same Sex Relations and Female Desires: Transgender Practices across Cultures*, New York: Columbia University Press.

Weston, K. (1991/1997) *Families We Choose: Lesbian, Gays and Kinship*, New York: Colombia University Press.

Wieringa, S. E. and Blackwood, E. (eds) (1999) 'Introduction', in *Same Sex Relations and Female Desires: Transgender Practices across Cultures*, New York: Columbia University Press.

Whitehead, H. (1981) 'The bow and the burden strap: a new look at institutionalized homosexuality in native North America', in S. B. Ortner and H. Whitehead (eds) *Sexual Meanings: The Cultural Construction of Gender and Sexuality*, Cambridge: Cambridge University Press.

Wittig, M. (1992) *The Straight Mind and Other Essays*, New York and London: Harvester Wheatsheaf.

Wolfe, S. J. and Penelope, J. (eds) (1993) 'Sexual identity/textual politics', in *Sexual Practice/Textual Theory: Lesbian Cultural Criticism*, Oxford: Blackwell.

Worton, M. (1998) 'Cruising (through) encounters', in J. S. Williams (ed.) *Gay Signatures: Gay and Lesbian Theory, Fiction and Film in France, 1945–1995*, Oxford: Berg.

Yanagisako, S. J. and Collier, J. F. (1987) 'Toward a unified analysis of gender and kinship', in J. F. Collier and S. J. Yanagisako (eds) *Gender and Kinship: Essays Toward a Unified Analysis*, Stanford: Stanford University Press.

Yannakopoulos, K. (2001) 'Andriki Tautotita, soma kai omofyles sxeseis: Mia proseggisi toy fylou kai tis seksoualikotitas', in S. Dimitriou (ed.) *Anthropologia ton Fyllon*, Athens: Ekdoseis Savallas.

Zinovieff, S. (1992) 'Ellines andres kai ksenes gynaikes: To kamaki se mia eparhiaki poli', in E. Papataxiarchis and T. Paradellis *Tautotites kai Fyllo sti Sygxroni Ellada: Anthropologikes Proseggiseis*, Athens: Ekdoseis Kastanioti.

Zinovieff, S. (1991) 'Hunters and hunted: Kamaki and the ambiguities of sexual predation in a Greek town', in P. Loizos and E. Papataxiarchis (eds) *Contested Identities: Gender and Kinship in Modern Greece*, Princeton: Princeton University Press.

INDEX